The Moment Is Now

Swedenborg Studies No. 22

The Moment Is Now

Carl Bernhard Wadström's
Revolutionary Voice on Human
Trafficking and the Abolition
of the African Slave Trade

Anders Hallengren
Editor

SWEDENBORG
FOUNDATION
West Chester, Pennsylvania

Debbie and Clive
I hope you find
this valuable
and an
incredible
piece of
writing —

luv from

[signature].

September
2019

Swedenborg Studies is a scholarly series published by the Swedenborg Foundation. The primary purpose of the series is to make materials available for understanding the life and thought of Emanuel Swedenborg (1688–1772) and the impact his thought has had on others. The Foundation undertakes to publish original studies, English translations of such studies, and primary sources that are otherwise difficult to access. Proposals should be sent to: Editor, Swedenborg Foundation, 320 North Church Street, West Chester, PA 19380.

Library of Congress Cataloging-in-Publication Data

Names: International Carl Bernhard Wadström Conference on Human Rights and
   the Abolition of Slavery (2015 : London, England) | Hallengren, Anders,
   1950-editor.
Title: The moment is now : Carl Bernhard Wadström's revolutionary voice on
   human trafficking and the abolition of the African slave trade / edited by
   Anders Hallengren.
Description: West Chester, Pennsylvania : Swedenborg Foundation, 2019 |
   Series: Swedenborg Studies, 22 | "This volume consists of the proceedings
   of The International Carl Bernhard Wadström Conference on Human Rights
   and the Abolition of Slavery held in London on June 2-4, 2015"--
   Acknowledgments. | Includes bibliographical references and index.
Identifiers: LCCN 2018040332| ISBN 9780877853176 (hardcover : alk. paper) |
   ISBN 0877853177 (hardcover : alk. paper)
Subjects: LCSH: Slave trade--Africa--History--18th century--Congresses. |
   Wadström , Carl Bernhard, 1746-1799--Congresses. | Abolitionists--Great
   Britain--Congresses. | Abolitionists--Sweden--Congresses. | Antislavery
   movements--Great Britain--Congresses. | Slavery and the church--New
   Jerusalem Church--Congresses. | Africa--Colonization--Congresses. |
   Sweden--Colonies--Africa--Congresses. | Colonization--Religious aspects.
Classification: LCC HT855 .I585 2019 | DDC 306.3/6209609033--dc23
LC record available at https://lccn.loc.gov/2018040332

Edited by John Connolly
Design and typesetting by Karen Connor

Printed in the United States of America

Swedenborg Foundation
320 North Church Street
West Chester, PA 19380
www.swedenborg.com

"'As o'er the past my memory strays,' I recall certain
reminiscences of a past generation ... which may possess
some interest to readers ... and, therefore, I will record
them, without delay, as my own generation is nearly past,
and the one prior to that, entirely gone, and soon there will
be no one either to tell or to listen with interest."
From "Some Reminiscences of the Warminster Society" (1914)
by MARY W. EARLY

~

"The Negro is lashed to death, alas! to sugar your tea."
From "England and France" (1806)
by ESAIAS TEGNÉR

~

"I sacrificed a tear on the altar of humanity."
From "Resa ifrån Stockholm genom Danmark" (1811–15)
by CARL BERNHARD WADSTRÖM

Contents

From the Preface to Observations on the Slave Trade *(1789)*

Carl Bernhard Wadström

Animated with a desire of defending the cause of suffering humanity . . . having been so fortunately situated, as to be enabled fully to inform myself of the nature of the slave trade . . . would I were endowed with powers to represent in colours sufficiently striking, the frightful picture I have formed to myself, of the above-mentioned traffick, and thereby to prove, that these detestable markets for human flesh, constitute the last stage of all false principles; the greatest of all abuses; the inversion of all order; and originate solely in that corrupted system of commerce, which pervades every civilized nation at this day. . . . This detestable abuse may be considered as proceeding from a degenerate love of *dominion*, and of *possessing* the property of others; which, instead of diffusing the genial influence of benevolence and liberty, produces, in their state of inversion, all the horrors of tyranny and slavery. . . .

I am not only ready to devote my own person in this cause, but also to excite all those in whose breast there still remains a spark of humanity, to unite with prudence and activity, to accomplish this grand work, which has for its end the extermination of every *evil* and *false* principle, preparing the way for the reception of *Goodness* and *Truth*, in every human society. . . . pleading at the bar of human sensibility, in favour of the most oppressed nations in the universe. . . .

In exposing to the world the atrocious acts committed in that part of the globe to which I have been eye-witness, it is not improbable, that both the nations and individuals who have countenanced them, may consider the writer in the light of a spy, and a divulger of those things which ought, in honour, to have been buried in silence. But if they can find no other appellation for the just and pure intentions of a friend to mankind, who dares to expose crimes and cruelties which the abusers of human right are guilty of, he then accounts it an honour in discharging the duty he owes to society, to be esteemed as such. But let it be well observed, that herein he speaks from a respect due only to truth, with a view to expose *Wickedness* and *Falsehood,* but not *Nations* or *Individuals.* ⌁

Source: *Observations on the Slave Trade, and a Description of some Part of the Coast of Guinea, During a Voyage, Made in 1787, and 1788, . . . By C. B. Wadstrom,* [1746–99]. London: Printed and Sold by James Phillips, George-Yard, Lombard-Street, 1789, iii, iv–v, vi, vii, viii–ix. [English pp. ix, [1], [3], 67. The Royal Library, Stockholm.]

Acknowledgments

ANDERS HALLENGREN

THIS VOLUME CONSISTS of the proceedings of *The International Carl Bernhard Wadström Conference on Human Rights and the Abolition of Slavery* held in London on June 2–4, 2015. Organized by the Centre for Scandinavian Studies Copenhagen–Lund in conjunction with The Swedenborg Society of London and the Anglo-Swedish Society, this event was a public research symposium on Swedish and British cosmopolitanism and philanthropy of the eighteenth century, with a particular focus on the life, work, and impact of Carl Bernhard Wadström (1746–99).

In 2013, the idea for the conference was proposed, formed, and developed by Anders Mortensen of Lund University—then vice director of the Centre for Scandinavian Studies Copenhagen–Lund—who planned and paved the way for the event in cooperation with Anders Hallengren of Stockholm University—then president of The Swedenborg Society of London and distinguished member of the Anglo-Swedish Society in London.

On June 26, 2013, the two were invited by Alexander Malmaeus, chairman of the Anglo-Swedish Society, to a tea party in the Mansion House, the official residence of the Lord Mayor of London. At the party, Mortensen and Hallengren took the opportunity to present their ideas to Alderman Sir Roger Gifford—then Lord Mayor—with Lady Gifford also being present. Sir Roger became so enthusiastic about the plans that he at once offered the Mansion House's Egyptian Hall to be used for the conference, and he right away brought Mortensen and Hallengren to see it. His support, encouragement, and sponsorship were invaluable up to the very opening evening of the conference in the Mansion House, at which both he and Her Excellency Ambassador Nicola Clase delivered welcome addresses. Malmaeus served as chairman and efficient organizer of this memorable event, which was attended by British and foreign dignitaries, high officials, sheriffs and their consorts, and embassy staff from Europe and Africa, including His Excellency the high commissioner of Sierra Leone.

The Swedenborg Society then acted as host to the two days of conference proceedings that followed. At Swedenborg Hall, in their headquarters at Swedenborg House in Bloomsbury, the proceedings were organized by their staff, which was headed by director Stephen McNeilly and the editor and librarian James Wilson, both of whom served as moderators along with then-president John Cunningham, Anders Mortensen, and Anders Hallengren. David Lindrooth—the director of General Church Outreach—and Brycchan Carey—then school director of research at Kingston University—were among those who contributed with important panel comments. Lindrooth also delivered one of the concluding speeches.

We also owe many thanks to the several supporters and sponsors whose contributions finally made this conference possible and who met all expenses for traveling, housing, rents, refreshments, Mansion House security, audiovisual recordings, photography and camerapersons, the conference dinner, and the publication of this research work: The Swedenborg Society (UK); Swedenborg Foundation (USA); Centre for Scandinavian Studies Copenhagen–Lund (Sweden/Denmark); Anglo-Swedish Society (UK/Sweden); Royal Patriotic Society (Sweden); Paul Carpenter Fellowship Fund, Academy of the New Church (USA); Letterstedtska föreningen (Sweden); Stiftelsen fil. dr. Uno Otterstedts fond för främjande av vetenskaplig undervisning och forskning (Lund University, Sweden); Helge Ax:son Johnsons Stiftelse; and the Centre for Languages and Literature (Lund University, Sweden).

A final credit must be given to Mortensen and Malmaeus for all their efforts to conclude the conference with the installation of a memorial blue plaque at one of Wadström's old lodgings in London. As the houses that we were able to locate were either destroyed by war, demolished, or restructured with new facades, this idea was turned down by the English Heritage and so, unfortunately, did not materialize. While this was a setback, the very idea was at least favorably received and accepted by the British authorities, since Wadström was considered a Londoner worthy of a memorial. ⁓

Introduction

ANDERS HALLENGREN *and* ANDERS MORTENSEN

THIS BOOK IS a multidisciplinary effort by leading international scholars to shed light on an unknown aspect of Swedish–British cosmopolitanism and philanthropy during the eighteenth century, with a particular focus on the life, work, and impact of Carl Bernhard Wadström (1746–99)—an internationally active abolitionist, economist, and author. Wadström settled down in central London in 1788, moving between several different addresses there (Goodge Place; Oxford Street; Poultry; and Upper Marylebone Street, where Thomas Paine was living) in the years that followed and making friends with leading reformers of the time.

Wadström was an important figure in Swedish and international affairs, and he played a significant role in helping to change the course of history. Unfortunately, English-speaking academics have, over the years, had little access to a wealth of Swedish documents, while Swedish scholars have until recently had little interest in the international history of the slave trade and abolitionist movement. As a result, Wadström's name has all too often been overlooked, with his achievements clouded in undeserved obscurity.

The present gathered research will remedy this anomaly, demonstrating all the while the same spirit of Swedish–British humanitarian cooperation that was instigated by Wadström in London in the 1780s and 90s. It accesses source materials in different languages that were hitherto scattered throughout English, French, and Swedish archives—materials that no single biographer has as yet been able to overview and assess.

The scholars involved have been brought together to investigate Wadström's work and influence in the fields of economy, science, abolitionism, travel writing, African colonial history, Swedenborgianism, philanthropy, utopianism, and human rights. In particular, they show the topicality of the slavery issue, bringing the account and the arguments up to contemporary history—the slave trade in our times, trafficking, illustrated and exemplified by the UK Modern Slavery Bill and the Modern Slavery Act of 2015—and presenting a number of historical arguments against racism and oppression.

This book is not just a history of the past; it is also a call to action and a primer for the present moment, a guide from which we can learn how to tackle the current issues of human trafficking and slavery—activities that affect perhaps even more people than did the horrors of the slave trade that Wadström sought to abolish.

❦

Carl Bernhard Wadström was a Swedish technologist, official, businessman, and entrepreneur who played a pivotal role in the human rights movement. In 1779, he founded an economic society in Norrköping, Sweden, which worked to form a colony in Africa that would be built on agricultural progress and trade as alternatives to the enslavement of natives. In 1787, the Swedish monarch Gustav III sponsored Wadström to lead an expedition to West Africa with the intention of establishing there a Swedish colony. On this trip, in Senegal, Wadström witnessed firsthand the brutality and atrocities of the slave trade. He began to work tirelessly for the abolition of slavery, writing two hugely influential works on the matter: *Observations on the Slave Trade* (1789) and *An Essay on Colonization* (1794–95), the latter of which would become the key text for the economic and humanist arguments against slavery, for free trade with Africans on their own terms, and for international development programs in the settlements.

Wadström's observations gained him an audience with the Lord Mayor of London, as well as with the British Prime Minister William Pitt, and brought him into close contact and collaboration with leading British abolitionists: William Wilberforce, Thomas Clarkson, and Granville Sharp. His testimony before the British Parliament is recorded in the *Minutes of the evidence taken before a committee of the House of Commons . . . appointed . . . to take the examination of the several witnesses . . .* (1790).

Wadström's campaigning against the slave trade and his utopian ideas were in part inspired by his Swedenborgian beliefs; and he was similarly influential in propagating the works of Emanuel Swedenborg, bringing many of the Swedish mystic's unpublished manuscripts to Britain for publication and translation and helping fund and issue the first Swedenborgian periodical, the *New-Jerusalem Magazine,* in which African affairs was a leading theme. As Wadström lived in London for a number of years, he was baptized into the nascent separatist New Jerusalem Church at Great Eastcheap (now Cannon Street) on Christmas Day, 1788—a religious institution that William Blake, among other prominent people, attended.

With declining health, exhausted and financially ruined by his idealistic projects, Wadström made his last shadowy appearance at the annual meeting of *La Société des amis des noirs* on January 4, 1799, commemorating the republic's abolishment of slavery in the French colonies (a decree later revoked by Napoleon), but he was not among the speakers. In the early days of spring at Versailles, on Friday, April 5, at the new moon, suffocating from an exacerbated asthmatic condition, he passed away. Despite Wadström's significant contributions to the abolition of slavery, his resting place is unknown. ≈

The Moment Is Now

Swedenborg Studies No. 22

Prospects and Retrospect: Mansion House and the Historical Role of the City of London[1]

ALDERMAN SIR ROGER GIFFORD

CHAIRMAN, YOUR EXCELLENCES, Ladies and Gentlemen,

Welcome to Mansion House. I can think of no better place in London, or the UK, Europe even, for this conference to be held; and I am personally delighted it was possible to make the arrangements to accommodate you here.

I would like to add that, in this year of anniversaries, it is highly appropriate that this conference is being held at this time—and we in the City of London are honoured to be hosting it.

The House

This house, the Mansion House, is first and foremost the residence and workplace of the Lord Mayor of London. She or he is the country's chief ambassador for financial and professional services and represents one of the oldest continuous and elected appointments in any democracy in the world. The current Lord Mayor is Alan Yarrow, and he is number 687 in an institution well over eight hundred years old.

This building is only 250 years old. It was built by the city merchants in the mid-eighteenth century at a time of great prosperity and riches for Britain, as with a number of European countries, rich through trade, rich through international commerce, rich through thriving business built upon things like . . . the sugar plantations of the West Indies.

Yes, I'm afraid the truth is inescapably ironic, as so often in life, that we are holding this conference in a building built, albeit indirectly, from the proceeds of a practice which relied on human "employment" of a nature which we look on today as completely unacceptable wherever we encounter it. Slavery.

But such was life then—I read only recently of how several notable figures of the early eighteenth century, figures of considerable humanity such as George Frideric Handel, were invested in companies directly reliant on the slave trade.

But the revolution in practices that came about up to and after 1807 was, I am glad to say, supported by the City and not least through this house—at least at home, if not always in the colonies. Evidence of this can be seen in the dedication of Carl Bernhard Wadström's most famous book, *An Essay on Colonization* (1794–95), to the merchant Paul Le Mesurier, M.P., then Lord Mayor of the City of London. The dedication states it is . . . "in testimony of his laudable and exemplary zeal in promoting the civilization of Africa."

The history of this house is therefore quite interesting.

When proposals were invited for plans for building the house in 1734, the Common Crier of the City demanded that the House contain "a cause or justice" room.

That "justice" room is now the Programme Office—there is still a gallery overlooking proceedings, though it's now used for nothing more dynamic than a photocopier.

Equally, the concept of the rule of law was already well established, evidenced by the stained-glass window in the Egyptian Hall depicting the signing of Magna Carta. Indeed, one can fairly say that the rule of law illuminates the room—even if at the other end is the depiction of another Lord Mayor slaying the hapless Wat Tyler during the peasants' revolt of 1381.

There are also cells from the nineteenth century beneath the House—in use as recently as 1982. Indeed, the final sitting of the Mansion House Justice Room took place on July 25, 1991. It was then amalgamated with the Guildhall Justice Room to form the City of London Magistrates' court, next door to this building (behind me). One of the cells beneath Mansion House was called "the birdcage"; it was suspended from the ceiling and used to hold female prisoners. One famous prisoner was the early twentieth century suffragette women's rights campaigner Emmeline Pankhurst, in 1912.

Oh, and this brings me to the first of my anniversaries. This year, it's one hundred years since the foundation of the Women's Institute in England, three years *after* Emmeline Pankhurst was in prison here and three years *before* women aged over thirty were given the vote.

2015 Celebrations

Yes, the year 2015 is very much one for anniversary celebrations here in the UK. There is much in the papers about the events of the First World War from one hundred years ago; it is two hundred years since the Battle of Waterloo in 1815 and four hundred years since the Battle of Agincourt. Naturally, I won't dwell on the anniversaries which we don't wish to celebrate—I'm sure there are a few.

It's also twenty-five years since Nelson Mandela walked to freedom after twenty-seven years in prison, and fifty years since the death of Winston Churchill. All of these events are being celebrated one way or another this year.

But perhaps more importantly in the context of this conference, we are celebrating eight hundred years since the signing of the Magna Carta or Magna Carta Libertatum, the Great Charter of Liberties, depicted in that window in the Egyptian Hall (next door) that I mentioned. It has had great significance here, not least because it established the independence of the City of London, the square mile, from the King. This principle is still in some evidence today in the way the city is administered and run—even though it has been written and reissued many times after the original version of 1215.

The Magna Carta is worthy of a much longer exposition than I could give it today; and I encourage you to go and see the Guildhall exposition on at the moment, with the city's own copy of 1297 on show.

City History

As I mentioned, the city has a claim to having played a prominent role in the antislavery movement.

- The prominent judge Lord Mansfield ruled in 1772 that a slave who deserted his master in Britain could not be taken by force to be sold abroad. This verdict led directly to the decline of slavery in Britain and the emergence of clandestine "black quarters," primarily in St. Giles in the Fields. By 1800, there were between fifteen thousand and twenty thousand black people living in the city, mainly as free men and women.

- On May 22, 1787, twelve men met in a room in George Yard in the City of London. Two months later, they took offices at 18 Old Jewry, and they called themselves the Committee for the Abolition of the Slave Trade.

- It took twenty years, but in 1807, England banned the slave trade in the British Empire—in particular, the Atlantic slave trade—and also encouraged British action to press other European states to abolish their slave trades, though it did not abolish slavery itself. This was swiftly followed in other countries: the United States, Denmark, and of course Sweden. It took a further twenty-six years before slavery per se was actually abolished—as you well know.

One of the founding members of the Committee for the Abolition of the Slave Trade was Granville Sharp, who had previously been deeply involved in the story of the slave Jonathan Strong. Strong had been brought as a slave from Barbados to London, where he was beaten by his master and left for dead. Strong crawled to the surgeon William Sharp in Mincing Lane, where Sharp treated the city's poor for free. Sharp's brother, Granville, asked Strong about his injuries. William Sharp arranged for Strong to be admitted to St. Bart's, where he received treatment for four months.

Years later, Strong's former master saw him by chance in the street and kidnapped him. Granville Sharp took the case to court. The action was heard here in this house on September 18, 1767, before the Lord Mayor, Sir Robert Kite, who discharged Strong. Later legal work by Sharp led to the conclusion that any person who came to England and lived there became subject to habeas corpus, allowing trial before internment and preventing forcible removal to another country. He also used humanitarian arguments—*"a toleration of slavery is, in effect, a toleration of inhumanity."* This was the first major antislavery work by a British author—in 1767.

Modern City and Conclusion

The modern city today owes an enormous debt to those men and women, priding itself as it does on its openness and respect for all religions, cultures, and races—not least, one extraordinary Londoner, John Wilkes, who served as Lord Mayor of London in the 1750s. A chancer, a libertine and wit, debtor, demagogue, and democrat—above all, a lover of liberty in all its forms, especially political and religious—he stood for votes for all in the 1780s.

He wanted to see, across London's skyline, "rising in the neighbourhood of a Christian Cathedral, near its gothic towers, the minaret of a Turkish mosque, a Chinese pagoda, and a Jewish synagogue . . ." Two hundred and fifty years ago! The success of the modern city is built on this openness. We are proud of the fact . . . that London is today home to 270 nationalities; three hundred languages; and all those cathedrals, churches, minarets, synagogues, and temples . . . let alone those other temples of human activity, restaurants. So that at the London 2012 Olympics, the top fifty countries attending each had ten thousand supporters already in place.

The binding language for us all is commerce and trade, in some sort of English, with no regard to religion or race. Indeed, I myself am a Scotsman working for a Swedish bank, no less—in England!

Ladies and gentlemen, thank you for coming; and again, you are most welcome to Mansion House and the City of London. ≈

On Human Bondage: An Overview of Slavery and the Slave Trade

NEIL KENT, *University of Cambridge*

The Background

THE ORIGINS OF the Atlantic slave trade are ancient, lost in pre-historical times; but throughout ancient history, slavery evidently thrived in such places as Egypt, the Greek city-states, and the Roman Republic and Empire. Greece, claimed as the cradle of modern western democracy, was built literally upon the backs of slaves, who, in general, made up the mass of the population and were granted no civic rights.

With the arrival of Christianity and its spread throughout the Middle Ages, slavery in Western Europe dramatically declined. Throughout most of the continent, it was increasingly considered immoral for Christians from Europe to be held in bondage. Therefore, many peoples, upon accepting Christianity—whether converted by the sword or by missionary activity—no longer became prey to European slave raiders. Serfdom—in which the majority of the farming population was not held as chattels but was bound to the land at a particular aristocratic estate—by contrast, continued to thrive in most places, even increasingly so during the seventeenth century. Continuing through the eighteenth century and culminating in the middle years of the nineteenth century, it was thereafter abolished in the era of industrialization, urbanization, and social reform. The desperate need for agricultural labor had previously been too great to stop it.

In the Nordic countries, slavery, which was ubiquitous in historical documents, largely ceased during the early years of the first millennium.

However, the Sámi people of the North were considered suitable for enslavement until their Christianization in the later Middle Ages. Serfdom, in this region, was a different matter; it was not until 1789 that it was abolished in Denmark, under the auspices of the then-Prime Minister Count Bernstorff, and its last vestiges in Sweden did not disappear until the twentieth century.

Yet the issue of the morality of human bondage was no new subject of interest. With at least the rise of humanism in the sixteenth century, it became a key topic of concern amongst theologians. Protector of the Indians in the Americas, the Spanish Dominican friar Bartolomé de las Casas joined in argument with fellow Spanish theologian and philosopher Juan Ginés de Sepúlveda, in the so-called Valladolid debate (1550) over the morality of Indian enslavement. However, at this time— although his views seem to have changed later in life—he actually encouraged the enslavement of black Africans, who he felt made suitable slaves, unlike the Indians. In any case, the de facto enslavement of the Indians had continued apace, the theological debate notwithstanding, and had so devastated their numbers that, in conjunction with the high mortality rate from European epidemics, there were hardly any of them left to put to work. Black Africans seemed to provide the only alternative as a reservoir of labor.

Indeed, the enslavement of black Africans for labor in the Americas seemed a necessity, if the economic enterprises they supported were to carry on. Within months of their arrival in the new colonies, white free farmers and their white indentured servants almost invariably succumbed to such insect-borne diseases as malaria and yellow fever. The Africans, by contrast, enjoyed at least a partial immunity. In consequence, the sugar, indigo, rice, tobacco, and coffee plantations on which they labored were able to thrive, bringing in vast wealth for their white European owners. This wealth fueled not only the well-being of the latter but also the Industrial Revolution itself, which sprung from a burgeoning middle class in Britain that had never before existed and that rarely, and typically only tangentially, came into contact with slaves or slavery. As shown in a fairly recent BBC television production,[1] many slaveholders were widows and children who had inherited individual slaves or even joint ownership of slaves from their husbands, businesses, or the bequests of other relatives. Thus, the institution of slavery was like the proverbial iceberg, with relatively little of it visible. Yet its infrastructure was powerful and efficient, functioning like a well-worn machine and bolstered by the shipping companies of Bristol and Liverpool and by the insurance companies of London.

The Classic Triangle of Rum, Slaves, and Molasses on the Middle Passage

The slaves, who were the principal commodities of this trade, were purchased at various points on the western and southeastern coasts of Africa, through local black African intermediaries—usually from such favored tribes as the Ashanti, located in today's Ghana—who had, in turn, captured them or bought them from other tribes in the interior. Local "criminals" and tribal enemies were the principal victims of the trade. Rum, weapons, and beads were prized commodities to the Africans for the exchange. The captives—invariably young and able so as to be fit for years of labor—were then held at coastal fortresses that were run by the Europeans.

One such place was the Swedish Carolusborg Fortress (now known as Cape Coast Castle), which was rebuilt by the British in the eighteenth century. It had originally been built by the architect Hendrik Caerloff for the acquisition of timber and gold but later came to be notorious as a slaving fortress. It was founded by the Swede Louis De Geer, who had made his money in the copper trade in 1649 for the Swedish Africa Company, which was based in newly founded Gothenburg. However, as Swedish military might waned, the fortress was later seized by the Danes and eventually from them by the British. The British transported the overwhelming majority of African slaves across the Atlantic, not only to their own colonies but also to those of the Spanish and Portuguese.

Black Africans were not the only enslaved peoples who were transported across the Atlantic. The Muslim Barbary pirates of North Africa, flying the Ottoman flag, carried on a thriving slave trade for centuries, attacking Christian European powers. Occasionally, even the southwestern coast of Britain was subject to their depredations. However, amongst their victims, Icelanders fared the worst. The most terrible attacks occurred at Grindavik, on the island's southwestern coast, in the summer of 1627, under sea captain Murat Reis the Younger, a Dutch-born Muslim convert who had sought alternative work with the Turks when the Dutch wars had ceased. Three hundred and eighty Icelanders were captured in Grindavik for slavery in the Maghreb. Hvalsnes was also attacked, with 110 captured, as was Vestmannaeyjar, where another 234 were seized, not to mention those who were killed, including the local priest. Up to nine hundred Icelanders were seized out of a total population of some sixty thousand. Ólafur Egilsson, another priest from Vestmannaeyjar, was captured and enslaved; although he was eventually released to plead at the court of Christian IV for a ransom to be paid in exchange for those who remained in Algerine captivity. One so freed as a result was Guðríður Símonardóttir, who was held as a sex slave. She eventually married the Lutheran priest Hallgrímur Pétursson, one of seventeenth-century Iceland's most famous poets.

Nonetheless, black Africans made up the overwhelming majority of the victims of the slave trade. They were carried across the Atlantic as part of the Middle Passage. The Danish slave ship *Count Bernstorff*, which during the 1780s plied the seas from Copenhagen to the Guinea coast to the Danish West Indies and back, made such a journey. (With perhaps unintentional irony, the ship was named after the Danish Prime Minister Andreas Bernstorff, who himself had emancipated Danish serfs in 1788.) It was Carl Bernhard Wadström (1746–99), by whose spirit both this conference and this book have been inspired, who brought us the clearest visual image of what such a voyage meant. This he conveyed in *Plan and Sections of a Slave Ship*, an illustration picturing the slave ship Brookes of 1789, which was published by Wadström in the second volume of his seminal essays on colonization, a work that was to have considerable influence on the ultimate abolition of the "peculiar institution." (See *Plate* 1.)

Scandinavia's greatest abolitionist, Wadström had studied at Uppsala University before first traveling out to Western Africa's Slave Coast. His *Observations on the Slave Trade* (1789) and *An Essay on Colonization* (1794–95) brought his views to the attention of the wider world, but in particular to the British Privy Council and the House of Commons. The images of the punishments meted out to slaves were harrowing; the amputation of limbs and hanging were just two of the gruesome practices used on recalcitrant slaves as warnings to others.

Of course, the everyday lives of African slaves were normally as regular and commonplace as they were toilsome; on special holidays, like Christmas, they were even festive. Once the slaves were auctioned in the American and Caribbean ports, life for them achieved a relative stability and order, with rural life developing its own regional rhythm. However, unlike those subjected to European serfdom, African slaves and their descendants were legally considered chattels, or material possessions, rather than people who were bound to the land. This distinction affected their family life dramatically, since slave marriages often had limited or no legal validity, especially in the British colonies. Intercourse was restricted; and for economic reasons, childbirth and family life were not encouraged.

On the formerly Danish Santa Cruz in the Virgin Islands, today known as St. Croix, is the Hogensborg Plantation. While remembered for its late-eighteenth-century grandeur, including its palatial mansion and stately gardens, it is also an illustrative and representative example of the hard rules and cost-effective measures that brought its owners considerable wealth and maintained their demand for unpaid workers. For the Africans who toiled there, life was short, and they had few children. Consequently, the slave trade needed to continue so that the white plantation owners could maintain their workforce.

Many Scandinavian planters had a voice in the famous and well-traveled botanist Carl Peter Thunberg. A former student of Carl Linnaeus, Thunberg supported Linnaeus's ideals and believed in a hierarchy of *Homo sapiens,* much as he did in other species. For him, Africans were the lowest form of human life, of whom the Hottentots he found to be "monstrous, abnormal," suspecting them of suffering from *monorchidism,* or having only one testicle. As for African women, in general, while he found them to be "cheerful," he thought they were exceptionally well suited to be slaves—so unlike Americans, he noted. Like Linnaeus, he thought that Asians occupied a higher level on the human scale, albeit far below that of Europeans. Therefore, just as he did with Africans, Thunberg supported the enslavement of Asians.

More and more, however, it was the abolitionist ideals of the British politician and activist William Wilberforce that came to the fore in Europe's ruling elite and mercantile forces. In 1792, Denmark abolished the transatlantic slave trade, the first country in the world to do so. France followed suit in 1794, only to reinstate it in 1802 under Napoleon. In the Caribbean, Haitians rose up in outrage, rapidly establishing in 1804 the only independent black and mixed-race state in the Americas. In 1807, Britain followed suit in outlawing the importation of slaves, and the United States did also in 1809. Slavery as an institution continued, however, as slaves continued to be imported, albeit illegally, right up to and during the Civil War. Slavery was only definitively abolished in the United States in 1865, since President Abraham Lincoln's Gettysburg Address of 1863 had only freed those slaves who were residing in states that were in rebellion.

As for the Danish and Swedish Caribbean colonies, it was not until 1850 that slavery came to an end. The king of the Ashanti people had to be deported to Copenhagen, Denmark—where he could be seen in top hat walking up and down fashionable Langelinie—in order to force compliance in what had at that time become a British, rather than Danish, West African colony. To deal with the so-called "unwanted" black ex-slaves, the states of Liberia and Gabon were founded in West Africa, with many ex-slaves transported to each by the United States and France, respectively. This nineteenth-century American emancipation left African and Asian slavery at home largely unaffected. As for Cuba—which was still under Spain—and Brazil, they were the last states to abolish slavery in the Americas; this happened as late as 1886 and 1888, respectively. In the former, the royal government had desired its abolition for decades, but the local Creole landowners had refused; in the latter, it was the coffee planters of the north who long objected to its abolition. Altogether, some twelve-and-a-half million black slaves had been shipped across the Atlantic during its centuries of activity, a third of whom were sent to Brazil alone.

The Eurasian Context

Bonded labor had, of course, existed for millennia in both the Eurasian context and the Atlantic littoral zone. Much of that, as we have seen, took the form of serfdom. Yet serfdom tended to have a more benign character than did chattel slavery. Indeed, in its rural setting, serfdom was often kinder to the laborers' physical well-being than it was to agricultural or industrial free laborers in urban settings. Russian serfs in the 1830s, for example, enjoyed better diets than did those free laborers who carried out agricultural work in urban areas at that time in Britain. They also played a greater role in their self-government, having limited self-determination in the mir, which was the unit of local serf self-administration. On the other hand, agricultural laborers in Britain at that time had no direct political representation of any sort.

Slavery also existed in Crimea, the Ottoman Empire, and other areas in that part of the world. For centuries, Crimea's primary significance was that of being a slave emporium. In excess of a million slaves were exported from today's Russia and Ukraine by Crimean Tatars between the fifteenth and late seventeenth centuries, usually to the slave markets of Constantinople and Baghdad. Up until the early modern period, blonde girls and boys, who were highly desirable in the Arab and Ottoman world, could be obtained cheaply and sold for huge profit by raiding parties. Indeed, the word slave comes from the term *Slav*.

But the slave trade could occasionally function in the opposite direction. African slaves might be brought to Russia for their novelty value. It was Peter the Great who abolished slavery there, albeit whilst reinforcing serfdom. The most famous and successful of all such slaves sent to Russia was Abram Petrovich Gannibal, a black African who was presented to Peter the Great as a gift. Emancipated, he became Peter's godson and went on to be educated first at the court of the Tsar and then with the military in France. Gannibal was eventually ennobled by the Empress Elizabeth, after which he became governor of Reval, which is Tallinn in today's Estonia. His great grandson was Russia's eminent literary figure Alexander Pushkin, the national poet; and his great-great-great granddaughter is Natalia, Duchess of Westminster.

In Recent Times

In the Americas, in particular their sugar plantations, slavery had ultimately come to be uneconomical. In the decades following the Napoleonic wars, rich planters more and more returned to their homelands, either selling their estates or leaving them to others, sometimes to mixed-race relations who were willing to run them on a lower margin. With the abolition of the slave trade and increasingly diminishing returns, the end of the "peculiar institution" was definitely on the horizon. Its end in the Americas, however, did not imply its demise elsewhere.

Indeed, in Africa and the Middle East, it continued under the auspices of Arab slave traders well into the twentieth century. According to British historian John Illife, in his book *Africans* (1995), 1910 was the year in which the greatest number of Africans was enslaved. Despite its suppression as a trade in Egypt since 1854, slavery persisted there, often under the radar of the authorities. In 1905, some 2,253 children were freed in the Europeanized city of Alexandria alone. Slavery carried on in the Ottoman Empire as well; and it was only in 1962 that Saudi Arabia, formerly under the empire's auspices, officially abolished the practice.

❧

But is slavery gone from the face of the earth in the way that smallpox epidemics have been eliminated, or does it continue to this day under other guises? If a plethora of statistics is to be believed, it remains with us: in ISIL-controlled Syria, Iraq, and parts of the Sahel region of Africa, slavery is occurring with as full a force as ever. And it has even reared its ugly head in First World countries. In Britain, for example, in 2015, it appeared in the form of human trafficking for prostitution and for the forced labor of those who were mentally and physically vulnerable enough to be unable to resist their oppressors.

It remains to be seen whether the world will ever be able to gather the social, legal, and military resources to finally defeat slavery, or whether it will remain, like poverty, an evil that will always be with us. ≈

It Happens Here: From the Slave Trade to Trafficking

MARK FLORMAN, *Chairman, Centre for Social Justice, London*

FOR MANY OF us, our crime is that we have a failing of the imagination: a willingness to participate as consumers in this fast-paced, supply-chain-dependent society without demanding stringent transparency or accountability and without questioning the army of global corporations, laborers, domestic and hospitality workers, and myriad others who provide us with services. It's a failing that has, for too long, given freedom to the traffickers and slave drivers who curtail the freedom of so many vulnerable people by means of violent force, fraud, coercion, and deception. This modern form of slavery deals directly in the recruitment and movement of these people with the aim of exploiting them.

Britain has long bathed in the afterglow of our proud abolitionist history; and it is this, perhaps, that for so long has prevented us from believing in and giving voice to the reality of these appalling crimes. But as the landmark 2013 report *It Happens Here* proved beyond a shadow of doubt, modern slavery happens on UK soil, affecting not only its natural-born citizens but also those vulnerable people who have been trafficked here from around the globe. It happens across Europe, empowered and legitimized by the free movement of people. It operates across borders. It happens to adults and to children, to men and to women. It manifests in a shockingly wide range of forms, from exploitation in the sex industry, to forced labor, to domestic servitude, to forced criminal activity. It breaks the lives of the susceptible and voiceless, many of whom are already living testament to the devastating effects of the five pathways to poverty: family breakdown, educational failure, economic dependency and worklessness, addiction, and extreme personal debt.

It Happens Here, produced by the Centre for Social Justice (CSJ), was enabled by the tremendous work of more than 180 charitable sources across all sectors who have worked tirelessly for the antislavery cause, often without recognition. The report gathered evidence on numerous cases of exploitation in factories, fields, construction sites, brothels, and homes. It uncovered shocking systemic failures at every level that left victims vulnerable to indifference, incompetence, arrest, or recapture.

It Happens Here identified a leadership vacuum at the heart of Westminster: a messy legislative framework; frontline professionals—however well-meaning and brilliant they were in some areas—forced to swim against a tide of apathy; official bodies failing in their duty of care, with little idea about the scale of the problem; a fragmented charitable sector struggling to work together; far too little support and care for survivors; and major supply chains within the business community devoid of basic transparency.

Hidden in Plain Sight

The UN's International Labour Organization estimates that forty million people are enslaved around the world, creating a market that generates more than $150 billion a year in profits.[1] While the full extent of the UK's share of this figure remains unknown, the Home Office estimated that there were up to thirteen thousand potential victims of modern slavery in the UK.[2] *It Happens Here* showed that a large proportion of cases is never recognized or reported; and as a result, these cases do not appear in any statistics that are capable of measuring the size of the problem. In 2014, only 2,340 potential victims were referred to the National Referral Mechanism (NRM).[3] This organization has, since the 2008 Council of Europe Convention on Action against Trafficking in Human Beings, been the primary gateway to support services for victims; but there has been no consistent grip on the numbers, and efforts to improve this have faltered at every attempt.

It Happens Here was a collective effort to breathe new life into the fight against modern slavery. It proposed a revitalization of every aspect of our country's approach to this battle by injecting new and effective leadership to match the seriousness of the crime; by developing better information about the prevalence and pattern of modern slavery in the UK; by equipping those on the frontline with the ability to recognize modern slavery and the capacity to act with competency and compassion; by ensuring that the business community plays its part to stamp out these crimes; and by improving critical services to help survivors rebuild their lives.

Filling the Leadership Vacuum

At the very highest levels, the report identified an urgent need to improve the UK's strategic leadership with regard to the fight against modern slavery. There was nobody leading such a fight in any cohesive and effective way, and responses to the call became unstable and stalled with changing governments and officials. Furthermore, government responsibility on this issue lay with the Minister for Immigration, who wrongly turned modern slavery into an immigration issue, resulting in severe implications for its victims. The report recommended that the remit for human trafficking and modern slavery be transferred to the Minister for Policing and Criminal Justice in order to reflect the serious criminality of the issue and undo its harmful association with immigration.

Unsurprisingly, in light of these discoveries, the report also uncovered enormous legislative confusion around these crimes. At the time of publication, legislation relating to human trafficking and modern slavery was represented by three different acts.[4] Confusion caused by this division of representation was compounded by the fact that offenses of human trafficking for non-sexual exploitation fell under immigration law, further putting trafficking victims at real risk of arrest as illegal immigrants.

To this end, the report called for the introduction of an Independent Antislavery Commissioner, an individual who would be free of political influence and endowed with a powerful remit to oversee an effective and consistent UK response to the problem. The Commissioner's team would be the single point of contact for the modern slavery agenda, independently driving improvements in strategy, awareness, training, and information gathering; and giving voice to, and shaping policy with, the testimony of victims, ultimately enabling a proportionate, unwavering, and effective response.

Lifting the Fog: Clear Data and Useful Information

The nature of modern slavery is insidious and shadowed, and the extent of its activity remains difficult to accurately gauge. Adding to this problem was the fact that, in 2013, the NRM was also the system through which either of the UK's Competent Authorities—the UK Human Trafficking Centre (UKHTC) or the UK Border Agency (UKBA)—decided on whether someone was a victim of trafficking, confusing both the data gathered and the issues of modern slavery and immigration themselves.

The report called for reforms that would enable a much more detailed picture of modern slavery to be developed, and it proposed a two-tier NRM that would better capture critical information. An anonymous "first-tier" referral would receive information on cases of modern slavery, regardless of whether a victim consents to a named referral. A "second-tier" referral would be for those who wished to formally access support through the NRM; this would be a named referral, as per the existing format.

Calls were also made for the UKBA to be stripped of its Competent Authority status. This would ensure that the first decision made about a victim of modern slavery would not relate to their immigration status; instead, it would become a welfare decision based solely on their need for support. In too many cases, the CSJ had been told that the UKBA involvement in the NRM process acted as a major barrier to victims making a referral, further damaging the UK's grasp of the problem's scale and fundamentally denying the victim's right to unbiased treatment. These calls for reform recognized that a single Competent Authority ruling on a person's trafficking status—regardless of their immigration status—was the only way to ensure that the UK's response was victim-centred, compassionate, and fair.

Lack of Awareness

Just as shocking as the political confusion was the lack of awareness among professionals, as demonstrated in their inability to deal competently with the problem of modern slavery. The report highlighted unacceptable levels of ignorance and the misidentification of victims among the police, social services, the UKBA, the judicial system, and others whose responsibility it was to identify victims and ensure their protection. These conditions gravely hindered the UK's response to both the victims hidden within its communities and the traffickers who seek to exploit them.

> In any room of thirty to forty social workers across the seventy local authorities we have trained, when asked if anyone knows what the NRM is, no more than one or two will raise their hand. (Children's charity representative, in evidence to the CSJ)

The testimonies gathered wove a picture of devastating ignorance. An appalling outcome of such failure on the frontline has been that numerous victims of modern slavery have themselves been prosecuted for offenses they committed *as a result* of being trafficked. These may include immigration offenses or—in cases where people, often minors, are trafficked into the UK to work on cannabis farms—drugs offenses.

> One girl escaped from a brothel and went to a police station to tell them that she had been trafficked. She had no passport. Under these confusing circumstances, we chose to arrest her for being an illegal immigrant. (Deputy Chief Constable, in evidence to the CSJ)

While the report found some impressive examples of work by local police forces, it revealed that in many areas police were unaware of the issue or treated it as a low strategic priority. The report recommended that the recently elected Police and Crime Commissioners be leveraged as a key way to ensure that modern slavery is kept on the agenda and that training be improved to ensure a strong understanding of modern slavery's myriad manifestations.

Human trafficking is not a performance indicator for police. Until it is, there is more incentive to investigate a shed burglar . . . than there is [to investigate] a human trafficker. (Anonymous former law enforcement officer, in evidence to the CSJ)

In addition, there could be a failure of ownership over investigations, with smaller area units often unaware of the evidence requirements and overwhelmed by the complex, international nature of the crime. The report recommended that each force have a simple and clear protocol—underpinned by a national strategy—to enable it to bring a consistent and effective investigative approach as well as to support victims through the NRM.

The Government previously stated that each police force had identified a responsible senior police officer for human trafficking— a Single Point of Contact (SPOC).[5] However, the report found that only half of the thirty-three forces that responded were able to give any information about their SPOC[6]—a state of affairs that was in clear need of urgent reform.

Social work training was also shown to be deeply inadequate. To this end, the report called for trainee social workers to be taught about the risks of child trafficking in the UK as part of their qualification; and as part of their continued professional development, existing social workers were trained effectively through an agreed-upon program.

The Disappeared: British Children in Modern Slavery

One of the most disturbing and unanticipated aspects of the report was the evidence of British children being trafficked within the UK for sexual exploitation.[7] In 2011, 42 percent of the UK citizens who were trafficked were girls trafficked for sexual exploitation. Even worse than the statistic itself, many of these children were viewed by authorities as being complicit in their exploitation—a grotesque point of view that powerfully demonstrates the deep lack of understanding surrounding modern slavery among those charged with protecting its victims.

The power of psychological enslavement—in situations where issues of control are highly complex, with dependencies being built and exploited over long periods of time—is often a far more effective shackle than are physical threats. It remains a core challenge of modern slavery, complicating questions of agency and often obscuring blame, to the horrifying detriment of victims and our integrity as a nation.

> Control of the mind is more effective than a pair of handcuffs.
> (Nick Kinsella, founder and former head of the UKHTC and board member of the United Nations Voluntary Trust Fund for Victims of Human Trafficking)

The report highlighted the variety of methods used to control trafficked children, including sexual or other forms of violence; physical or emotional abuse; threats of violence against family members; and threats of public shaming, perhaps with the publication of humiliating photographs of the abuse that has taken place. In the midst of such abuse, one of the perpetrators will play "good cop," becoming the victim's main controller through a misplaced loyalty or the semblance of a relationship. In this way, the victim becomes beholden to the perpetrator's demands, however abusive, demeaning, or illegal they may be. It is crucial that social workers are able to adequately identify and respond to this horrific commodification of children.

> The controls I have seen exerted on British children who have been trafficked for sexual exploitation are virtually the same as those I see on adult victims who are trafficked to the UK from abroad for sexual exploitation. (Mike Hand, former Tactical Adviser at the UKHTC, in evidence to the CSJ)

Rebuilding the Lives of Adult Survivors

In addition to the inadequacy of the mechanisms used to identify and extract victims from their enslavement, a severe dearth of specialist aftercare support for victims was also uncovered. Survivors need help to recover from their experiences and—in light of the strong psychological bonds that often remain—to ensure that they do not fall back into exploitation. While some support services existed at the time of the report, there remained a pressing need to rethink the approach to reintegration and resettlement for survivors of modern slavery and to develop standardized, effective long-term provision to enable survivors to rebuild their lives.

Similarly, survivors who returned to their home country were found to be in dire need of better protection from re-trafficking. Shamefully, there was no guaranteed assistance for those from outside the EU who were returning home through the UKBA returns program, and there was no returns assistance at all for EU nationals who wished to go home.

> These are some of the most faceless, voiceless, helpless people that we have in the country. (Chief Superintendent John Sutherland of the Metropolitan Police, in evidence to the CSJ)

The report recommended that all trafficked EU and non-EU victims be offered the support of a return and reintegration scheme when returning home. It further recommended that the Antislavery Commissioner work with the Government to ring-fence international assistance, with financial conditions and sanctions, for countries that are persistently the top sources for victims of modern slavery in the UK—marking a key development in the UK's recognition of the international nature of this human rights abuse.

Rebuilding the Future for Children

One of the most scandalous aspects of the report was the discovery of the shockingly high number of trafficked children who go missing from local authority care. It is estimated that 60 percent of trafficked children in the care of local authorities "go missing and are not subsequently found."[8] Between April 1 and August 31 of 2011, for example, twenty-five potentially trafficked children went missing from care in one local authority alone—five children per month during that timeframe.[9]

The psychological bonds of modern slavery are such that trafficked children who go missing are very likely to return to exploitation. Those working on the frontline have time and time again encountered children who are so terrified and "brainwashed" by their traffickers that they would leave at the first possible opportunity to return to them. In one particular case described to the CSJ, a boy in local authority care who had previously been trafficked into the UK disappeared on a visit to the dentist; he had climbed out of the window in a desperate attempt to return to his abuser.[10]

> If they're still with you in two weeks then you've achieved something. (Children's Services Manager, in evidence to the CSJ)

A serious barrier for professionals in children's services, police forces, and non-government organizations was the complete lack of appropriate accommodation for trafficked children. Secure accommodation, especially for the most serious cases, can go some way to ensuring the safety of a trafficked child in the first instance. In cases where absconding or re-trafficking are a serious risk, a welfare placement in a secure children's home while a long-term protection plan is formulated may be in the best interests of the child. The report, however, found that empty beds were common in secure children's homes—even in those that were solely for welfare placements and not for young offenders—because many social workers viewed these homes as punitive.

This misguided perception must be dispelled, and secure accommodation must be more widely considered as an option for keeping a child victim of modern slavery safe in the immediate and short term. To this end, the report identified excellent practice in the Barnardo's Safe Accommodation Project, which uses trained and specialist foster caregivers to look after children who have been trafficked, and recommended that this model be replicated in the UK, with more specialist foster placements made available.

But the needs of trafficked children go beyond physical security. For child victims, especially for those who are desperate to return to their abusers, physical security can never be assured until their psychological trauma has been addressed. Therapeutic services, however, were shamefully scarce. Specialist foster caregivers spoke of their exasperation at the lack of available and appropriate support for trafficked children. One foster caregiver spoke of taking it upon herself to chase up appointments and find a counsellor, eventually deciding to pay with her own money for a private counsellor rather than wait any longer. Making available quality therapeutic care tailored to the needs of trafficked children was rightly emphasized by the report as a key area that must be prioritized in order to break the psychological bonds of abuse and allow the healing process to begin.

The Modern Slavery Act: The Battle

In light of its shocking findings, the report—harnessing the extraordinary efforts of so many who have fought this battle on the frontline for many years—called for the introduction of the Modern Slavery Act: a simplification of all human trafficking and slavery offenses under one act that *powerfully declaims the criminality of human trafficking and any form of exploitation* and makes provisions to ensure that victims of human trafficking are not prosecuted for crimes they may have committed as a direct consequence of their trafficking situation.

On March 26, 2015, the call was met, and the Modern Slavery Act was introduced. It was one of the last bills to receive royal assent before Parliament was dissolved ahead of the General Election. *The first of its kind in Europe,* it represents a major step forward in beginning the work that must be done to fight slavery, once again putting Britain at the forefront of the global battle against this crime to humanity.

The Modern Slavery Act consolidates and simplifies existing offenses into a single act, empowering officials to take action with clarity and focus. It ensures that perpetrators can receive suitably severe punishments—including life sentences—for these appalling crimes. It strengthens the court's ability to restrict individuals where necessary in order to protect people from the harm caused by modern slavery offenses.

Crucially, the act has led to the appointment of the first Independent Antislavery Commissioner (IASC) to improve the response to modern slavery. It has placed on the secretary of state a duty to produce statutory guidance on victim identification and victim services, and it strengthens regulation in these areas.

The Modern Slavery Act makes provision for independent child trafficking advocates, and it introduces a new reparation order to encourage the courts to compensate victims in cases where assets are confiscated from perpetrators. It closes gaps in the law to enable law enforcement to stop boats on which slaves are suspected of being held or trafficked.

The Modern Slavery Act also supports supply chain transparency by requiring any UK business turning over more than thirty-six million pounds—not limited to UK-incorporated or UK-registered companies—to disclose their annual actions by publishing them, according to the IASC, "in a prominent place" on their website. Such disclosure is a way of ensuring that there are no instances of modern slavery in their business or supply chains.

The Duty of Business

It is impossible to over-emphasize the role of business in leading the war on modern slavery. It is essential that businesses combat the dangers of the supply-and-demand mentality with the highest levels of rigor and accountability, ensuring that supply and product chains as well as business practices are slave-free. It is no longer enough to be satisfied with the barest standards of "ethical" packaging—the terrible ironies of which were captured in 2013 by *The Sunday Times* journalist George Arbuthnott's investigation into the British food industry:

> The authorities had gathered evidence that the workers had been trafficked to Britain and forced to work for a gangmaster on chicken farms run by Britain's largest egg-producing company.... From those farms, premium free-range eggs were sent on.... The GLA said the workers were suffering from exploitation "so extreme" ... they had to immediately revoke the gangmaster's licence.

> Legitimate food-producing companies ... employ the victims, unaware their pay and freedom is being seized by a trafficker operating in the shadows. This makes it very difficult for stores to guarantee the food on their shelves is not the product of slave labour—whatever they say about their ethical practices.[11]

The reporting requirements of the Modern Slavery Act have been modeled on successful legislation passed in the state of California, where companies such as Walmart and ExxonMobil have engaged with this new transparency agenda.

Eighty-two percent of the individuals polled by the report supported the Government's requirement for large companies to report on their efforts to battle modern slavery.[12] With the implementation of the Modern Slavery Act, forward-thinking businesses are recognizing the mutual benefit of committing to such standards of transparency. These standards allow consumers and investors to make informed decisions, give space for companies already doing good work to showcase their efforts, and enable all businesses to proactively manage and improve their public reputation.

The tide of public demand means that businesses resisting these changes are fighting a losing battle. As the Government has acknowledged, commercial competition will make doing nothing an unattractive and potentially more expensive option. These changes have the potential to revolutionize the commercial landscape of Britain, lending powerful support to the good business movement that has, for some time, been led by B Corp—first in the US and now through its UK branch, which launched in January 2015 and which I now support as president.

For this revolution to be a success, it is vital that transparency be embraced in the spirit of opportunity, not regulation. It should not be seen as a forcing of hands but as a chance to address problems and share best practice, ultimately increasing the positive social impact of business in general.

Continuing the Fight

Great steps have been taken in the fight against slavery, but they are just the beginning. Legislation is only part of the answer. Slavery may be centuries old, but modern slavery is a distinctly modern phenomenon. Enabled by modern technology, it is now a global industry, managed by organized criminal gangs across borders with the efficiency of any modern corporation.

These highly sophisticated illegal businesses show a detailed understanding of how to avoid detection and prosecution by Europe's law enforcement agencies when moving men, women, and children across international and national borders. Criminals will exploit victims in the most profitable of ways and by the easiest of means; and as technology evolves and methods change, much work will need to be done to fully understand the extent of these groups and their business models.

Modern slavery is a truly cross-border crime. As Britain becomes a more hostile environment to traffickers, and criminal gangs shift their base, there will need to be a concerted and coordinated action from law enforcement in different countries, working together in a spirit of open collaboration.

> It is absolutely critical that we recognize and respond to the need for ongoing support and that we get it right so we do not fail yet another generation. (Sheila Taylor, Director, National Working Group for Sexually Exploited Children, in evidence to the CSJ)

The CSJ wrote a report entitled *A Modern Response to Modern Slavery,* which lays out the next steps that must be taken by Europe—working as a united entity—to sustain the fight. As we focus on the urgent Europe-wide issues of free movement, mass immigration, instability in the Eurozone, and widespread youth unemployment—all themselves partially tied to modern slavery—we must not forget to ensure that action is taken to end the injustice and ongoing failures revealed in this report's pages.

With the Modern Slavery Act, we in Britain have chosen to look directly into the face of this crime. We have given it a name and recognized its reality, and this time will be the last time that we ever again will be able to say that we did not know. For too long, we have been guilty of having a culture of complacency—as leaders, as businesses, as professionals, and as individuals—and we must not return to such a place. *It Happens Here* is proof of the change that can happen when the collective pulls together to challenge the status quo and rattle the bars of resignation, and we must move forward in this spirit if we are to succeed in the long road ahead. A society is judged on the basis of how it treats its weakest members, especially its hidden and its voiceless ones. *Slavery has not been banished to the past; it is here today, now, in our midst. But it is not inevitable; its eradication must be the work of all of us.* ⌁

Knowledge, Silence, and Denial: The Late–eighteenth–century Debate on Slavery and Colonialism in Sweden

Fredrik Thomasson, *Uppsala University, Department of History*

THE FIRST LINE of a 1797 review of the Swedish translation of Thomas Clarkson's (1760–1846) abolitionist tract *An Essay on the Slavery and Commerce of the Human Species* (1786) states: "Here is another important subject, generally less related to the advantageous conditions of our country; however it will not therefore lack the warm compassion of the philosopher and friend of humanity."[1]

The reviewer, court poet Carl Gustaf af Leopold, seems oblivious to the fact that since 1785, Sweden itself was a slaveholding nation. Swedish merchants were trading slaves, albeit on a small scale, and Swedish officials at the Caribbean colony of Saint Barthélemy had in the decade prior put in place a draconian justice system that governed the island's black population, both enslaved and free. Nonetheless, Leopold was certainly aware of the debate on slavery and the slave trade, and he joined Clarkson in his condemnation of this sordid business.

Leopold's remark highlights the main question of this essay: how were slavery and colonialism discussed in Sweden during the second half of the eighteenth century? It also reminds us of how Sweden has been silent about its own colonial ventures and participation in the Atlantic slavery system—a silence that to a certain extent is still with us.

While Carl Bernhard Wadström (1746–99) made a significant contribution to the international abolitionist movement, he was also a great promoter of colonization. My students sometimes have difficulty understanding how these two seemingly contradictory convictions could be part of the same worldview. Wadström studied and began his career in Sweden at a time when both slavery and colonization were being discussed. He was of course not alone in either his distaste for slavery or his enthusiasm for colonization. Most well-known among his fellow abolitionist Swedes was the botanist and physician Anders Sparrman (1748–1820), who not only criticized slavery but also early in his career advocated for Sweden to colonize parts of Australia.

My aim is to show that Swedes like Wadström and Sparrman were participating in a debate that had already been highly prevalent in Sweden. While their joining with the abolitionists, arguably one of the earliest transnational political movements, attested to their position on these issues, many of their opinions were probably already formed before they left Sweden.[2]

I do not intend, however, to make any detailed comparisons between the international debate on slavery and the Swedish debate in particular, as this would entail a study of much greater scope. I do hope to be able to publish a book-length study on that subject in the future. Since the recent literature on abolition is vast, this essay offers only a brief account of the debate in Sweden during Wadström's lifespan, situating him and other Swedish abolitionists in their Swedish context.

Colonial Propaganda

Sweden never became an important overseas colonial power, but this was not for lack of ambition. The most prominent result of its colonial ambitions was New Sweden (1638–55), which was its attempt to gain a territory in the Americas. The Swedish colony, located in today's Pennsylvania, Delaware, and New Jersey, was a brief interlude in the battle between the more successful colonial powers, Britain and the Netherlands. The Swedish Africa Company's fort at Cabo Corso, located in today's Ghana, was an even briefer episode (1650s–60s).[3]

Notwithstanding these experiences, a range of more or less realistic plans were discussed and investigated all throughout the eighteenth century. Among the more fantastic projects were the establishments of

Swedish colonies at Madagascar and in the Orinoco delta, located in today's Venezuela.[4]

Swedish merchants and statesmen were inspired by, for instance, neighboring Denmark's more successful ventures in both Africa and the Caribbean. The rise of the Atlantic sugar economy did not go unobserved, and Swedish governmental economic discourse was turning increasingly mercantilist. One of the main professed aims of this new colonial interest was to find new markets for Swedish products. Having made his early career in the Swedish mining sector, Wadström was aware of such economic thinking.[5] In a 1768 trade manual, for example, among a plethora of goods, slaves were described as a potential form of Swedish merchandise. It was underlined that such Africans were used for purposes of both agriculture and mining.

> These African peoples are bought by Frenchmen, Englishmen,
> Dutchmen, Portuguese and Danes on the Guinea coast. . . . They
> are used by the Europeans in their mines and on their plantations in
> the Americas.[6]

One of the reasons for Sweden's 1757–62 participation in the Seven Years' War was to gain a foothold in the Caribbean; this time, the plan was to acquire the island Tobago, but Swedish diplomats were later instructed to try to obtain several other Caribbean territories, including Puerto Rico.

The colonial discourse can be followed in state papers, an example of which is an undated document (most probably from around 1780) proposing that a colony be established in Africa. The proposal contains a detailed budget, which states that out of the total sum of twenty-five thousand Swedish *riksdaler,* ten thousand were set apart for the purchase of 250 slaves. This was justified in the following way:

> As the climate does not permit Europeans to be used for hard work,
> and the low initial number of them is only sufficient for guarding
> and supervision, it is necessary to purchase at least 250 negro slaves.[7]

This shows that the purchase of slaves was not a foreign idea in the circles promoting Swedish colonization.

Colonization propaganda was also printed. Ulrik Nordenskiöld's (1750–1810) *Treatise on the Benefits of Commerce and Colonization in the Indies and Africa for Sweden,* which he published anonymously in 1776,[8] strongly argues on behalf of Swedish colonies, containing budgets and plans for such enterprises. It is clear that Nordenskiöld knew the international literature on the subject. In 1778, Anders Sparrman, who traveled with James Cook (1728–79) around the world in the first part of the 1770s, proposed in print that a part of New Holland's (Australia) southwest coast should be claimed by Sweden, as "it is still unseen by Flag officers . . . [and] an altogether unknown part of our globe . . . which I especially would like to see . . . named after Swedish places and Mæcenases."[9] Another example of the promoting of colonization was Johan Henric Kellgren's (1751–95) anonymously published *Proposal: On the Founding of Colonies in the Indies and on the African Coast* (1784), which contains an enthusiastic program for Swedish overseas ventures.[10]

Wadström's own account, *Observations on the Slave Trade* (1789), was informed by his voyage to Africa. Published in Swedish in 1791,[11] the first half of the tract is indeed a critique against slavery and the slave trade, while the second half is an exhortation for establishing African agricultural colonies. How Swedish readers perceived this message is hard to reconstruct, but it is not impossible that Wadström was foremost considered a promoter of colonization. It should also be noted that Wadström and his fellow Swedes' publications in English reached some Swedish readers as well. Of the 284 names in the list of subscribers to Wadström's *An Essay on Colonization* (1794–95), more than 130 of them are Swedish.[12]

Later commentators, including historians, have had problems in taking Swedish colonial ambitions seriously. Indeed, some of the Swedish projects do appear bizarre in their disregard of both geographic and political realities. Nonetheless, the small Antillean island Saint Barthélemy was acquired from France in 1784 in exchange for French trading rights in Sweden. It may well also be possible that pre-revolutionary France considered advantageous the presence of a friendly Swedish island in the highly volatile Caribbean archipelago.[13] This is not the right context to discuss the history of the acquisition, suffice it to underline that the preceding decades' debate indicates that Swedish government circles and the upper echelons of society had an abundant interest in and showed a great deal of preparedness for overseas colonial ventures. Sweden took possession of the island in March 1785, becoming the last entrant in the quest for Caribbean colonies (the United States's later forays not included). This also made Sweden a slaveholding nation for the first time, since serfdom, human bondage of ancient date, largely had lost its grip on peasants since the late Middle Ages.

The Debate in the Newspapers

While colonization was being promoted and discussed by litterateurs, merchants, and statesmen, there was a vivid debate going on over this issue in the Swedish newspapers.[14] In 1781, one of the capital's main newspapers—*Stockholms Posten*—bleakly predicted the following:

> Yet there are countries on earth to be discovered. . . . Yet there are riches to be stolen, counties to plunder, heads to be baptized, throats to strangle, blood to shed.[15]

In 1782, the culprits were specified in another newspaper.

> Spaniards, Englishmen, Dutchmen and Frenchmen call themselves Christian, and yet they keep thousands of humans prisoners in this gruesome state [of slavery], and trade them as dumb animals.[16]

In 1786, yet another newspaper added economic and demographic rationales to the critique.

> It is a shame for the enlightened world that slave trade is still conducted by peoples of the Christian faith. This trade hinders the sciences, industry and population increase.[17]

There was great interest in Sweden for the fledgling United States, and opinions were mostly enthusiastic. The praise was not always unconditional, though; several authors did not fail to point out the discrepancy between its constitution, which is probably what the writer here means by the term *religion*, and its practice of slavery:

> Yet, in this moment, there is no country where humanity is more humiliated than in America, Mr. Franklin's native land. A friend of

humanity must either close his eyes or shudder at a country, where contrary to its religion that proclaims that all humans are brothers, you can at every plantation see seven to eight hundred humans reduced to servitude, and indeed, counted as members of the animal kingdom.[18]

The above quotations summarize the mainstream opinion in the Swedish newspaper debate concerning these issues at that time: colonialism and slavery make up a sordid and exploitative business; hypocritical "Christians" treat slaves like animals; and these practices are not even conducive to the growth of commerce and population.

This discourse was not isolated to only the Stockholm newspapers. Gothenburg journals lambasted the cruelty of Caribbean slaveowners, and they eulogized slaves who, notwithstanding their brutal treatment, preserved their dignity and sense of justice.[19] In a story retelling an event purportedly set on the Caribbean island Saint Christopher (St. Kitts) in 1756, one such noble slave by the name of Quazy had been wrongly accused of theft. During a fight with his owner— a childhood friend—rather than hurting his master, Quazy committed suicide.[20] This article is also an example of how such stories circulated in the Atlantic world; it had already been published in the United States in 1788 and might have come from the British press originally.[21] Swedish newspapers gathered a good deal of their international news and information from foreign newspapers. Sometimes a source is given, but most of the time it is not. Nevertheless, it would certainly be possible to trace the origins of a large number of the Swedish articles in French, British, and German press, the main sources of foreign news in Sweden. And while there were articles in the Swedish press that promoted commerce and took a more sanguine view on slavery, even the authors of these articles felt the need to justify slavery by claiming that it gave slaves the means of survival: "Yes, it is through commerce . . . that we can feed the porcelain worker in China and the despondent slave at the sugar plantation in the West Indies."[22]

I do not yet have enough material to ascertain a chronological development of what was published, but it is certainly the case that the number of articles concerning slavery increased during the 1780s–90s. This might have been a function of the growing foreign abolitionist material, especially in the British press. It should also be emphasized that the distinction made here between newspapers and books is a highly fluid one. Many newspapers and journals were short-lived, as the commercial conditions were difficult on the restricted Swedish market. In addition to economic problems, especially during the late 1780s and the early 1790s, censorship and political circumstances made continuous publishing a challenge. (See "Reporting about Saint Barthélemy" on page 41, below.)

Travelogues and Literature

The second half of the eighteenth century saw an international boom in the publication of travel books and descriptions of foreign lands. Almost all books concerning Africa and the Americas in some way mentioned or described slavery. A number of Swedish authors also endeavored to satisfy the readers' curiosity. Pehr Kalm (1716–79), one of Linnaeus's so-called apostles, visited North America from 1748 to 1751. His comprehensive travel account (1751–63) included detailed descriptions of the conditions of slaves in British America.[23] Anders Sparrman spent almost two years in the Cape Colony in the 1770s. He traveled inland and experienced the almost warlike conditions on the edges of the Dutch colony. The first volume of Sparrman's account of his travels in Africa and around the world was published in 1783. He was highly critical of how the black populations were treated, of slavery, and of the slave trade.[24] Botanist and physician Carl Peter Thunberg (1743–1828), another Linnaean, spent three years in the Cape Colony in the 1770s. He also described how the black population was treated; but contrary to Sparrman, he saw colonialism and slavery as a fact, and he was considerably less sympathetic about the Africans' plights.[25] Kalm's, Sparrman's, and Thunberg's books were immediately translated into several languages. In *An Essay on the Slavery and Commerce of the Human Species,* Clarkson cited Sparrman's account of how the Dutch colonists hunted Hottentots to enslave them,[26] which goes to show how quickly knowledge circulated at that time.

Slavery and its terrors were also touched upon in songs and popular literature. The following rhymed example is taken from a travel account by a ship chaplain who visited the Cape Colony on route to China:

"Should we, as slaves, be shipped to an unknown isle, away from homeland, girl and friend, no please, let us rather die!"[27]

Other scientists who traveled overseas saw the effects of slavery and commented upon it in texts that were predominately directed toward a learned audience. Botanist Olof Swartz (1760–1818), who traveled to the West Indies in the 1780s, made important contributions to the study of the Caribbean flora. But Swartz also wrote about the conditions of the slaves on the islands he visited, and he did not mince words when he criticized slaveowners, referring to them as barbarians and executioners. One of the examples he gave was the following account of an execution, although it seems improbable that he actually had witnessed the scene:

> A Negro that had killed his master was executed at Cavaillon at St. Domingue. His thumbs were cut off, and he was put on the breaking wheel without shedding a tear. You could only hear him saying: "When I murdered my master, it was bad for him: now I have to die for his sake, which is bad for me."[28]

Similar stories were repeated by other Swedish writers, who had not themselves traveled or witnessed atrocities in the Caribbean but instead had picked them up in the foreign literature that reached Sweden. Jöran Fredriksson Silfverhjelm (1762–1819), for example, made the following observation:

> If a Negro kills one of the whites, for whatever reason, he is burned alive; but if a white kills his slave, this misdeed is atoned for by an insignificant fine, which is seldom collected.[29]

A surprising amount of travel literature was translated into Swedish, especially in the last two decades of the century. A great number of the international successes were promptly published in Sweden, often in abridged versions. The strong presence of travelogues in late-eighteenth-century circulating libraries attests to the popularity of the genre at that time. These types of books, as well as novels and biographies, were considered to be part of the "lighter" reading material.[30]

Sometimes, reviews of travelogues were scathing in their critique of the circumstances that foreign writers described. A passage in the Swedish edition of Mungo Park's (1771–1806) *Travels in the Interior Districts of Africa* led to an irate comment by a reviewer who condemned the author's compatriots who traded in slaves and human misery.[31]

Forewords were a common place to air opinions or underline the horror of the descriptions in the translated book. C. G. A. Oldendorp's (1721–87) book on the Moravian mission on the Danish Caribbean islands was translated twice into Swedish. In the first abridged version (1784), the editor cited a Swedish informant—just back from the Americas—to prove that Oldendorp's descriptions were not exaggerated:

> A Swedish officer who had served with distinction in the entire sea campaign in the most recent war in the West Indies told me that he had seen a French Officer in Martinique who while playing billiards crushed the skull of a negro boy with his cue stick just because of a slight mistake in the marking. The negro collapsed, and the officer said coldly: *I can pay for him.*[32]

A few lines from another foreword offer insight into just what a Swede might have known about slavery around the year 1800. Samuel Ödmann (1750–1829), the translator and abridger of John Gabriel Stedman's (1744–97) narrative on the Maroon wars in Surinam, underlined how accessible knowledge about slavery was in Sweden during that time:

> The translator imagines that most readers will find the cruelties against Surinam's slaves given account for here exaggerated, against nature, impossible. But he cannot support such a consoling thought. The information he has on the manner which the Dutch and English treat their slaves in the West Indies paints a picture that does not in any sense make these unfortunate beings' fate in Surinam unbelievable.[33]

While a list of quotations such as these could be made very long, the above selection gives an idea of the rhetorical strategies that were employed. The books in Swedish that mentioned slavery and the slave trade were critical.

Slavery on the Stage and in Poetry

While reading through newspapers in search of the above material, my attention was drawn to an advertisement for a play that was staged at one of Stockholm's theatres. Entitled *The West Indies Traveler, or Virtue's Reward [Westindiefararen, eller Dygdens Belöning]*, with the author given as Herr Björn (i.e., the playwright Didrik Gabriel Björn [1757–1810]), the play was an adaptation of Louis-Sébastien Mercier's (1740–1814) *L'Habitant de la Guadeloupe,* which was first staged in Paris in 1786 and premiered in Stockholm in 1791. I immediately started to peruse bibliographies and Swedish theatre history. Plays with slavery either as a central theme or in some way touched upon turned out to be common on Swedish stages, and several of them were successes. *Westindiefararen* was performed more than 170 times. Other plays included abolitionist dramas, such as August von Kotzebue's (1761–1819) *Die Negersklaven [Neger-slafvarne],* which premiered in 1796. In the foreword to his play, Kotzebue underlined that many events had been omitted from the performance in order to spare the audience. Such cruelties would be too gruesome to portray on the stage, but in the printed version, he was truthful in his depiction of the slaves' terrible fate.[34]

Some plays were set in the Orient, and the slavery depicted was thus Ottoman, or Oriental. But this did not stop the playwrights from referring to issues of the Atlantic world as well. Sébastien-Roch Nicolas de Chamfort's (1741–94) *Le Marchand de Smyrne [Slafhandlaren i Smirna]* was first staged in Stockholm in 1775, exactly a year after its Parisian premiere. Significantly, the Swedish translation of the title underlined that the goods traded were slaves. In the play, when the slave trader Kaled is criticized by a French prisoner for selling him as a slave, Kaled retorts: "But what do you mean? Do you not sell negroes? I sell you for the same reason. . . . Is it not all the same? The only difference consists in that they are black, and that you are white."[35]

We have little information about the theatrical performances, but judging from some of the preserved role lists, black characters were played by white Swedish actors, as using white actors only was the rule in European theatre at that time. Similarly, there is scant information on how these exotic settings were represented on the stage. Fascinatingly, the 1793 "pantomime-ballet" *Mirza and Lindor,* which was set in the newly acquired Swedish colony ("The scene is the island St. Barthelemy."[36]), included several slaves on its role list. Swedish slaves were thus represented on Stockholm stages for at least some productions.

The bibliography concerning slavery in theatre has recently grown, but there is no Swedish work treating the subject.[37] The large number of such plays and their performances, however, is just another confirmation of the importance of slavery in public debate. It is difficult to estimate readership of books and newspapers, but the commercial success of some of these plays is tangible proof that the slavery question was ever-present in society and, importantly, not only among the upper classes. The Stockholm theatres catered to a fairly varied audience, including the middle class and lower classes of city workers, such as shop assistants and craftsmen.[38]

Learned poetry could not be claimed to be a popular art form, as it was printed in small editions that catered to an educated and highly literate audience. A typical exponent of this tradition was Count Johan Gabriel Oxenstierna (1750–1818), who along with a career in government also wrote poetry. Among his most famous poems is his 1796 epic poem "The Harvests" [Skördarne], in which he in the sixth song eloquently criticizes the greed of plantation owners and merchants, pitying the African slaves who can never benefit from their own work. Nils Lorents Sjöberg (1754–1822) expressed similar thoughts in his 1791 poem "Commerce" [Handeln]. While commerce is hailed as the fount of contemporary riches, he criticizes the excessive greed that has created inhuman slavery, its worst aberrations being the slave trade and the plantation system in the Americas. Oxenstierna and Sjöberg are prime examples of how the antislavery rhetoric was expressed in poetry.

Reporting about Saint Barthélemy

Court poet and litterateur Carl Gustaf af Leopold (1756–1829), the reviewer of Clarkson's abolitionist tract, was a central figure in the capital's literary scene.[39] When he stated that slavery and slave trade were "generally less related to the advantageous conditions of our country," was he at the same time saying that Sweden had no connection to Atlantic slavery? It is impossible that he was not aware of the Swedish Caribbean colony. The acquisition of this colony in the 1780s was celebrated by King Gustav III (1746–92), who had been instrumental in the negotiations with France, and it was hailed as a triumph for Sweden. This message was repeated in Swedish newspapers. In 1785, the island was declared a free port, granting merchants the freedom to come to trade at the island. Both this and other royal ordinances were read in churches; and as a result, especially poor peasants from the Finnish part of Sweden started to inquire about the possibility of moving there. A rumor about a possible future in the Swedish colony started to circulate. So to stymie these rumors, another royal proclamation was issued, this time prohibiting moving to Saint Barthélemy without royal permission.

This episode made it clear that the dissemination of information about the new colony could have unforeseen consequences. Censorship had become progressively stricter during Gustav's reign; and though there is no tangible proof that news either from or about Saint Barthélemy had been censored, there are many examples of self-censorship by writers, journalists, and editors during these years.[40] It appears highly likely that any Swedish litterateur would have known that writing about the colony might displease the king or a member of his entourage. The public opinion was, as shown above, critical of slavery; and the many nobles and important merchants who were shareholders in the Swedish West India Company were aware of this fact. The company was instituted in 1786, and one of its professed goals was to trade slaves using Saint Barthélemy as a transit harbor. The king encouraged merchants to join this lucrative commerce. In *An Essay on Colonization,* Wadström succinctly summarizes not only his own interests but also those of both his colleagues and royalty: "But the truth is, that the King loved gold, my worthy companions loved natural science, and I loved colonization."[41]

Silence is difficult to interpret; however, the fact remains that after the flurry of publications celebrating the acquisition, there was very little news arriving from Saint Barthélemy. A brief period of freedom of the press followed the assassination of the king in 1792, but censorship was again introduced in 1794. The 1790s was a tumultuous decade in Swedish politics; and while the international campaign against the slave trade grew in intensity, it seems that the implicit prohibition on writing about Swedish involvement was observed. In 1793, news from France was restricted; and in 1794, it was prohibited to report on anything concerning the United States or French constitutions. The political reporting only restarted in earnest in 1809, when the Swedish constitution went through radical change and a modicum of freedom of the press was reintroduced.[42] During these two decades—sometimes called "the iron years"—the only news reported in Swedish newspapers about Saint Barthélemy were shipping and commercial news.

One of the very few publications about the colony was naturalist Bengt Anders Euphrasén's (1756–96) description of the island published in late 1795. Euphrasén visited the island in 1788, on behalf of the Royal Swedish Academy of Sciences, and he was instructed to investigate its flora and fauna. But as in other scientific travelogues, he included many passages on the island's population. Euphrasén wrote several pages on the island's legal system, which, as in all slave colonies, differed substantially from the public law of the mother countries. As soon as the Swedes arrived in 1785, they began adapting to the surrounding archipelago's traditions of controlling the black population, both enslaved and free. The first major Swedish slave law was proclaimed in 1787. Euphrasén was a perspicacious observer, who in 1788 already understood perfectly how this system functioned. He described it over several pages in his book, writing in plain terms about how slaves were punished:

> The punishment is usually executed in the following manner. The criminal is laid with face down tied to the wheels of a cannon and his legs stretched out and tied to two poles in the ground, his clothes are removed until he is nude, the one that hits him has a whip with a short handle, but the whip is 6 to 7 ells [c. 3 meters], he hits the nude slave violently from some distance, each lash sounds like a pistol-shot and big pieces of skin and flesh often come off the back. The slave has to endure 30, 50, or 100 such lashes according to the nature of his crime.[43]

In the beginning of the Swedish period on the island, slaves were punished at one of the island's forts, which explains the detail about how slaves were "tied to the wheels of a cannon."

Knowledge in Sweden of the black population's conditions on Saint Barthélemy was certainly not widespread during this period. Newspapers did not write about it, and Euphrasén's travel account probably never gained a broader audience. The only way for those in Sweden to assess the situation would be to apply what they knew about conditions in other colonies to the situation at Saint Barthélemy. This is what

Ödmann, the translator of Stedman's work, did when he commented upon the terrible fate of the slaves in Surinam.

Conclusion

During the late eighteenth century, due to the relatively high Swedish literacy rate, readers of newspapers—and sometimes books—were more common in Stockholm than they were in many other European towns and cities. The reading public there at that time could easily inform itself about both the cruelty and the economic significance of slavery and colonization. In addition to this group, we may add the theatre audiences, who albeit in a different and often less direct way, were introduced to some of the facets of slavery, both Atlantic and Oriental.

This demographic consists only of those who had access to sources in Swedish. The Swedish upper classes, where knowledge of German and French was common, could also become informed by reading the international literature on the subject. An example of this is French writer Abbé Raynal's (1713–96) famous colonial history, which although eventually banned in Sweden was nevertheless widely read.[44] While knowledge of English was less common, it was increasing during the period.

People like Wadström and Sparrman, for example, would have had ample opportunity before leaving Sweden to inform themselves about slavery and the situation facing black populations in Africa and the Americas. I have provided examples only from 1750 onward; but of course previous literature, such as geographic manuals, earlier travelogues, and so forth, was also available to the capital's educated inhabitants.

While the opinions voiced in the majority of newspaper articles and other writings were predominately against slavery, this critique never seems to have been addressed in conjunction with the fact that Sweden had its own slave colony. Censorship and the protection of political and commercial interests are certainly part of the explanation for this silence. Even more intriguing is how this silence remained the state of affairs at least until the debate on the Swedish abolition of slavery started in the 1840s, but that goes beyond the scope of this essay.

There were, of course, people who did know what was happening—first and foremost, the Swedish colonial officials in the Caribbean and the administrators of colonial affairs in Stockholm. The judges of the Swedish Supreme Court were also aware of the situation, as they had to confirm the island's legislation and sometimes preside in court cases that involved slaves.

It is probably unrealistic to pretend that the general reading population in Sweden could have connected their Caribbean colony, about which they knew very little, to the antislavery propaganda that had been present for decades. But Anders Sparrman could certainly have made the same analogous conclusion as did Ödmann in his foreword to Stedman's book. In Sparrman's case, though, it would have been based on personal experience. In 1784, when he was offered the position of government doctor at Saint Barthélemy and declined, it is possible that he did not want to partake in the foundation of the Swedish slave colony.[45] ~

Labor and Money: Wadström's and Nordenskiöld's Utopian Ideas

Ronny Ambjörnsson, *the Royal Swedish Academy of Sciences*

THE YEAR 1789 is one of the most important in European history. It was when the French Revolution began, which shook the foundations of Western Europe and in the long run would change the political map, but it was also the utopian year. The collapse of the division of France into three Estates created both hope that could not be realized in the immediate political situation and dreams of a way of life quite different than the aims of the leaders of the Revolution. These dreams had their origins in the intense discussion of ideas that had taken place in the decades leading up to the Revolution, in the debates that were had during the radical Enlightenment, and in the new religious movements that were being formed. Such ideological movements are rarely uniform, as they contain elements that are divergent from their original aims, thoughts, and ambitions and therefore can only materialize in another historical context. This was particularly true of the late-eighteenth-century radical political debate. The exclusive devotion to reason that we see in Enlightenment tracts is weighed against both Romanticism and utopian mysticism, which were fully developed in nineteenth-century radical movements.

Published in London in 1789, the Swedish utopian pamphlet *Plan for a Free Community upon the Coast of Africa, Under the Protection of Great Britain; But Intirely Independent of all European Laws and Governments. With an Invitation, under certain Conditions, to all Persons desirous of partaking the Benefits thereof. . . .* is a prospectus for a colonial settlement project. While authored by August Nordenskiöld, Carl Bernhard Wadström, Colborn Barrell, and Johan Gottfried Simpson—two Swedes, an American, and a Prussian—it is generally thought to have been written by Nordenskiöld alone.[1] This is a sketch for a free society, where political power is based on labor, and marriage is based on love—"the very Pillar of the Community." Religious belief is important for the project, since mandatory in the new community are the rules, as the disciples of Emanuel Swedenborg described them, for a New Jerusalem. As we shall see, their Swedish Utopia was wholly modeled on Swedenborgian concepts and ways of thinking.

Plan for a Free Community was printed in London by the Swedenborgian publisher Robert Hindmarsh. One reason for this was the rigorous Swedish censor, whom Nordenskiöld was constantly trying to avoid. Other reasons for printing in London were that there was an active Swedenborgian community there, and, more important, there was an interest in colonial business and expansion. For those who, like Nordenskiöld, wanted to set sail from Europe, London was the embarkation point, the gateway to the unknown world, with all its hopes and dreams. For both Nordenskiöld and Wadström, England was the ideal country, as ideal a place as was possible in a Europe dominated by an aristocracy that lived on other people's labor and was corrupted and driven by what these radicals considered to be "the tyranny of money" and "the lust for power."

Vanguards of Freedom

In her biography of Carl Bernhard Wadström, Ellen Hagen calls him "a son of the age of freedom." He was born in 1746 and grew up in Norrköping, a town south of Stockholm.[2] His first impressions of the world must have been from the intensive production and commerce that took place there. He graduated as a surveyor and was apprenticed at the Board of Mines in Stockholm, where he was to be commended for his work at the Falun and Dannemora mines. Wadström's social circle consisted of the sons of industrial managers, young men on their way up. He made several trips to continental Europe, filling his travel journals with descriptions of "practical inventions," from door handles to bellows. Of course, it was primarily ironworks, mines, and metallurgical techniques that attracted his interest. After taking part in several industrial projects, he was made a member of the National Board of Trade and was appointed senior manager of the National Precious Metals Board. His business career was marked by his continuous effort to develop the steel industry, reduce the export of raw materials and semi-manufactured goods, and encourage domestic production.

But Wadström's objective in business also had more far-reaching goals. In 1787, he traveled to West Africa at King Gustav III's expense to investigate the possibility of establishing a Swedish colony there. The project was abandoned, in large part due to his confrontation on this trip with the dreadfulness of the realities of slave trade. On his way back to Europe, Wadström stopped in England and testified to a parliamentary committee on the abominations of this institution. As a result, he was drawn into the abolitionist movement that was growing there at that time.

He went into business in Manchester, where he ran a textile factory. At the same time, he became known as an author, writing primarily about the abhorrence of human enslavement. Most well-known of his writings is the massive *An Essay on Colonization* (1794–95), an early classic in the literature on international colonization.

Wadström's criticism of the slave trade did not lead to any immediate success, however; and after his textile factory in Manchester experienced economic difficulties, he transferred his activities to France, where he opened a china factory in Chantilly. As a result of this move, he ended up spending the last years of his life in revolutionary circles. Shortly before his death in 1799, the Directory, which was at that time the government in revolutionary France, made him an honorary citizen.

Unsettling the Financial Markets

While Wadström's life seemed to have run quite smoothly, with optimistic up-and-coming stages between each setback and rift, that of Nordenskiöld is more difficult to account for, full of sudden changes, hurried journeys, and secretive intervals.[3] He turns up here and there, but for the most part he is on the move along a triangle whose angles are in Stockholm, London, and Nyland—the region in southern Finland where he grew up and where his family lived. His passion was geology, which he studied at the university in Åbo (Turku), Finland. There he went on to write his thesis on pewter and its constituent ores. As was Wadström in 1769, Nordenskiöld was apprenticed to the Swedish Board of Mines in 1773, where after only a few months he was appointed as a special officer. In 1777, in competition with considerably older candidates, he was appointed Assessor at the Department of Ore Investigation. What then transpired creates a picture of a young man on the rise in his career, hard-working and promising.

But that is only the official aspect of Nordenskiöld's story. There is another aspect, one that eventually was to overshadow the first. Nordenskiöld was an alchemist and was obsessed with the mission that he felt was his calling: to create gold from other chemical elements and to do so in such quantities that it would no longer be valuable. As he saw it, in the long run, this would lead to the collapse of "the tyranny of money"—that is to say, capitalism—by undermining the international gold standard. This mission drove him into a double life, one that makes him appear as a character in a sensational novel.

Nordenskiöld's problem was finding the time and money for his ambitious alchemical experiments, and his own money problems run like a thread through this strange story of his efforts to extirpate "the tyranny of money." In 1779, he applied for a leave of absence to study mining in central Europe, but he instead went to London. There he began to publish a treatise entitled *A Plain System of Alchemy*. He also applied to King Gustav III, through an intermediary, to return secretly to Stockholm and continue his alchemical research in His Majesty's service. The king accepted, and in the autumn of 1780, Nordenskiöld began his work in an unused section of the Royal Mint in Stockholm.

The following years were successful for him. He was alternately in Finland and in a house close to the king's summer palace at Drottningholm. His laboratory was moved to this house, and a loyal friend assisted him with the project. He also had time to work with theological questions, and in the Swedenborgian tradition, he prepared a treatise against the doctrine of the Trinity—the humanity of Jesus was conceived as altogether divine. He participated in the Swedenborgian circles, taking part in their discussions on colonization. He also engaged in debates in the daily newspapers; and in 1784, he contributed an article to the *Afton-bladet*, then a Swedenborgian journal, entitled "On how communities should be organized" (*Om sammansättning af samhällen*). This article can be seen as a rudimentary form of what would later become *Plan for a Free Community*. In 1783, he wrote the following in a letter:

> Here it is just a matter of endless determination and perseverance, developing one's ideas, running around with them, talking about them and turning the world upside down.[4]

His dual career situation, however, turned out to keep him trapped. Officially, Nordenskiöld was traveling abroad; unofficially, he was the royal alchemist, responsible only to the king and to the Governor of the Royal Palace, Adolf Fredrik Munck. His alchemical research was carried out in the strictest secrecy, and each step and phase was supervised. A draft contract in Munck's own handwriting regulates how this special undertaking was to be carried out. Nordenskiöld was required to hand over all his scientific manuscripts when the project was completed. He was not allowed to mention his methods or results to anyone else. He was not to receive visitors. He was not permitted to leave the laboratory until late in the evening. He was required to always be dressed like a farmer, with long hair and a long beard. He was not allowed to take a swim in the Mälar Lake, adjacent to the laboratory, without the governor's consent.[5]

As these conditions increasingly became a burden for him, he finally decided to escape. At the beginning of 1789, Nordenskiöld traveled to London, where together with Wadström and others, he published *Plan for a Free Community*. For the remaining years of his life, he traveled continuously, between Stockholm and London, with occasional visits to Copenhagen and Paris. During this time, he tried to remain on good terms with the king, but he must have understood more and more that the new life that he envisioned was not going to be realized in the immediate future. So his interests turned further afield. He celebrated the French Revolution by dancing on the ruins of the Bastille on the first anniversary of its being stormed. He regarded England as being nearly a paradise, and during this period, he seems to have become an international enthusiast for revolutions—a modest, Swedish version of Thomas Paine or Lafayette. In July of 1791, he wrote to his younger brother Carl Fredrik:

> Last year I celebrated the French Revolution in Paris. This year I am in brilliant company in Manchester, and we drink toasts that would have condemned us to death in Sweden.[6]

But, of course, Nordenskiöld was not just a revolutionary. He was above all a utopian thinker. The community he hoped for was impossible in late-eighteenth-century Europe. He wanted to build the "New Jerusalem," a community created not by human endeavor but by God, through his prophet Emanuel Swedenborg. Wherever he went, as long as the censor did not stop him, he publicized the divine program. With the same energy that he had previously spent on synthesizing gold, Nordenskiöld now spread this gospel.

In fact, he saw these two activities, alchemy and political activity, as part of the same mission—two sides of the same gold coin. In a pamphlet printed in London in 1789, *An Address to the True Members of the New Jerusalem Church, Revealed by the Lord in the Writings of Emanuel Swedenborg,* he explained these two aspects. Just as Swedenborg had revealed to us "the touchstone of spiritual wisdom," alchemy was going to reveal to us "the touchstone of material wisdom."[7] The first was going to eliminate what was ethically wrong; the second would eliminate what was against the laws of nature. In Nordenskiöld's rendering, the first meant loveless marriages and other relations, while the second meant "the tyranny of money." Nordenskiöld wanted to eliminate these two wrongs by building a fundamentally new civilization, one that would be based on *love* and *labor.* When he sailed from Europe in 1792, he brought bundles of plans, both in rough and edited form, containing information on how this was to be done; but he appears to have given priority to the haphazard idea of building this new society somewhere outside Europe.

The African Destiny

The great plan to establish a free community in Africa was not an idea that Nordenskiöld and Wadström came up with on their own. As were many other notions made by Swedenborg enthusiasts, it was inspired by the man himself, in whose celestial writings Africa holds a special position.[8] In Africa, Nordenskiöld thought, the Bible's original message had been handed down through the times, uncorrupted since the earliest communities. Swedenborg knew from the spiritual world that Africans were more spiritual than other pagans and that they were inherently more capable of easily accepting the tenets of his New Jerusalem.[9] Moreover, Swedenborg was sure that a new Enlightenment was spreading from the middle of the African continent out toward the coastal regions. Naturally, information of this sort, even if it referred to conditions in the spiritual world, was of immense value for those who were beginning to despair of the situation prevailing in their own countries. They could put their hopes on Africa.

Provinces of Freedom

In a strange way, these hopes were nurtured in the 1780s by the admittedly modest ambitions that the Swedish state then showed for creating a colonial empire. In 1784, Sweden acquired the West Indian island of Saint Barthélemy; and in 1786, the Swedish West India Company was formed, with Wadström and Otto Henrik Nordenskiöld, August's elder brother, as shareholders. As was the case on the other islands of the West Indies, Saint Barthélemy's economy depended on plantations, so the Swedish West India Company included slave trading in its program. This being the case, the Company was interested in West Africa, and its contacts with the Swedenborgians were thus very appropriate. At this time, August Nordenskiöld was in Finland, but Wadström devoted his usual energy to the new Company. He wrote a memorandum on a reconnaissance expedition and secured royal approval for it. In strict secrecy but at the king's expense, he traveled in 1787 to France and at Le Havre embarked on one of the Senegal Company's ships. This trip only lasted a few months, but it soon became obvious that Wadström's interests in the colonial project did not coincide with the colonial policy of the Swedish West India Company. The Company had in mind, of course, the triangular trade, which other European countries had so profitably carried on for more than a hundred years: firearms to Africa, slaves to the West Indies, and produce from the plantations to Europe—all on the same voyage. This was an exceptionally profitable trade route.

This apparently attractive scheme also appealed to Wadström. He seems not to have been such a sworn enemy of the slave trade at the outset, but he became one as a result of both first-hand experience and the change of course in economic and ethical debate at the time. In the British Parliament during the 1780s, for example, a fierce discussion was taking place between the supporters and the opponents of the slave trade. The latter, known as the Abolitionists, often made their case using moral arguments, describing the ideas of a law of nature, and showing the contemporary delight in understanding primitive cultures and ethnic groups. Their ideas could give rise to serious philanthropic projects designed to found colonies in Africa for emancipated slaves and Africans who had been transported to Europe. One such project was Henry Smeathman's proposal to found a colony in Sierra Leone that was to be called the Province of Freedom and was to be based on democracy and racial equality.[10]

Such was the environment into which we must place *Plan for a Free Community*: a London seething with different schemes and ideas, where the echoes of the Revolution's preliminary skirmishes were beginning to be heard across the Channel. In Swedish society, far from London, the unfamiliar growth of Swedenborgianism was the background against which we have followed the destinies of an alchemist and a factory manager. Up to this point, we have only glanced at what was happening around them. But how could Swedenborg's rather ethereal theosophy inspire radical politics and practicable community projects? Clearly these social reformers were not directly inspired by Swedenborg's scattered and brief ideas on how a community ought to be. Their inspiration came rather from the general attitude behind Swedenborgianism and from the underlying structure of basic concepts discernible in Swedenborg's mysticism.

Communitarian Vistas

Swedenborg's heaven can best be described as a sort of petit bourgeois artisan Utopia, with streaks of learned studies and spiritual delights. Heaven contains all sorts of workshops, an extensive administration, and a magnificent library with every sort of science and art.[11] The angels are exemplary family beings and know how to combine their work with learned conversation.

Swedenborg writes that the heavenly delights are based on doing something that is useful for oneself and for other people. The angels' whole existence depends on being useful in some way, and human beings are born to be useful to society. In his book *Conjugial Love*, Swedenborg states that social relations exist to be useful. Here he has in mind a usefulness in all the senses that he describes: from the heavenly and the spiritual to the moral and social, without which no community can survive.

An existing society can, of course, be criticized from such a point of view, as we may ask whether it is more or less adapted to take advantage of useful actions. Such an analysis of society was what the Swedenborgians attempted to provide in their journals and publications.

But one can also sketch an ideal society on the basis of usefulness. *Plan for a Free Community* begins with an argument that illustrates how Nordenskiöld considered usefulness as fundamental for a society:

> Society is no other than a conjunction, a combination of uses; or, in other words, of men formed into a vast variety of useful occupations. Its life consists of uses, and the perfection of that life is according to the excellency of those uses.

This statement recalls literally what Nordenskiöld had written in the Stockholm journal *Afton-bladet* five years before:

> A society is nothing less than a collection and an organization of useful activities. . . . Usefulness is created by those who live there and the quality of life depends on the quantity and quality of useful actions.[12]

In the Swedenborgian context, usefulness is a complex concept. For Swedenborg, usefulness binds all Creation in a sort of ecological system. It is to be found everywhere in Creation, in the mineral world as well as in the vegetable and animal worlds. All created things, living or inert, are useful for one another, and their exchange is "the root of life." In this way, Swedenborg regards all created things anthropomorphically, considering humanity to be a microcosm, or a miniature, of all Creation. But this image transcends the material world and includes both the spiritual and heavenly worlds. It is the sum of humanity's good deeds that constitutes goodness. When a human being does good deeds or works or thinks usefully, he or she comes nearer to God. God is for Swedenborg the perfect human being, and this is the basis of his radical humanism.

According to Nordenskiöld, the alchemist is the true human being, the one who consummates Creation's plan. More modestly, we could say he felt that human beings had a duty to process and transform nature. In his article in *Afton-bladet,* Nordenskiöld maintains that an inactive person is a body without life. He sees the connection between person and activity as sacred, as long as the activity is beneficial to humankind. A society constructed on these lines would, for him, be a paradise, the Garden of Eden of labor, "full of domestic animals and adorned with a wealth of trees and herbs, which appear to compete with one another on how best to develop the greatest usefulness." [13]

It is just such a dream of paradise that Nordenskiöld would like to implement in Africa. His goal is a community based on "an unbounded active industry, in what is useful." [14] This cannot be realized in Europe because there "political and economic slavery" currently prevail. Above all, Nordenskiöld sees two circumstances to be at the root of all evil: marriages not based on love—the moral evil—and "the tyranny of money"—the economic evil. By "the tyranny of money," he means the situation whereby the quantity of money in circulation does not correspond to the productive labor: "The root of this <u>evil</u> is exclusively that the <u>accession</u> of money is entirely independent of the <u>production of commodities</u>." [15] Money has become simply an asset, one of many commodities, instead of being a receipt for labor. Thus, money is now an idol that is worshipped all over the developed world, "the whole deformed temple of idols."

What Nordenskiöld wants to draw attention to here is the antagonism between labor and capital, which to him seems to be an antagonism between reality and illusion. It is symptomatic that he often describes this antagonism in terms of how "the true order of things" is opposed to "chimaera" and "lie." However, he does not relate this antagonism directly to general oppression, "the tyranny of one man over another," of which he is nevertheless aware. Instead, he sees oppression as the result of a personal attitude, that is to say, the desire to own and to dominate, which he in turn, according to the Swedenborgian tradition, explains as a love for the world or for oneself, which is evil. Nonetheless, he does describe contemporary Europe as a class society, where generations grow up to be either tyrants or slaves.

Nordenskiöld in no way suggests a classless society to replace the current order of things. On the contrary, his Utopia can be described as an inverted class society. Following Plato's example, he regards society as an image of the human body. Three social classes correspond to the head, the trunk, and the feet. But Nordenskiöld turns Plato upside down. The class, which is the term Nordenskiöld uses, corresponding to the head he calls "the Producers," which consists of those who produce raw materials directly from nature.[16] Since society cannot survive without this class, it is to be considered the most superior of the three. The other classes live from these Producers. The class that refines the raw materials, "the Manufacturers," consists of artisans of all sorts and comes next in priority. The last of the classes is "the Merchants." The status of the different classes is reflected in the distribution of political power. In the governing and executive assembly, twelve of the twenty-four shall be from the Producers, eight from the Manufacturers, and four from the Merchants.

Nordenskiöld consequently defines his three classes according to their relationship to the production of goods. He is not interested, however, in what they own but rather in their place in the chain of production. His plan hardly mentions ownership, and it is evident that for him the ideal society is one composed of self-owned small-scale producers. It is the rights of these that he wants to protect, principally against the manipulations of capitalist finance. He neither takes up wage-earners, which suggests that the working class has disappeared from this utopian society. As a Producer would be disenfranchised for accepting paid employment from the government and would no longer be regarded as "a private citizen," we might also infer that Nordenskiöld considered wage-earners and rentiers to be inferior citizens.

Wadström's Vision

Plan for a Free Community is a rather sketchy outline of the proposed community. As we search in vain for a more thorough treatment of all the problems that are involved, we neither find them in other of August Nordenskiöld's utopian writings. We meet an altogether different attitude, however, in this Utopia's other Swedish author, Carl Bernhard Wadström. Here we leave the visionary atmosphere and come down to a more conversational environment. Wadström's magnum opus, *An Essay on Colonization*, includes two maze-like volumes that are full of parentheses, footnotes, and associations. There we encounter in closer detail ideas found in *Plan for a Free Community*, which was published five years earlier.

As in *Plan for a Free Community*, the reasoning in *An Essay on Colonization* starts from the value of labor. Wadström confirms that someone who lives without working is of no use to the community. From this he goes on to criticize what he calls "the monied interest." Here he seems to refer not only to merchant business but also to capitalist finance in general. Wadström states that financial speculation, along with industry, has made us dependent to a degree near slavery. This dependency exists in different forms, from domestic service—"what we are pleased to style a gentle state of service"—to the slavery in the sugar plantations.[17] All this has made a few people enormously rich, at the expense of the working class.

Thus, in contrast to *Plan for a Free Community*, the condition of the working class is here treated. Capitalism's profit-maximization is consistently contrasted with the labor of the majority, in a way that shows that Wadström is aware that the object of speculation is labor. However, as in the earlier utopian writings, Wadström sees the world around him not as the outcome of a necessary and logical development but as a world of lies and illusions.

> In this unnatural chaos of money-speculation . . . in this forced and artificial state of things, could it be surprising that men should find their labours speculated upon, or monopolized, their time engrossed, their social and domestic comforts abridged, their persons degraded, their minds darkened, and their children brought up, as machines, to

spin cotton and grind scissors? And all for what? But to enable a few monopolists to accumulate *money*.[18]

Here the stage is set for William Blake's England, with its slag heaps and humiliated families with their emaciated children. We are reminded that Blake's poetry was written in the same Swedenborgian intellectual environment as were the writings of Wadström and Nordenskiöld.

Wadström directs his wrath primarily toward monopolization and speculation. But, more theoretically, at the center are the characteristics of the credit system, as described in *Plan for a Free Community*. Wadström writes that inasmuch as money has become a commodity, it has pushed out all useful production. This artificial, money-based credit ought to be replaced by a credit based on "a real knowledge of the useful ability and activity of men." He does not explain in more detail what he means by this, but a footnote in this context refers to a book by Granville Sharp entitled *A Short Sketch of Temporary Regulations*...[19]; and this gives us an indication of the direction in which Wadström's thoughts are pointing. Sharp's book outlines the constitutional principles for the Province of Freedom, the proposed colony in Sierra Leone. Here the political power was to be put in the hands of a self-owning agricultural peasant class. Instead of a currency based on the gold standard, payments were to be made in hours of work and registered in a publicly owned bank. Wadström refers to Sharp's proposal in the affirmative, but he does so without going into detail.

Two years after the publication of *An Essay on Colonization*, he returns to this idea, this time in a brochure addressed to the Directory entitled *Quelques Idées sur la Nature du Numéraire* . . .[20]; but here we learn that the reform is postponed. Ideally, money should be replaced by labor-inputs, he says, but such a change can only be made in stages; Wadström suggests that in the meantime, grain should be the security for a value-check currency. Otherwise, the language in this brochure is as it is in the previous publication. It is labor that is considered really valuable in a community, because work is what is useful. To consider money as the thing of real value is a chimaera that only leads to perdition. The question confronting the Revolution now under way is ultimately one of who shall triumph, the useful citizen or the despicable.

Freedom's Basis Is Labor

The great importance of labor that we meet in Nordenskiöld's and Wadström's writings can be seen against the background of the contemporary development of the ideas on political economy. The economic debate during the latter part of the eighteenth century is foremost characterized by the development of the theory of the value of labor. According to this theory, a commodity's value is determined by the work required to produce it. The theory of the value of labor is, of course, in the first place a scientific theory; but in the classical texts, the basic idea is often given an ethical bite and has ideological overtones that are related to the political debate.

One idea that is continually and emphatically put forward is that humanity's most valuable resource and property is our ability to do work and the very work that we perform. This is sometimes considered a sacred and unassailable right. As Adam Smith expresses it in *The Wealth of Nations*, his classic work of economic liberalism, "the property which every man has is his own labour, as it is the original foundation of all other property, so it is the most sacred and inviolable." [21] But this sentence might well have come from *Plan for a Free Community* or from *An Essay on Colonization*. In fact, Wadström often quotes *The Wealth of Nations* in his essay.

In this context, we should also take a look at Wadström's campaign against both the slave trade and slavery in general. While the classical liberals were, generally speaking, spokespersons for the interests of industrial capital against financial capital, they were fundamentally against the slave trade and against slavery as a social institution. Both were considered counter-productive to a country's economic development. Late-eighteenth-century England was the scene of a growing conflict concerning the purpose of the colonies: the mercantilists saw the traditional combination of slave trading and plantation agriculture as the source of the country's wealth; and those affiliated with the more liberal perspective saw the colonies as both exporters of raw materials to the mother country's industries and potential markets for the mother country's products. The liberal doctrine was not immediately fully developed. To begin with, it saw the slave trade as destroying a social structure that might have promoted the colony's economic development. Later on, it became evident that all sorts of slave economy arrest economic development.

In this spirit, Wadström maintains that colonies based on the mercantile system always tend to be dominated by some form of slavery. This is for him the inescapable consequence of a mercantile policy. A colony should instead be based on the production of raw materials. In the case of Sierra Leone, he visualizes a colony of small-scale growers of sugar cane. All of them, both colonists and "natives," should have access to advantageous loans from the colonial management. In this way, labor and freedom would replace sloth and compulsion. The economic structure of several of today's independent African countries may appear similar to Wadström's outline: an emphasis on the production of raw materials, with former colonialists and indigenous Africans on an equal footing under the economic preponderance of Europe. ≈

Enlightenment, Scientific Exploration, and Abolitionism: Anders Sparrman's and Carl Bernhard Wadström's Colonial Encounters in Senegal, 1787–88, and the British Abolitionist Movement

KLAS RÖNNBÄCK, *Dept. of Economy and Society, University of Gothenburg*

IN THE AUTUMN of 1787, three Swedish scholars—Anders Sparrman, Carl Bernhard Wadström, and Carl Axel Arrhenius—traveled from Sweden to Senegal on a mission of scientific exploration and reconnaissance. In Senegal, their scientific explorations soon came to an end due to a number of unforeseen factors. Instead, two of the men (Sparrman and Wadström) became observers of and witnesses to the transatlantic slave trade. After returning to Europe, these two scholars would give voice to what they had seen when testifying before special committees of the British Board of Trade and the House of Commons at a key moment in the history of the British abolitionist movement. In that role, they would make a contribution to the breakthrough of this movement in Britain that later would be cited and emphasized by some of the leading abolitionists in the country.

Christopher Leslie Brown has argued that the British antislavery campaign was built upon three different, but related, phenomena: the development of an *antislavery ideology,* the development of a political *abolitionist movement,* and the outcome of *power struggles,* in which this movement took part that eventually led to abolition and later emancipation.[1] The main aim of this article is to study how Sparrman's and Wadström's encounters in Africa contributed to the latter two of these phenomena: the development of the abolitionist movement and, most importantly, to the success of this movement in Britain in actually achieving abolition. I will argue that the role of the scientist in the Age of Enlightenment has been neglected in previous studies of the abolitionist movement. The case of the two Swedish scholars' contribution to the British abolitionist cause shows that a rhetoric based upon the status of science was one of the factors that contributed to the success of this movement. This sort of rhetoric complemented the *sentimental rhetoric,* which Brycchan Carey has shown was common among many other abolitionists.[2]

From the minutes and abstracts of these hearings, we are able to get a good insight into the two scholars' experience in Africa and the testimonies they provided at the hearings. Some scholars studying the Linnaean apostles have taken note of the fact that Sparrman, together with Wadström, were called to testify before these British committees after their joint journey to West Africa.[3] No historian has, however, actually used these hearings as a source for a historical study of these scholars and their contribution to abolitionism. This article therefore studies the testimonies given by these two Swedish scholars.

A Failed Expedition

Who were these Swedes? Anders Sparrman (in the British sources often spelled Andrew Spaarman) was one of the so-called disciples of the internationally renowned Swedish natural scientist Carl Linnaeus, having been a student of his at the University of Uppsala in Sweden. Sparrman had, by the time of this expedition, himself undertaken a number of travels to distant continents, including China and the Cape (1772–76), as well as participating on Captain James Cook's journey around the world, and had for that reason acquired some fame in intellectual circles.[4]

Carl Bernhard Wadström (often spelled Charles Wadstrom in the British sources) was an engineer by training, specializing in the science of mining. In his employment at the Swedish Board of Mines

(*Bergskollegium*), he had been involved in a number of important construction works in Sweden. By the time of this expedition, he had not traveled much abroad. On a more personal note, Wadström was also a part of Swedenborgian circles in his small hometown of Norrköping in Sweden.[5] Much later in life, Wadström would also claim that he had been one of the initiators of an abolitionist society—the Exegetic and Philanthropic Society (*Exegetiska och Philantropiska Sällskapet*)—in his hometown in 1779. Modern-day historians have, however, so far not been able to find much evidence (apart from Wadström's claims) that any such society even existed, let alone its activity.[6]

Finally, Carl Axel Arrhenius had made a career in the Swedish military and was by this time a lieutenant of the artillery. He had also undertaken and published scientific studies in chemistry, which presumably was the basis of his gaining a place on the expedition.[7]

Sparrman and Wadström—together with the third companion Arrhenius—spent three months on the West African coast, from October 1787 to January 1788. They were sent there by the king of Sweden, Gustav III, officially on a scientific journey of exploration and discovery, since "the king of Sweden [was] a great lover of natural history, of antiquities, and other curious subjects relating to discoveries," as Wadström put it.[8] Secretly, the king of Sweden also seems to have had colonization in mind when financing the project, hoping that the scientific expedition could contribute to such a project.[9] Due to a number of unforeseen events, the three companions were unable to cross the African continent.[10]

After returning to Europe, Arrhenius soon left his two companions and returned to Sweden. The somewhat cryptic reason for his early return was that his two companions had "strange motives" ("*mystiska syftningar*").[11] The other two Swedes returned to Europe through France, but eventually ended up traveling to London. Thomas Clarkson, one of the most prominent figures of the British abolitionist movement, wrote: "It so happened, that by means of George Harrison, one of our [abolitionist] committee, I fell in unexpectedly with these gentlemen. I had not long been with them before I perceived the great treasure I had found."[12]

Clarkson was already acquainted with Sparrman's travel account from the Cape: a translation of volume one had been published in

Britain just a couple of years earlier. In a book Clarkson published shortly after the publication of Sparrman's travel account, he had cited long passages from these accounts and commented upon them. [13]

The two Swedes arrived in London just at the time of some key hearings at the Board of Trade regarding the slave trade. Because of their supposed great knowledge of Africa, Clarkson managed to get the two scientists to be called to testify before the hearings. This would eventually come to be one small, but nonetheless important, step for the British abolitionist movement.

The British Committee Hearings as a Source

The testimonies of the hearings were taken down by secretaries and survive in the form of published minutes, abstracts, or summary reports. The surviving sources contain a varying degree of detail: the most detailed source is the record from the House of Commons, while the records from the hearings of the Board of Trade are significantly so. [14]

A number of people from various backgrounds were called to testify before the committees about the slave trade in Africa. Among the other witnesses, one can find people who were or had been shipmasters and merchants trading in slaves or goods on the African coast; various officers from the Royal Navy; governors from the British forts in Africa; a former chaplain on a slave-trading ship as well as a couple of ships' surgeons. [15] The two Swedes were the only scientific scholars that were heard. Anders Sparrman was to testify only once before the committee of the Board of Trade in 1788. Carl Bernhard Wadström would also testify before a committee of the House of Commons the following year. An additional source is a further testimony by Wadström, taken down and published by Thomas Clarkson, and a pamphlet on the same topic Wadström published himself. Finally, Wadström's personal travel account from Senegal was published posthumously in Sweden. The contents of the travel account are very similar to the testimonies Wadström gave during the British hearings, but are on many issues more detailed. We thus have considerably more sources related to Wadström than to Sparrman. When asked about the same topic, the two Swedes do, however, give very similar evidence. It therefore does not seem unreasonable to treat the evidence given by the two together.

We only know what language the two scholars spoke during the hearings in one case: Wadström's testimony before the committee of the House of Commons. In this case, the minutes state explicitly that Wadström asked whether the committee would accept that he answered questions in French, since his knowledge of English was "imperfect." The committee, however, denied this request, which Wadström accepted.[16] It is not recorded what language the two scholars used in the hearing before the Board of Trade. On the other hand, the records do not state that a translator was used. Wadström's posthumously published travel account was published in Swedish.[17]

The two Swedes based their evidence on a number of different sources. They had talked to slave traders, the French company's director in the region, as well as a number of African kings. They had themselves witnessed slave raiders leave and later return with newly enslaved victims. They had also visited the slave dungeons of Goree, seen the slaves themselves, and on some occasions talked to slaves (sometimes using an interpreter, sometimes in French). In the hearings, the two were often very clear about what they had seen themselves and what information they had gathered from secondary sources or from hearsay.

". . . such an infernal scene"

The two men stated that they spent much of their time in the coastal town of Joal in western Senegal. They also traveled inland up the river by the same name as well as staying on the island of Goree, at the time one of the important nodes for the transatlantic slave trade. Sparrman and Wadström also visited St. Louis, another French settlement which by this time was the home of perhaps one thousand European settlers, by the River Senegal, and yet another of the important nodes of the transatlantic slave trade.[18]

Visiting these nodes of the slave trade, Sparrman and Wadström became witnesses to how the trade was conducted. They learned that thousands of slaves were sold from the region annually. Just from the region around Joal, their informants told them that around 1,200 slaves were sold annually (even though Wadström later maintained that the figure might be somewhat exaggerated). From the area around the

Senegal River, they got information that around two thousand slaves were sold annually.[19]

One of the questions during the hearings concerned how the Africans were enslaved. Wadström summarized:

> Three ways particularly came to my knowledge, by which Slaves were obtained on that part of the Coast where I was [around Joal]. The first is what they call General Pillage, which is executed by order from the King, when slaving vessels are on the Coast; the second, by Robbery by individuals; and thirdly, by Stratagem or Deceit, which is executed both by the Kings and individuals.[20]

During the time they spent in Joal, hardly a day passed without the king ordering a new slave raid.[21] Wadström maintained that he had taken down notes about many slave raids. When asked, Wadström could therefore describe a couple of such raids in quite close detail.[22] On one occasion, for example, the raiders returned with a large number of victims—men, women, and children:

> The men, as they were brought in, exhibited marks of great dejection. One of them, however, appeared to be quite frantic with grief. [...] The women, on the other hand, vented their sorrows in shrieks and lamentations. The children, in state of palpitation, clung to their mother's breasts. Their little eyes were so swelled with crying, that they could cry no more. During all this time, the captors, to shew their joy on the occasion, and to drown the cries of their unfortunate fellow-subjects, were beating large drums. To this was added, all the noise that could be collected from the blowing of horns, and the human voice. Taking in the shrieks and agony of the one, and the shouts and joy of the other, with the concomitant instruments of noise, I was never before witness to such an infernal scene.[23]

This sort of slave raid was not uncommon. Often, they took the form that Wadström called "General Pillage," which were raids sanctioned by the local king. When the Europeans arrived at the coast off Joal to trade in slaves, the Swedes state in the hearings, they sent a number of gifts to the king of Sin. To show his gratitude, the king then was expected to return slaves, and was thus forced to sanction slave raids in order to acquire a large enough number of slaves to present as a gift in return. From the minutes of the hearings:

> *Did the king appear willing and disposed thus to harass his subjects?*
> No; he was excited by the French officer and the Mulattoes that accompanied the embassy, by means of a constant intoxication, to send out the above mentioned parties for pillage. [24]

Sparrman also gave evidence of alcohol as a driving factor behind the "General Pillage" before the committee of the Board of Trade. When they visited King Barbessin of Joal one night, the king was so intoxicated that he hardly could speak. As soon as the king was sober, on the other hand, he was unwilling to participate in the slave trade. [25] Wadström continued on the same topic, stating that the king—when sober—complained about the slave traders arriving from the island of Goree, presenting him with worthless gifts he neither wanted nor needed, and then expecting gifts in return in the form of slaves. [26] The European traders certainly seemed to have been cynical enough to try to exploit a king who perhaps was devoted to drinking as well as exploiting the local culture of gift-giving.

Royal slave raids were not the only sources of slaves. Individuals could and did also participate in slave raiding, through kidnapping or deceiving victims. The victims were then sold to traders from Goree. A French slave trader from Goree also told Wadström that they often used individual Africans to "go into the interior country, and steal as many of the inhabitants as they could." [27]

In the region around the fort of St. Louis, which Wadström and Sparrman visited after Joal, the most common mode of acquiring slaves was through wars. These wars were certainly encouraged by the French, according to the statement made by Wadström. The French traders again presented gifts to local rulers for them to provide the traders with slaves. The French agents also provided local rulers with both guns and ammunition. [28] This evidence, in particular, was something that many of the summaries of the hearing carefully noted. It thus seems to have been among the more interesting and potentially controversial claims made during the hearing.

At the same time, there were African rulers who completely refused to participate in the slave trade. Wadström gives one detailed and vivid example of this: the king of Almammy, who had prohibited all slave-trading in his country shortly prior to the Swedes arriving in Africa.[29] Representatives of the French Senegal Company nonetheless tried to persuade him to resume the trade by presenting him with a range of gifts. The gifts were, however, returned by the king. Wadström happened to be present at the company director's house when the gifts were returned: "[The Director] seemed very sorry that such a heavy expence should arise from the detention of the vessels in the River for so long without a cargo."[30]

The French company instead tried to bribe "Moors" to kidnap the subjects of the king and sell them to the company, so that the ships could fill their holds and leave. When the Swedes arrived on January 12, 1788, fifty people had already been sold and more were arriving every day they stayed there.[31] Most of these people were severely hurt by raiders' muskets and swords, Wadström told Clarkson:

> One of them was dreadfully mangled. His arms and shoulders were almost cut to pieces. Mr. ——— [Wadström] visited this man in the prison where the slaves are lodged, and found him a dreadful spectacle. He saw others also lying chained in their own blood, and in a very dejected state.[32]

Since the slaves were in so "dejected" a state, the company director asked Anders Sparrman to visit them, since he was experienced in medical science. Wadström also got the chance to accompany Sparrman to the slave dungeons. Wadström was horrified by what he saw: "Their situation was very pitiful—I found a great part of them, and particularly one, who was lying in his blood, which flowed from a wound from a ball in his shoulder."[33]

Such a cruel treatment of slaves was rather common, according to the two witnesses, not the least the treatment of women. Wadström described briefly an auction at Goree of young women "who were sold for acts of petty larceny, which scarcely deserved the name of crimes."[34] In a footnote to this paragraph, Wadström adds: "The treatment the [female] sex experience from the white traders on all occasions, is such, as decency forbids me to describe." [35] Anders Sparrman also testified to the slaves' emotional suffering:

> The slaves he [Anders Sparrman] saw expressed the greatest
> Concern and Apprehension at the Loss of their Liberty. Many of
> those he witnessed in his physical Capacity, on his feeling their
> Pulse and examining them, trembled with Fear, thinking he was a
> Purchaser, and would send them to the Islands, which they dread. [36]

Observing the slave trade seems to have made a deep impression on the two Swedes. This is perhaps most evident in the case of Wadström. In his personal travel account, he on one occasion wrote down his deeply personal response to the slave trade:

> A couple of days ago, a Frenchman bought a slave for 450 livr. and
> he believes that he can get 2,000 livr. for him in the West Indies.
> This Negro has a beautiful figure, and he is big. [...] I saw the
> wretched one, bound in chains, in deep thought, and—I sacrificed
> a tear on the altar of humanity. [37]

"Is that your serious opinion?"

When presenting their evidence during the hearings, the members of the committees were most interested in the two Swedes' observations concerning the slave trade. However, another issue that seemed to intrigue the members of the committees were their observations concerning African societies. In the minutes from the hearings with Wadström, we can follow the questions and answers:

> *What opinion have you formed of the capacity of the Negroes?*
> I consider their understanding as not yet being fully improved, but
> is as capable of being in all respects brought to the highest perfec-
> tion, as those of any white civilized nation.

> *What opinion did you form of their temper and dispositions?*
> They were honest and hospitable; and I had not the least fear in
> passing often days and nights quite alone with them; and they
> shewed me all civility and kindness, without my ever being
> deceived by them. [38]

The idea that Africans were not "fully improved" (presumably compared to Europeans) was an issue that Wadström had argued otherwise in his travel account (ostensibly written at the time, but only published posthumously).[39] The members of the committee seemed somewhat surprised at how highly the Swedes rated the Africans' economic development: they observed cultivation of maize, sugar, tobacco, cotton, rice, and indigo—exotic goods in high demand in Europe.[40] Many of these goods were furthermore refined or worked into manufactures by the local population—often very fine work indeed, they claimed: "they work in gold very ingeniously, and so well, that I never have seen better made articles of that kind in Europe."[41]

Wadström also claimed that the Africans he met "have an extraordinary genius for commerce; and their industry is in all regards proportionate to their demands."[42] That Africans had an extraordinary genius for commerce, and were on a par with Europeans in a number of fields, was one of the things that the committees would emphasize in their reports and abstracts of the hearings.[43] Still, it seems as if many of the members of the committees had a hard time believing this part of the testimonies. They kept coming back to the issue of African economic development, requiring further information on specific details: Do they dye and print their own cloths? From what are the dyes produced? Is their cloth neatly manufactured? How do they forge iron? Time and again Wadström explained and clarified, persisting in his statements.

But was all this not something that the Africans had learnt from the "Moors," the British members of the committees asked? No, replied Wadström: they might have learned it from the "Moors" once upon a time, but were at the time so skilled in these arts and crafts that they certainly could compete with most European manufacturers. This statement seems to have been very provocative to the people asking the questions, so provocative that one of them finally felt compelled to ask:

> You have said "that the Negroes work ornaments in gold so well, that you never have seen better made articles, of that kind, in Europe;" Is the Committee to understand that that is your serious opinion of them?
> Yes, in regard to fillagrees [sic], and even other articles; I have seen

buckles that could not have been better made by any European goldsmith, except the chapes, and tongues and anchors; and there are scarcely any officers at Goree and Senegal that do not bring to Europe some samples of such manufacture. [44]

The African societies were thus highly developed, according to the Swedish observers, but the slave trade prevented further social and economic development. The slave trade also made traveling or even working in the fields dangerous for the local population, since there was the risk of being kidnapped. If the slave trade were to be abolished, Wadström believed, these societies would develop rapidly, especially if some Europeans with an entrepreneurial spirit chose to settle among the Africans.[45]

In his travel account, Wadström furthermore took notice of the details of everyday life in the regions of Senegal he visited. He noted the practice of scarification; moreover, he was fascinated by African music and dance and described both in words and by an illustration the games that the people played. [46] He furthermore observed such details as the greetings the local population gave each other when meeting. [47]

Anders Sparrman was likewise asked questions about his experience of African societies. Unfortunately, the sources are not as detailed in his case, but one of the questions concerned the issue of happiness:

> Dr. Spaarman being asked if the Inhabitants of these Countries appeared to him to be happy? replied, Very much so, if Idleness, Ease, Plenty of Food, and few Wants, constitute Happiness. [48]

"The tide began to turn in our favour"

During the following debate about the slave trade and abolitionism, the evidence provided by Sparrman and Wadström was to gain a certain prominence. This was not least due to the fact that William Wilberforce had been deeply impressed by what the two Swedes had testified. In a long speech before the British Parliament, where Wilberforce was arguing in favor of a total prohibition against the trade in slaves, he cited the evidence of the two Swedes as highly reliable. Wilberforce argued that the audience ought to give more weight to their impartial testimonies than they did to different British witnesses, since the latter often had some economic interests in the trade.[49]

The evidence of Sparrman and Wadström would thus, at least according to Thomas Clarkson, sway members of the special committees in favor of the abolitionist movement. Sparrman's contribution was of the utmost importance, Clarkson claimed: "Dr. Spaarman was a man of high character; he possessed the confidence of his sovereign; he had no interest whatever in giving his evidence on this subject, either on one or the other side; his means of information too had been large; he had also recorded the facts which had come before him, and he had his journal, written in the French language, to produce."[50] This was at least how Clarkson remembered it some twenty years later, when writing his history of the abolitionist movement. That both Swedes made a lasting impact was clear to Clarkson, who summarized the importance of their testimonies: "The tide therefore, which had run so strongly against us, began now to turn a little in our favour."[51]

"These detestable markets"

That Thomas Clarkson remembered Sparrman's contribution in particular during the hearings might seem somewhat ironic. While Sparrman soon returned to Sweden, Wadström would stay in Britain for a number of years and take a quite active part in the struggle to abolish the slave trade. He got to know many of the prominent characters of the abolitionist movement, including Thomas Clarkson, William Wilberforce, Granville Sharp, and Olaudah Equiano (and is among the subscribers to Equiano's famous book, *The Interesting Narrative of the Life of Olaudah Equiano; or, Gustavus Vassa, the African*).[52] Wadström also published a number of pictures of the slave trade that he had drawn himself during his travels in Africa. These were printed in large print-runs so that the movement could make use of them as part of the campaign against the slave trade.[53]

Wadström's perhaps most important contribution to the abolitionist cause in Britain was, apart from the testimony before the committees at the Board of Trade and the House of Commons, the publication of the pamphlet *Observations on the Slave Trade*. Just a year after arriving in

London, the pamphlet was written and published, although Wadström apologized in the introduction for the hastily published product.[54] The printing of the pamphlet was partly financed by the abolitionist committee, spearheaded by Clarkson.[55]

In the pamphlet, Wadström explicitly positioned himself as an abolitionist. He was a zealous man writing about the slave trade: "These detestable markets for human flesh, constitute the last stage of all false principles; the greatest of all abuses; the inversion of all order; and originate solely in that corrupted system of commerce, which pervades every civilized nation at this day."[56] He did not censor his words, calling the slave trade an "execrable traffic," "evil," built upon "false principles." All those "in whose breasts there still remains a spark of humanity" ought therefore to unite in order to exterminate evil, and prepare the way for "*Goodness* and *Truth, in every human society*."[57] Substantively, Wadström mainly repeated what he had stated during the committee hearings, but he was now aiming at a more general public. Wadström thus not only remained an impartial witness to the slave trade; he also actively and explicitly chose to side with the victims by participating in the abolitionist movement.

Even though returning to Sweden, Anders Sparrman would also continue to make some contribution to the abolitionist cause. When asked by Clarkson, Sparrman willingly agreed to bring some abolitionist literature home to Sweden to deliver to the Swedish king. Sparrman was also handed a letter to be delivered to the king "in which they should entreat his consideration of this powerful argument which now stood in the way of the cause of humanity, with a view that, as one of the princes of Europe, he might contribute to obviate it, by preventing his own subjects, in case of the dereliction of this commerce by ourselves, from embarking in it," as Clarkson put it.[58]

The Scholars' Description of Senegambia and Modern-Day Historiography

Wadström and Sparrman were not the first European scientific travelers to West Africa. Some previous eighteenth-century scholars, such as Michel Adanson, Paul Isert, or Henry Smeathman, had also been more interested in studying ethnography systematically than the two Swedes.[59] A pro-slavery member of parliament, John Ranby, also denounced the evidence on the grounds that the Swedes, and Sparrman in particular, only generalized from a few odd examples (and furthermore examples from the French slave trade rather than the British).[60] On the other hand, Thomas Clarkson, in his history of the abolitionist movement, proclaimed that he had learnt more about African societies from Sparrman and Wadström than he had done from all the people he had previously met taken together.[61]

To what extent do their testimonies then correspond with what is today known about the history of the transatlantic slave trade in the region and of Senegambia in particular? On some accounts, the testimonies provided by the two scholars fit well with the picture that historians paint of late-eighteenth-century Senegambia. Wadström and Sparrman, for example, stated that the number of slaves transported from the coast amounted to some 3,200 from just two ports in the regions in question. The estimate by historians is that approximately twenty-four thousand slaves were embarked from the Senegambia region alone (including the fort of St. Louis and Goree Island as two of the important nodes) in the years 1786 through 1790. This amounts to an annual export of almost five thousand slaves from the whole region.[62] Sparrman's and Wadström's informants' contemporary estimates are thus not very far off from modern-day estimates of the slave trade in the region they visited.

The two scholars also seem to comprehend some of the social implications of the slave trade quite well. Most importantly, they describe the intimate connection between the slave trade and violent conflicts. The two scholars talk much about slave raiding, how the slave trade contributed to an increase in regional warfare in Senegambia in order to acquire slaves, and how Europeans armed various African parties, so that they could purchase slaves captured from wars. Many historians have found the same relationship between the slave trade and violent conflicts supported in a number of different sources, in many—if not necessarily all—parts of both Africa in general and Senegambia in particular. In the case of Senegambia, Philip Curtin claims, the main share of the slaves were indeed captives from slave raiding and wars, rather than judicial slaves (a practice he claims was more frequent in central Africa).[63] Carl

Bernhard Wadström furthermore explicitly argued that the slave trade was holding back African economic development by increasing the level of risk in African societies and thus depressing economic activity. Again, this is an analysis many scholars agree with.[64] Scholars have also recognized the high quality of much local craftsmanship and manufacture, including the Senegambian gold filigree praised by Wadström.[65]

At the same time, the two scholars seem to remain ignorant of, or at least silent about, many aspects of African society and history. To some extent, this reflects the questions asked during the hearings and the aim of the pamphlets published, which were focused upon the slave trade in particular. Against this background, many issues related to life at the European settlements in Africa or on the African continent at large might have been of limited interest.[66] Nonetheless, there are many issues directly related to the slave trade where the two scholars seem quite ignorant. For example, neither of them makes any reference at all to the connection between the slave trade and the transformation and intensification of domestic slavery in Africa.[67] On an even more basic level, they make little reference to the means of exchange, and only refer to a few of the trade goods exchanged for African slaves—most importantly alcohol and arms—but make no mention at all of the goods that historians believe to have been the most important ones, such as textiles and iron.[68] When describing the slave raiding, the Swedes also adhere to what James Searing has claimed was a common metaphor for Europeans describing Senegambia, namely the king raiding his own people—in this case further reinforced by the factor of alcohol driving the process of raiding. This was a metaphor, Searing argued, that Europeans later often would use as an excuse for colonizing the African continent.[69]

Colonial Encounters in the Contact Zone

P. J. Marshall and Glyndwr Williams have argued that European early-modern travel accounts of Africa initially gave much attention to the exotic nature of the continent. Starting in the seventeenth century, however, more detailed accounts of particular West African societies did become available for interested readers.[70] The descriptions, Marshall and Williams show, were often highly condescending, claiming that the African societies and people were primitive and inferior, but at least according to some writers capable of development if imitating the superior European ways.[71] Mary Louise Pratt has argued that a qualitative change in how Europeans would see indigenous peoples took place during the early modern period. In Pratt's view, it was particularly the work of the Swedish natural scientist Carl Linnaeus (and his work *Systema Naturae*, first published in 1735) which "would have a deep and lasting impact not just on travel and travel writing, but on the overall ways European citizenries made sense of, their place on the planet."[72] According to Pratt, the eighteenth-century Linnaean revolution led to what she has termed a vision of "anti-conquest" in much European scientific travel writing:

> [Linnaean-inspired] natural history asserted an urban, lettered,
> male authority over the whole of the planet; it elaborated a
> rationalizing, extractive, dissociative understanding which overlaid
> functional, experiential relations among people, plants and animals.
> [...] The system created [...] a utopian, innocent vision of
> European global authority, which I refer to as an *anti-conquest*.[73]

This "anti-conquest" would naturalize and *deculturate* many naturalists' descriptions of non-European parts of the world. According to Pratt, issues such as slavery virtually disappeared from European scientific travel writings as an effect of the Linnaean revolution's emphasis upon the writing of natural history (only to return again in the form of "sentimental" travel writing of the late eighteenth century). Indigenous peoples were furthermore almost never allowed to make their voices heard in the late-eighteenth-century accounts.[74]

One important piece of evidence for Pratt's analysis is from Linnaeus's disciple Sparrman and his travel to the Cape that preceded the journey analyzed in this article. If anyone felt the impact of the Linnaean revolution, one might expect that Linnaeus's own disciples did. According to Pratt's reading of Sparrman's travel account from the Cape, he adhered to the vision of "anti-conquest." Most of the account of the Cape is devoted to describing the natural history of the region. To the extent that the human world figures in the account, however, it is largely naturalized and deculturated. Pratt argues that Sparrman above all described the indigenous Khoikhoi as "bodies and appendages," denuded and biologized.[75] Colonial relations were also reproduced in the traveling party and the description given of it: Khoikhoi servants were never even given individual descriptions or referred to by their names in Sparrman's account, thus showing their subaltern status.[76]

It is not surprising that a naturalist such as Sparrman would devote much attention to the study of natural history.[77] Linnaeus often gave his "apostles" detailed directives and lists of what to study when traveling abroad. Given Linnaeus's background, these lists naturally included many questions related to natural history. They could, however, also include other issues such as local agriculture or economics.[78] In an article criticizing Pratt, William Beinart has argued for an alternative reading of Sparrman's travel account from the Cape. Beinart claims that Sparrman adopted much more humane positions, including an explicit criticism of the institution of slavery, an issue that Pratt ignored in her reading. Sparrman also exhibited a "questioning intellectualism" to a much higher degree than Pratt's reading shows, according to Beinart.[79] It is important to note that Sparrman's travel account was published many years after his journey, so it is probable that his writings reflect many years of reflection and consideration over—as well as certain obliviousness to—the issues dealt with.

As has been shown in this study, Sparrman would return with Wadström and Arrhenius to the "contact zone" eleven years after returning from his travel to the Cape, again with the intent of further scientific explorations. During their time in the "contact zone" in Senegal, the Swedish scholars certainly perceived the sorry plight of the African slaves and the horrors of the slave trade. As Christopher Leslie Brown has put it: "Slavery often was out of mind because it was very much out of sight."[80] Once traveling in Africa, the issue was no longer out of sight for the Swedes. They observed—sometimes with a stunning eye for details—how the slave trade was conducted and the miserable situation of the enslaved Africans. The Swedish travelers furthermore to some extent noticed the workings of the African societies they visited. The evidence shows quite conclusively that even though the Swedes were naturalists, and at least in Sparrman's case clearly following in the Linnaean tradition, they were in general not narrowly limited to seeing the world through deculturating "imperial eyes" only.

At the same time, there is one aspect in their description that deserves a comment in this context: the slaves were hardly ever described in close personal detail. Only the African kings, and on some occasion a more infamous slave raider—but never the slaves—were identified by individual names. The slaves largely remain nameless, pitiful victims. [81] On this issue, the evidence from the testimonies might seem to give at least some support to Pratt's view of a deculturated description of the indigenous peoples. Whether this *deculturation*—or perhaps rather *anonymization*—was a consequence of the Linnaean revolution is not entirely clear. The scientific study of human societies was comparatively undeveloped by the late eighteenth century, still largely an appendix to the study of general systems of nature. The methods of natural history—and its search for universal, systematic patterns to the order of nature—influenced how many scholars observed and described humans and human societies. [82] On the other hand, it seems as if the two Swedes also followed in an older tradition—reaching back to some of the oldest European travel accounts, and still alive for example in contemporary publications in the Royal Society's *Philosophical Transactions*—of generalizing stereotypes and searching for "national characteristics" of the exotic "Other." [83] In such a tradition, ignoring individual characteristics or personalities of the people talked or written about was not very surprising. It is furthermore noteworthy that the testimonies on this issue stand in contrast to how Sparrman previously had written about the Khoikhoi he met in the Cape. [84]

Certainly, the two Swedes were never exempt from some of the stereotypes of Africans so prevalent in European thinking at the time. For example, the scholars described the Africans as happy and skilled in many arts and crafts. At the same time, at least Wadström explicitly shared the common, patronizing view of Africans, arguing that they were less "improved" in their intellectual capacity than Europeans (even though they certainly could be perfected, Wadström added). He would return to the same line of thought in much of his later writings, including *An Essay on Colonization,* using this claim as an excuse for the necessity of colonization in Africa.[85] On this issue, Wadström's thinking reflected the idea of European superiority so prevalent in contemporary European thought, including in Linnaeus's hierarchical classification of the human races as a part of the classification of nature in general.[86]

Apart from this issue, however, the two Swedes make few condescending remarks about Africa and Africans. In general, and, in comparison with many other travel accounts from Africa, they seem quite sympathetically inclined toward the African "Others" that they meet or observe in Senegal. This was perhaps no coincidence. The disciples of Linnaeus constituted a quite heterogeneous group of individual scientists. Anders Sparrman in particular distinguished himself from many of the other disciples of Linnaeus, and many scholars have noted that Sparrman had been critical of slavery already in his travel accounts from the Cape.[87] Wadström, for his part, was involved in Swedenborgian circles while living in Sweden, and might certainly have been influenced by the positive description of African peoples and societies that Swedenborg had presented in some of his books.[88]

Hanna Hodacs and Kenneth Nyberg have argued that many European overseas scientific expeditions were transformative for the involved individuals: they set off as students, but returned home as scientists.[89] What the two Swedes encountered in Africa was perhaps transformative in another perspective: they set off as scientific explorers, but returned to Europe to become both witnesses who spoke out in public about the horrors of the slave trade that they had seen with their own eyes and abolitionist activists (especially in the case of Carl Bernhard Wadström), devoting time and effort to the abolitionist cause. To use Christopher Leslie Brown's distinction: it seems as if both Sparrman and Wadström shared—or at least were sympathetic toward—an antislavery ideology already at the start of their journey. Becoming actively supportive of the abolitionist movement was then perhaps a relatively small step.

Comparing the cases of Sparrman and Wadström to that of their third travel companion—Captain Arrhenius—is therefore perhaps illustrative. There is no evidence that he shared any antislavery ideology prior to the journey. On the contrary, he thought that the other two Swedes had "strange motives" when going to Britain instead of returning home to Sweden after leaving Senegal. That Arrhenius never seems to have shared in the antislavery ideology of his former co-travelers is potentially the reason why he did not support the abolitionist movement, but instead parted company with Sparrman and Wadström when returning to Europe.

Scientific Exploration and the Abolitionist Cause

There has been a long debate among historians as to the extent that the slaves themselves, as well as other economic factors, contributed to making slavery a less profitable institution during the late eighteenth century. Many scholars have agreed with Seymour Drescher in arguing that the organized abolitionist movement was a main driving force behind the process of abolition of the slave trade in Britain. Religious societies and networks, as well as bourgeois humanitarianism, all contributing to the emergence of this abolitionist movement, pioneered new techniques of political organization. Christopher Leslie Brown has furthermore argued that the success of this movement also included timing, requiring "rethinking the relationship between coerced labour and empire"—something, he argues, that became a reality only after the American Revolution.[90]

The hearings that Wadström and Sparrman participated in at the British Board of Trade and House of Commons were one step toward the political breakthrough of the abolitionist movement by the late eighteenth century. Much of the substance of Wadström and Sparrman's testimonies regarding the slave trade per se was, however, not unique. On the contrary, Seymour Drescher has claimed that few travel accounts of the eighteenth century failed to mention the brutality of the slave trade.[91] To the extent that the two scholars made any substantial contributions regarding factual evidence, it was perhaps in the part of their testimonies concerned with life and society in West Africa more generally. Philip Curtin has argued that during the late eighteenth century, the most prominent pro-slavery argument was "the intractable and unfamiliar conditions of tropical life." According to this line of argumentation, life in Africa was so degraded that even slavery was preferable. Many abolitionists eagerly sought evidence to counter this pro-slavery claim.[92] Here, the testimonies of the two Swedes provided more substantial evidence, when they claimed that Africans generally were civil, kind, and happy and that West African societies were quite advanced economically despite the negative effects of the slave trade. Since these ideas challenged the common contemporary image of Africa, it is not surprising that some of the committee members felt obliged to inquire whether this was the serious opinion of the two scholars. But even on this issue, the two Swedes probably could contribute little new information beyond that of many of the other informants (many of whom had stayed considerably longer in Africa) during the hearings. In essence, they contributed little or nothing new either theoretically or empirically to the development of an antislavery ideology. So why did leading abolitionists such as Clarkson stress the contribution of these two Swedes in particular?

Some of the abolitionists claimed that Wadström and Sparrman could be considered impartial regarding the issue of abolishing the slave trade, since they came from a nation purported or perceived to have little involvement in the transatlantic slave trade. This was to some extent an exaggeration. By the late eighteenth century, the king of Sweden had tried to enter into the transatlantic slave trade, establishing a chartered West Indian Company after acquiring the small Caribbean island of St. Bartholomew in 1784.[93]

The case of the two Swedish scholars illustrates a different factor behind the success of the propaganda war of the abolitionist movement: *the role of science and scientific scholars.* The journey to Senegal took place around the peak of the Age of Enlightenment. This age did not only produce a number of advocates of the Rights of Man—a discourse that sometimes included not only the rights of Europeans, but also the rights of Africans, and in those cases contributed to the development of an antislavery ideology.[94] The Age of the Enlightenment also witnessed the growing prestige and influence of both science and scientists.[95] This latter factor has received very little appreciation and attention by previous scholars studying the abolitionist movement, but is of the utmost importance to understand the impact that Wadström and Sparrman had.

Many abolitionists, from poets to politicians, made use of what Brycchan Carey has called a *sentimental rhetoric*—depending on emotions and feelings of mutual sympathy—in order to favor the cause.[96]

The testimony of the two Swedish scholars could have enabled a different and complementary rhetoric to be used, one less appealing to emotions and more to evidence, reason, and logic—in short, a science-based rhetoric. This was a form of rhetoric many abolitionists eagerly sought after at this time.[97] Sparrman and Wadström were both academic scholars of intellectual standing. They were also the only two people to be called to the witness stand of the committees who could lay claim to such a title. This clearly distinguished the two Swedes from all the other witnesses called to give testimony before the British committees. On account of this scholarly status, the two Swedes were thus well suited to take on the roles of epistemological authorities.[98]

Indeed, getting the two scholars to act these roles seems to have been the specific aim of the British abolitionists, both in advance, when striving to get the two Swedish scholars invited to the hearings, as well as afterward, when citing specific evidence from their statements. That their empirical evidence did not always live up to scientific standards—sometimes seeming quite non-systematic and impressionistic, not to say subjective—was in that context perhaps a lesser concern. Essentially, it was thus not the *content* of the testimonies as much as the *status* of the observers as supposedly impartial, academic scholars, which made their testimonies cited and discussed by influential abolitionist activists and politicians. Many of the people citing their testimonies favorably—including Thomas Clarkson and William Wilberforce—emphasized this academic background in particular when citing the evidence that they had provided. A pro-slavery critic such as John Ranby, on the other hand, sought to attack this scientific credibility by belittling the value of the evidence, emphasizing that it was made up of odd, non-representative examples.

In reality, the way the two scholars presented their observations was not always very detached from a sentimental rhetoric. Wadström, especially in his pamphlets published after the parliamentary hearings, made frequent use of these types of argument. This could also help to explain why Thomas Clarkson, when writing his history of the abolitionist movement later in life, particularly remembered the contribution of Anders Sparrman (rather than Wadström, who in reality seems to have put a lot more effort into the abolitionist struggle). In the end, it might have been Sparrman's particular status as a scholar, in combination with his less sentimental rhetoric, which at the time really stood out not only from Wadström's but also from many of the previous contributions in the field.

The abolitionist struggle required the joint effort of many different agents and forces at work, including the slaves themselves and a strong and well-organized humanitarian movement in Europe in order to succeed. However, in their role as representatives and voices of supposedly objective science, scholars such as Sparrman and Wadström could make humble but welcome contributions to the breakthrough for the abolitionist struggle. ≈

An earlier version of this research work was first made public in *Slavery and Abolition: A Journal of Slave and Post-Slave Studies,* vol. 34, no. 3 (2013). Published by permission.

The Swedenborgian, or New Church, Foundations of Carl Bernhard Wadström's Plan for Colonization in Africa

Jane Williams-Hogan, *Bryn Athyn College*

Deeply influenced by the religious writings of Emanuel Swedenborg, particularly his discussion of the celestial nature of Africans, Carl Bernhard Wadström (1746–99) and others formed an antislavery society in Norrköping in Sweden in 1779. This meeting changed the direction of Wadström's life, and he began to focus much of his energy on antislavery and colonization. Under the patronage of Gustav III, Wadström left Sweden in 1787 and traveled to Africa to pursue these goals. There, he made firsthand observations of both the slave trade and the geographical and cultural possibilities for colonization. He even sketched drawings of Africans at work, which he later used in his testimony about the African slave trade to the Privy Council and the House of Commons in Great Britain. The focus of this essay is Wadström's plan for colonization and the fundamental role that Swedenborg's new Christianity played in shaping both the values and the form of the new community that he envisioned. Some attention is paid to the sociological question of the workability of the Plan both then and now, particularly to its emphasis on the importance of the institution of marriage within the colony.

In 1792, Carl Bernhard Wadström reprinted a document titled *Plan for a Free Community upon the Coast of Africa* . . . . Originally written by August Nordenskiöld (1754–92) in 1789 and endorsed by Wadström at that time, the 1792 *Plan*[1] was somewhat amended by Wadström and, significantly, was published under his name. The first amendment placed the proposed free community specifically in Sierra Leone—a West African region known since Portuguese explorers of the fifteenth century as *Serra da Leoa*—with Wadström using the current Spanish spelling, *Sierra Leona*. The second amendment to the Plan was the addition of "Hints to the Reader," which Wadström wrote in four parts and added to the end of the document. With these changes, Wadström made this document a plan of his own. This is significant, because Nordenskiöld died in Sierra Leone on December 10, 1792.

In "Hints to the Reader," Wadström made four points:

1. Although the Plan was finished at the beginning of "this present year," the Embarkation was postponed until another year, allowing for more preparations.

2. The ideas presented in this section are contrary to common opinion, and thus the reader ought to weigh them carefully. The reader should also bypass the current standards of self-interest and pride as the measure of duties toward the Creator and the community—these destroy all "Ties of Union," which require instead that "good Uses, Order, and genuine Conjugal Love" in fact form the basis of Creation. For further illustration of this point, Wadström suggests that those interested should read extracts from the enlightened Emanuel Swedenborg offered by Wadström in a small work he published called *A sketch of the chaste delights of conjugal love, and the impure pleasures of adulterous love.*

3. Additional anecdotes on the natives of Africa, along with all that Swedenborg has written on the subject, are soon to be published.

4. Wadström would be interested in receiving any letters related to the Plan, and he gives an address to where they should be sent.

These "hints," as he calls them, make evident Wadström's interest in carrying out the Plan and that it should have a Swedenborgian foundation firmly rooted in the concept of "chaste married love."

❧

First, I would like to begin this analytic account by connecting Wadström with Swedenborg's teachings through a review of his biography from 1779 to 1792. Second, I would like to bring attention to the parts of the Plan not only that mention Swedenborg but also that are intimately connected to his teachings. In the process of doing this, I will highlight the connection between the Plan and Swedenborg's religious writings, touching on doctrines and some of Swedenborg's works that are foundational to the Plan, such as *The Lord, Life,* and *Conjugial Love.* Third, I would like to indicate why, sociologically, many of the Swedenborgian principles outlined in the Plan are sound ones for establishing a community, while some of the principles of the author's may be problematic.

Wadström's Relationship to Swedenborg's Teachings

Given our knowledge of Wadström's biography, the first formal connection that he had to the writings occurred at a meeting of Swedenborg admirers in Norrköping in 1779, a meeting that would prove to be life-changing. Prior to that meeting, there were several ways in which Wadström could have encountered Swedenborg's religious writings. Alfred Acton identified Wadström as a candidate in the Royal Academy of Sciences as early as 1766. In the mid-1770s, this academic connection could easily have brought him into contact with the Nordenskiöld brothers, August and Carl Fredrik, both of whom were readers of Swedenborg. August states that he became a reader of Swedenborg's writings in 1775. He soon was in correspondence with Gabriel Beyer (1721–79), an ardent Swedenborgian in Gothenburg, who had been put on trial in 1769 by the Consistory for his heretical beliefs, only to be exonerated by the courts in 1778. Beyer was well-versed in Swedenborg's works, and he could answer the many questions put to him by inquirers. Beyer may have alerted August to the trove of Swedenborg materials located in a chest at the Royal Academy. August converted his younger brother Carl Fredrik, who soon became not only a correspondent with Swedenborgians both in Sweden and in Europe but also a translator of Swedenborg into English. The Nordenskiöld brothers became extremely active in bringing to light manuscripts of Swedenborg's that they had discovered at the Royal Academy, and then they transcribed, translated, and published them. Since Swedenborg's works were banned in Sweden, this had to be done abroad.

In addition to Alfred Acton, the Board of Mines was another possible path of connection between Wadström and the Nordenskiölds.

Wadström was named an *Auskultant,* or apprentice, to the Board in 1769, with the right to advance in mining mechanics. In this position, he was ordered to work for the famous mining engineer Sven Rinman (1720–92) and also to oversee the continuation of the long-lapsed work on the Göta Canal near Trollhättan, a project that was started during the reign of Carl XII by Swedenborg and Christopher Polhem (1661–1751). In 1774 and close to the time that August Nordenskiöld became the superintendent of mining in Dalarna, Wadström became a stipendiary in mechanics on the Board of Mines.

Still another possible source of Wadström's connection to Swedenborg's writings was the fact that in 1776, he was asked to be the tutor of Adolf Ulric Grill (1752–97), son of Claes Grill (1705–67), someone with whom Swedenborg had business relations. Swedenborg for many years used the brothers of Claes Grill, who were residents in Amsterdam, as his bankers. Swedenborg was also invited to the family's summer home in Svindersvik, when he was living in Stockholm in the early 1760s. While there one evening, as reported by Count Fredrik Sparre (1731–1803), Swedenborg captivated the other guests with a discussion of his ideas about spiritual things.[2] In Wadström's capacity as tutor, he traveled with Adolf in Germany, France, Holland, and England. It is possible that during this trip he may have come across Swedenborg's writings at booksellers in both Amsterdam and London, or he may have been exposed to them in conversation with Adolf as they traveled throughout Europe.

In any case, by 1779, it appears that Wadström was already a deep reader of Swedenborg's religious works, and he had adopted them as his faith. What seemed to have been one of his primary interests in Swedenborg's writings were his teachings on the African people. In a reflection in the *New-Jerusalem Magazine,* which Wadström edited, he wrote:

> In the year of 1779 a Society of affectionate admirers of the writings
> of that extraordinary man Emanuel Swedenborg, assembled at
> Norrköping in Sweden, in consequence of reflecting on the
> favourable account this eminent author gives both in his printed
> works and manuscripts, of the African nations.[3]

It is clear that Wadström was not referring to a random sentiment here or there in Swedenborg's writings, because Swedenborg wrote hundreds of passages about the Africans. The following is an example of one such passage from *Conjugial Love* (1768) that Wadström used as an illustration in the *New-Jerusalem Magazine*. This material is found in what Swedenborg called *memorabilia,* which are events that he witnessed and then recorded from his experiences in the spiritual world. In this instance, Swedenborg observed a debate, arranged by angels, about the origin of married, or conjugal, love and its vigor and potency. Assembled were spirits from many of the nations of Europe. Each group of men—from the countries of Spain, France, Italy, Germany, Sweden, Denmark, Poland, Holland, and England—after discussing the question among their fellow countrymen, was asked by an angel to write down their opinion on a piece of paper and place it in a silver urn beside the gold table upon which sat the jeweled miter that was to be the prize. The angel then departed but said that he would return. Each group, in turn, submitted written statements, each piece of paper labeled with an initial identifying their country. The angel returned and then drew the papers from the urn and read them aloud. Then some men from Africa arrived, and they called out to the Europeans, saying, "Permit someone of us also to offer an opinion concerning the origin of conjugial love, and its virtue or potency." All agreed to let one of them speak. And so one of the Africans stood beside the table on which the miter lay and said, "You Christians deduce the origin of conjugial love from the love itself. But we Africans deduce it from the God of heaven and earth." [4] With regard to the question of virtue or potency, the African said that Christians deduce this "from various rational and natural causes. But we Africans deduce it from the state of conjunction of man with the God of the universe. This state we call a state of religion, but you a state of the church." [5] When he finished speaking a window opened behind the gold table, and through it a voice was heard, saying, "The [miter] shall be for the African." [6]

Wadström and the others in attendance at the meeting in Norrköping were impressed by this report and by many others, including some reports that claimed the following:

The African people are more capable of enlightenment than all other peoples on this earth, because they are of such a character as to think interiorly and thus to accept truths and acknowledge them.[7]

~

According to Wadström's recollection in the *New-Jerusalem Magazine*, the first aim of the conference in Norrköping was focused on developing a settlement "for a new and free community" somewhere on the coast of Africa.[8] However, it soon became obvious that this would be very difficult unless the slave trade could be abolished. As a result of the meeting, all of the attendees were resolved to address both matters.

> I esteem it as one of the happy events of my life, the being present on this remarkable occasion, and moreover to have seen, how wonderfully Providence has since disposed other concurrent circumstances to assist in promoting this grand design. . . . Before this memorable meeting was dissolved, every one present expressed his warmest and most cordial assurance to labour each in his particular station, unceasingly to exert his utmost abilities in concerting, and carrying into execution, a plan, not only for the abolition of the slave trade, but for the general civilization, founded on true Christian principles, of these uncultivated and hitherto abused nations.[9]

Wadström and his associates immediately petitioned King Gustav III to support the establishment of a farming and commercial community, but this was unsuccessful due to the international uncertainty, at the time, caused by the American Revolution. Another attempt was made in 1781, and this one was successful. The king granted them a charter on September 27 of that year with his "gracious consent."[10] They were, however, not "to affront and disturb others" by their undertakings, otherwise they would have no hope of the king's protection.[11] In addition, according to Wadström:

> By this deed, they were empowered to organize their own government, to enact their own laws, and to establish a society in all respects independent of Europe, and even of Sweden itself, by

which, however, they were to be protected, during the infant state of their community.[12]

During this period of his life, Wadström was not only dreaming of his colonization project, but he was applying his mechanical skills to develop a spinning and carding machine—the first of its kind in Sweden—and continuing to deepen his understanding of Swedenborg's writings. In 1779, Wadström was granted a monopoly by the Board of Commerce for the use of the machine that he had spent fifteen years building. That same year, he was also commissioned by the king to establish a factory for surgical instruments to be used by the army.

In 1781, August Nordenskiöld wrote to his brother Carl Fredrik about Director Wadström:

> [He] is one of the most solid receivers [of Swedenborg] of whom I know, and engages in much activity and conversation in all companies, wherever he can bring up the subject. He also gives his testimony modestly and frankly.[13]

In 1782, the king appointed Wadström chief director of the Assay Office. This office entailed considerable responsibility. All the while, efforts were being made to spread the knowledge of the "new teachings."[14] These efforts were, for the most part, unsuccessful. Thus, in 1786, Wadström joined with Nordenskiöld to form the Exegetical and Philanthropic Society. Initially, this venture was very promising, attracting many prominent members of Stockholm's highest circles, including counts, barons, and bishops. At its height, the Society had more than one hundred members. During that same year, Wadström attempted to publish and circulate books of Swedenborg's writings and collateral literature. He had good relations with the printer, who was willing to take risks, given the fact that Swedenborg's works were censored. Eight different works were published, including a catalog of Swedenborg's books and manuscripts. The catalog was prepared by Johan Beronius, ennobled Björnstjerna (1729–97), King Gustav III's librarian.[15] Wadström was the driving force behind the publishing efforts of the Society. He left Stockholm at the end of April to go at last on a scouting mission to the coast of West Africa with the support of the king. No new titles were brought forward at that time, although existing titles continued to be printed.

Members of the Society, including the king's brother Frederick Adolf (1750–1803), also began to explore spiritualism and Mesmerism, which led to attacks on the Society by the poet and private secretary to the king Johan Henric Kellgren (1751–95) in *Stockholms Posten*. The attacks were not made so much because they were printing material by Swedenborg or endorsing Swedenborgianism per se but because many advocates of the Enlightenment associated Swedenborgianism with the antirational forces of mysticism and occultism.[16] This did not bode well for the growth of Swedenborgianism in Sweden. The movement was forced to go underground and was maintained by devoted followers until the 1870s, when genuine religious freedom arrived and the church could have a public face. This, however, had little impact on Wadström, because he returned only briefly to Sweden in 1787 to report to the king about the expedition to the west coast of Africa—and perhaps to bring additional manuscripts of Swedenborg's abroad to publish.

When he returned to London toward the end of 1788, one of the first things Wadström did was to become baptized into the New Church on Christmas day. That event seemed to spur a period of intense involvement with the New Church in London. As already mentioned, he became an editor of the London *New-Jerusalem Magazine*. While only four issues were published, it was nonetheless an impressive achievement and is noted as being the first Swedenborgian journal in the English-speaking world. At this time, he also became deeply involved with both antislavery and colonization efforts in England, and he gave many pages of testimony to the Privy Council, the Board of Trade, and the House of Commons.

⮌

At the end of 1790, Gustav III made it clear to Wadström that he must return from his leave of absence or resign his post as director of the Assay Office. Expecting to leave for Africa very soon, he chose to resign. He soon learned that the Parliamentary Charter for the new African venture was not to be granted in the near future, so he decided to start a cotton factory in Manchester. It was at this time that he married Ulrika Westerberg, a young woman from Norrköping, whose father was a wealthy wholesale merchant. In May of 1791, Wadström worked from Manchester on the last issue of the *New-Jerusalem Magazine,* and then he devoted his energies to his business, hoping that it would serve as a model for future enterprises in Africa.

The French Revolution of 1789 led to war with England in 1793, and it brought with it the disruption of the cotton trade and so the ruin of Wadström's enterprise. This blow to his venture came on top of the death of his dear friend August Nordenskiöld in 1792. When his daughter was born in 1793, Wadström honored Nordenskiöld by naming her Carolina Augusta. She was baptized, according to Acton, most probably at the New Church in Great Eastcheap, and William Wilberforce was her godfather.[17] In the following year, his important work *An Essay on Colonization* was published, at great expense. The cost was not fully covered by subscription, requiring Wadström to assign the work to the printer in order to cover the expenses, without any profit for himself. This and other factors led him to go to France in 1795, where he continued both his antislavery work and the pursuit of his colonization plan. Ever active and again in some economic distress, he fell victim to consumption and died on April 6, 1799.

The Swedenborgian Foundations of the Colonization Plan

While the introductory section of the Plan includes many concepts taken directly from Swedenborg's religious writings, the advertisement at the beginning of the actual Plan specifically mentions Swedenborg and his "remarkable Anecdotes in regard to the Natives of Africa" that could not be published in that work. The reader is appraised, though, of Wadström's intent "soon to publish, as a Companion to this Work, all that the Honourable Emanuel Swedenborg has written upon this important subject, as well in those Works of his which are published, as in sundry Manuscripts, wherein he has been still more particular."[18]

These remarks highlight the indisputable fact that the central inspiration for the vision of the Plan, and the necessity to abolish the African slave trade as key to its realization, came from Swedenborg's commentary on Africa and Africans in his religious writings. It is my contention, however, that not only was the vision inspired by Swedenborg but that much of the essential framework of the Plan originated in his works. Among many other concepts and ideas taken from Swedenborg's teachings, the doctrines of the Lord, use, and love most clearly animate the Plan. Altogether there are at least seventy instances in the Plan where references are made to concepts or teachings from Swedenborg (e.g., the use of numbers with significant correspondences, such as four and twelve). It would be difficult to discuss them all in an article of this size and scope, so I will choose a number of significant ones to illustrate the Swedenborgian foundation. The discussion will focus on the Lord, use, and conjugal love.

The Lord

In discussing the active power of a free community, the Plan states:

> The grand Council Board is to be thus disposed: At the East end must stand a chair of state upon a throne, with the HOLY WORD upon it, to signify that there is no King in this Community but the LORD JESUS CHRIST, whose Divine Will and Wisdom are revealed to Mankind by the Word. Before this chair, on the table, must lie the Laws of the Community, which are founded upon the Word.[19]

Here it is plain that the Lord Jesus Christ is the governor or supreme ruler of the community and that he is the source of its order. The laws of the land are drawn from him through his Word, and they are subordinate to him. This concept is drawn from *The Lord* §1, which is headed "The Entire Sacred Scripture Is about the Lord, and the Lord Is the Word."

This concept is reinforced in section IX ("On the best Religion in a Community"[20]) of the section of the Plan called "OBSERVATIONS." The doctrine of the New Jerusalem Church revealed by Swedenborg is called the best because, first and foremost, it states "THAT NO OTHER GOD EXISTETH IN HEAVEN OR ON EARTH, BUT THE LORD JESUS CHRIST" and that "this is founded on the three following Principles, (1.) That there is only One God. (2.) That Jesus Christ is his only Son, or the Manifestation of that God. (3.) That He and the Father are One, just as the Body and Soul in Man are One."[21] This is also taught throughout *The Lord,* but a specific reference can be made to §45, which is headed "God Is One, and the Lord Is God." This idea is foundational to Swedenborg's religious writings. It is discussed in the very beginning of *True Christianity,* for example, in order to mend the idea of God that was current in the Christian world:

> This mending will occur when human reason is convinced from the Word and its light that there is a divine Trinity [and] that it exists within the Lord God the Savior Jesus Christ like the soul, the body, and the effect of one person.[22]

Swedenborg goes on concerning the state:

> The very essence and soul of everything in a comprehensive theology is the acknowledgment of God [arising] from a concept of him.[23]

Thus, it is not surprising that the Plan continues by saying:

> In a Political sense this may be considered as meriting the first rank in the point of Utility in a Community; for can any *Religion* have such a tendency to connect Society together in one band of Union, as that which inculcates the Worship of One Visible God in a Human Form, and as One Person? In such a Community no despotic Monarch is requisite to keep together the many thousands of individuals of which it may consist. Their God, their King, their First Man is the same.[24]

With these teachings in mind, it is important to note that according to *Plan for a Free Community,* there are four chief magistrates—two who guide the people and two who guide the country—not just one. The organizational focus appears to be modeled on the concept of marriage, which will be discussed more fully in the section on conjugal love.

Use

From my perspective as a sociologist, it is delightful to read on the first page of *Plan for a Free Community*—under the first heading,

"COMMUNITY"—the idea that "nothing is more confirmed by experience than that [Humanity] is born for Society; and that thence [it] derives all [its] Happiness, or all [its] Misery."[25] According to Swedenborg, unlike animals, human beings do "not have any knowledge inborn in [them], but only a capacity and inclination for acquiring such things as have to do with knowledge and love. And if [they do] not acquire them from *others*, [they remain] worse off than an animal" (emphasis mine).[26] Swedenborg continues that human beings are born without such innate capacities, "to the end that [they] may attribute everything not to [themselves] but to others, and finally may attribute everything of wisdom and of the love thereof to God alone and may thereby be able to become an image of God."[27]

Clearly to become human requires others and otherness. As I wrote in "The Swedenborgian Perspective on the Social Ideal: Society in Human Form,"

> Human beings are not social as an afterthought, or when they want to be, or when they think about it; human beings are social as such. To be an individual means that one is, or was at some point in time, a member of a group; to be a member of a group means that one is expected to do one's part, which is to be an individual. Self and other are inextricably bound together, and are inherently reciprocal. They can only be defined in terms of each other. The one requires the other to exist. The two form one whole, which socially cannot be separated, even though any particular self, once socialized, can discard all others as unessential. This reciprocity is the foundation of society, understanding the meaning of this reality is the key to our humanity.[28]

Suggesting that reciprocity is the foundation of society is perhaps another way of stating what is found in the very next paragraph of the section on "COMMUNITY":

> Society is no other than a Conjunction, a Combination of Uses; or, in other words, of [Human Beings] formed into a vast variety of useful Occupations. Its Life consists of Uses, and the perfection of that Life is according to the excellency of those Uses, and at the same time according to their multiplicity.[29]

The perfection of society, according to Swedenborg, is found in the wonderful truth that society has a human form. Since this is true in heaven, it should be true among the peoples of the earth. In *Heaven and Hell*, he states that:

> It is a secret not yet known in this world that heaven, taken in a single all-inclusive grasp, reflects a single individual. . . . Since angels do know that all the heavens, like their communities, reflect a single individual, they refer to heaven as *the universal and divine human*— "divine" because the Lord's divine nature constitutes heaven. [30]

This thought is echoed in the Plan, in the very next paragraph:

> The Strength of Society consists in the order and connection of those Uses, in one Form or body, and the Perfection of it is according to the ordination and subordination thereof. The Form of Society derives all its excellence and beauty therefrom. For what is the Form without Strength, or Strength without Life? Consequently the more numerous and various the parts, and the greater the harmony subsisting among them, the more perfect and complete is the whole; like the human body, whose components are innumerable, but whose action is unanimous. [31]

According to the Plan, the prosperity of the people springs from the useful employment of each person's will and understanding. Thus, it is imperative to cultivate "those two supreme faculties, which constitute the very Life of Man." [32]

The performance of uses requires individuals, groups, associations, collectives, or—in the words of the Plan—people. And according to the Plan, those people require, in the final analysis, a country. Wadström sees this relationship between the people and the country as reciprocal. The people require both cultivation and order, as does the country. The people require cultivation—or, in more sociological terms, socialization—because, as stated earlier, they have "only a capacity and inclination for acquiring such things as have to do with knowledge and love." Their minds, or their understanding, need to become vessels of truth, and their hearts, identified with their will, need to become vessels for doing good.

Thus, to become truly human, they need to be socialized spiritually, socially, and bodily. Or, as the Plan also states, they require instruction in religion, education, and health. These are essential useful tasks that need to be performed by members of the community for the sake of the people, as a whole, and for the well-being of the country.

⟿

In order to instruct the understanding, freedom is essential. In section II of "OBSERVATIONS," Wadström notes that "in all happy Communities, *Liberty* and *Intellectual Light* must exist." [33] He also believed that while liberty requires contracts bound by mutual agreements that specify rewards and punishments, intellectual light, on the other hand, requires that the understanding be unconfined. Thus, everyone is permitted "to speak, to write, and to print whatever [they please], as well against as for the Religion or the Laws of the Community." [34] The will, as it darts into action, however, "should be rigorously bridled by the Laws, and by the stipulated Contracts, otherwise the Community could not be kept together." [35]

In the passage below, Wadström cites principles almost directly from Swedenborg's writings:

> It is agreeable to Divine Order that Man ought to compel himself in regard to his *Will*; but that the *Mind* may freely think both against or for God: but who can think freely, if he is not at Liberty to speak, write, and print freely? This Order is founded on the Combination of *Causes* and *Effects*, wherein *Efflux* ought always to follow upon *Influx*, else the latter is stopped, and Man in the same proportion degenerates into stupidity. [36]

In *Divine Providence* §129, which is headed "It Is a Law of Divine Providence That We Should Not Be Compelled by Outside Forces to Think and Intend and So to Believe and Love in Matters of Our Religion, but That We Should Guide Ourselves and Sometimes Compel Ourselves," Swedenborg elaborates, considering topics that are related to freedom, external compulsion, and self-compulsion:

No one is reformed by threats or by punishment, because they compel. No one is reformed in states where freedom and rationality are absent. Self-compulsion is not inconsistent with rationality and freedom. Our outer self has to be reformed by means of our inner self, and not the reverse. [37]

It is possible that Wadström's discussion on *efflux* and *influx* was drawn from a discussion in *True Christianity,* where Swedenborg explains that in a country where freedom of expression is restrained by the government, freedom of thought is likewise restrained. He likens it to a

fountain with a basin of such high sides that the water level in the basin is actually above the point at which the stream of water comes out, so that what should be a jet of water leaping up in the air does not even break the surface of the water standing in the basin. In this analogy, the stream of water symbolizes what people think, and the basin of standing water symbolizes what they say.

Briefly put, what flows in adapts itself to fit what flows out. Our higher understanding, then, adapts itself to fit the amount of freedom there is to say and do what we are considering. [38]

While proposing the development of the will and understanding of the people, Wadström, in order to interiorly develop the human "raw material" for a productive society, was aware that it was necessary for the people to be open to shunning evils as sins against God. In his consideration of religion, as it relates to the cultivation of the people, he states that "the Will is led to do good only in Proportion as Evil is removed; consequently, the true object of all Religion is to shun Evils as Sins against God, which cannot be done without Humility, and Obedience to his Commandments." [39]

In *Apocalypse Revealed,* we find the following discussion of shunning evils as sins against God:

All these falsities exist in those who do not do the work of repentance, that is, shun evils as sins against God.

These things are signified in the spiritual sense by idols which
were graven images and molten images [found in countless passages
in the Old Testament].[40]

Wadström is interested in the interior order of the people, and this
can be achieved by setting forth the laws that must be mutually observed
for the sake of the community. These laws are found in the contracts
outline in the third section of "OBSERVATIONS." Wadström states that
there are "two most essential Contracts. The first and most important of
all *Contracts* in a Community is the *Decalogue*, which teaches, (1.) Not to
worship more than One God."[41] And then he goes on to list the remaining nine in abbreviated form, ending with "(10.) That he who indulges
the proud desire of domineering over others, yields himself up to the
devilish Principle which deprives him of all genuine Liberty."[42]

"The second and like sacred *Contract* is that which should subsist
between the *Man* and the *Woman* in every Marriage in this Community."[43] With regard to this contract, Wadström includes a very interesting list of ten items, which I will address later when I turn to the
discussion of marriage. What is important to note here, though, is the
last statement in this section:

> No Person ought to be permitted to participate in the protection
> and privileges of this State, but such as sign both these *Contracts*,
> and promise sincerely and faithfully to live according to them; the
> former in common Life, and the latter within his own Family.[44]

It would seem that if someone were to sign the above two contracts,
then they would be able to be part of the compact between the people
and the government. For that compact to work, there needs to be:

> (1.) The *Spiritual Alliance* of a Community, which is between the
> Lord and his Church ... (2.) The *Conjugal Alliance* of the Commu-
> nity, which is between the Sexes, or between the Understanding in
> the Man and the Will in the Woman; or, Man's Wisdom and
> Woman's Love, because upon this depends entirely the improvement
> of the very elements in all Communities ... (3.) The *Civil Alliance* in
> a Community, which is between the People and the Country.[45]

These alliances are essential "before anyone can be competent for composing a Constitution."[46]

In a way, one could see these contracts as measures of mutual good will and charity that Wadström felt were necessary to bond the people together in the new and common enterprise of founding a new country and a new civilization. These agreements form the basis through which a community could devote itself to useful activities, both spiritual and material: from worship, education, and healthy well-being to the cultivation of raw materials out of which one could manufacture goods to trade within the community and with nations outside the community. Government with judicial, political, and economic functions is required to maintain the well-being and integrity of the community; and in order to protect the community in the world at large, government must have a military, a financial system, and an office of foreign affairs.

All of the above are examples of useful activity from or within a Swedenborgian framework. Wadström puts at the forefront his understanding that God designed the universe for the purpose of accomplishing these types of useful actions. In his pamphlet on the Swedenborgian concept of "usefulness," Wilson Van Dusen expressed that the universe is not only a place of useful activity—in Swedenborgian terms, a "use"—but "even series within series of uses. Our bodily form is an example of this; hence, we are an image of the whole. Swedenborg uses 'man' or 'Grand Man' or the 'Divine Human' as the form of all uses."[47] As stated in *Divine Love and Wisdom:*

> At this point I need only . . . to call attention to the fact that God as
> a person is the very form suited to all kinds of [use], the one in
> whom all useful functions in the created universe find their source.
> This means that in terms of its useful functions, the created
> universe is an image of God.
>
> By "useful functions," I mean those processes that were created
> by . . . the Lord, as part of the design. I do not mean activities that
> derive from our own self-concern. That concern is hell, and its
> activities violate the design.[48]

As Wadström stated that "the very life of Civil Society is Marriage,"[49] it would now be useful to turn attention more specifically to it.

Conjugal Love

In the introduction to *Plan for a Free Community*, Wadström describes what he saw as the state of marriages in all the communities of Europe. He writes:

> Marriages constitute the very elements of Society, and every Marriage is a representative, in miniature, of the Civil Society in its principles or beginnings. In every Community we find great multitudes of Men mature for Marriage, who remain unmarried, and rove about the Community, like robbers, only serving to promote the Anti-conjugal Life; likewise vast multitudes of Women, designed by creation to constitute the felicity of Men, wholly neglected by the Community, and passing their time in a criminal indolence, and many in the miseries of prostitution, without ever tasting the pure endearments of affectionate Wives and tender Mothers. But this is not all; how affecting is it to come nearer, and reflect upon the present state of Marriage Unions; instead of considering them, as they should be, the most intimate and strongest ties, as the very Pillars of the Community, we find them in general the most neglected, and considered as the most insignificant and unsafe ties. It is distressing to observe it, but Marriages in their present state are but Seminaries for a corrupt Generation; instead of a sincere Friendship, which ought to subsist in the Union, we find nothing but Indifference, proceeding from dissimulation; instead of Liberty, Constraint; instead of tender Love, cold Disgust. [50]

Wadström makes the observation that prior to the emergence of nation states or civil societies, people lived in what he called "conjugal societies." He made the further observation that those conjugal societies can exist without the aid of civil societies, but civil societies cannot continue without the support of marriages. He is convinced that all the goodness and order of society derive from marriages. Thus, if the state of marriages in a society is strong, then the community itself is strong. However, if the reverse is the case, then:

> Without the Spirit of Prophecy, that Society draws nigh to its destruction, and so much the faster, as its higher Members are

found living in such [an Anti-conjugal] manner. . . . But this is not all; Marriages are unhappy, the Anti-conjugal Life is common, in all its enormously deadly branches, and the moral and political Evils from these baneful sources are continually extending their over-whelming destruction like a flood. [51]

Given Wadström's dire sense of the state of marriage in Europe, it would be worthwhile to first explore Swedenborg's perspective in *Conjugial Love* and then report on the marriage contract mentioned earlier, examining how Wadström hoped it would remedy the situation and lead to the flowering of successful, healthy, and happy communities.

Perhaps the clearest view of the state of marriage in Swedenborg's day can be found in an observation he made and recorded in the form of *memorabilia*:

Awaking from sleep at midnight, I saw, on an eminence towards the east, an angel holding in his right hand a paper which, from the inflowing light of the sun, was seen in a bright radiance. On the middle of the paper was a writing in letters of gold; and I saw written there: THE MARRIAGE OF GOOD AND TRUTH. From this writing flashed a splendor which spread out in a wide circle around the paper so that the circle or ambit seemed like the dawn as seen in spring-time.

After this, I saw the angel descending with the paper in his hand. And as he descended, the paper seemed less and less bright, and the writing, which was THE MARRIAGE OF GOOD AND TRUTH, changed from the color of gold to that of silver, then to that of copper, afterwards to that of iron, and finally to that of iron and copper rust. Finally, the angel was seen to enter a dark cloud and to descend through the cloud and alight upon the earth. There the paper, though still held in his hand, was no longer visible. This was in the world of spirits where all men first come together after death. [52]

Swedenborg was then asked by the angel to question those from all quarters of the spiritual world who passed by him, asking them whether or not they saw the angel or the paper in the angel's hand. Both the learned and all those who put faith in the words of the learned said they saw nothing. However, others who had been standing in the rear and "who in the world had been in simple faith from charity . . . said that they saw a man with a paper."[53] The man was in becoming clothing and held a paper that read "THE MARRIAGE OF GOOD AND TRUTH." They then asked the angel what those words meant.

> The angel then said: "All things in the whole heaven and all things in the entire world are nothing but a marriage of good and truth; for created things, both those which live and breathe and those which do not live and breathe, are one and all created from and into the marriage of good and truth. . . . Alone, the latter and the former are not anything; but by marriage they exist and become a thing of like quality as the marriage. In the Lord the Creator is Divine Good and Divine Truth. . . . They are also in their very union; for in Him they make one infinitely. Since these two are one in the Creator, therefore they are also one in each and every thing created by Him. Moreover, by this the Creator is conjoined with all things created by Himself in an eternal covenant as of marriage." . . .
>
> After this the angel spoke of THE MARRIAGE OF GOOD AND TRUTH as it is with married partners, saying that if their minds were in that marriage, the husband being truth and the wife the good thereof, they would both be in the delights of the blessedness of innocence, and thence in the happiness in which are the angels of heaven.[54]

As can be seen by what Swedenborg describes in the spiritual world, few in his day saw marriage as anything important at all. Yet, according to him, the marriage of good and truth is the origin, foundation, and life of the entire universe. Thus, it is not surprising that when Wadström and Nordenskiöld embraced the teaching of the New Jerusalem, they embraced the idea that marriage was the very life of civil society. Therefore, just as the underlying contract for the community was the Ten Commandments (Decalogue), they attempted to create a sacred contract for marriage based on the teachings concerning marriage that are found in *Conjugial Love.*

> (1.) That the Husband shall not love any other Woman but his own.
> (2.) That he shall not violate or lightly esteem the Laws of

Marriage. (3.) That he keep sacred the Union with his Wife, by a diligent observance of the ultimate endearment. (4.) That the Lord and the Church, or in other words, the Word and Doctrine therefrom, be loved and respected as their Father and Mother. (5.) That the Wife ought not to be without religious Doctrine. (6.) That the Wife ought not to live contrary to her received Doctrine of Religion. (7.) That she ought not to be of a different Religion from her Husband. (8.) And that she ought not to be deceitful or hypocritical in her Religion. (9 and 10.) That in Order that Love and Wisdom, Innocence and Liberty may prevail, the Lusts of Dominion and Possession ought not to exist either in the Husband or the Wife. [55]

This contract could be viewed as being more or less in keeping with the prevailing ideas concerning men and women at the end of the eighteenth century. However, underlying Swedenborg's understanding of marriage is a union based on mutual love and affection, looking toward an internal marriage of minds as the married couple becomes more and more one in affection and thought, and in word and deed. These sentiments are not codified in the rather legalistic contract above—perhaps because such sentiments describe the life that is lived if one were to abide by the contract.

At the moment, I am unsure about either how many families ever subscribed to this particular colonization plan or what those who did not subscribe had as their reasons for not doing so. Certainly, embarking into the unknown was then and is now a radical move. While the continent of North America had been an attractive destination for religious dissidents and adventurers in the seventeenth century, Africa in the eighteenth century remained not only relatively unknown but also foreign and exotic. Thus, the draw may not have been there for many. However, questions that I have, which, at the moment, I cannot answer are: Was the Plan in and of itself attractive? Who read the Plan, and how was it assessed and judged? In what way, if any, did the focus on marriage either attract or repel potential emigrants? And, of course, in what way did the focus on the doctrine of the New Jerusalem *in toto*, including the doctrines of the Lord and of use, have an influence?

I can certainly imagine answers to these questions, but while I cannot assess why families did not flock to join this amazingly wonderful and radical project, I can turn my attention to assessing it sociologically.

Sociological Assessment of Wadström's *Plan for a Free Community*

While I am a sociologist, I taught political science for many years during my career. In that capacity, I came across a book by Robert MacIver titled *The Web of Government,* which was first published in 1947 and then revised in 1965. Parts I and II of his book are thoroughly sociological, and they provide good tools for assessing a plan such as the one presented in *Plan for a Free Community at Sierra Leona.* In Part II, labeled "The Bases of Authority," MacIver begins with the following statement:

> Without law there is no order, and without order men are lost, not knowing where they go, not knowing what they do. A system of ordered relationships is a primary condition of human life at every level. More than anything else it is what society means. [56]

To be human is to live in relationship—to live within one or more ordered, patterned, or predictable relationships. Without instincts to guide us, human beings can exist only in patterned connections with other human beings, only in a web of relationships. Wadström's plan has taken this reality into account. The Plan is ordered and focuses on two fundamental relationships: our relationship to the Lord and Creator and the marriage between a man and a woman. And from these, it also focuses on the intervening relationships in the community and in the state that are described in and illustrated on the various charts provided. [57]

It is clear that the intervening boards and associations at the district and parish levels draw their vision from the relationship between the community and the Lord and from the strength found in families formed from loving and harmonious marriages. A community that is ordered around the Ten Commandments and that lives according to them would be socially strong and secure. It would be subject to a minimum of crime and disorder. The same would be true if, indeed, wandering sexual loves and disorders were kept in check. This would certainly be true for a passionately committed first generation. Two problems, however, could arise: the imperfect transmission of the communal ideals and the absolute necessity for freedom. *Everyone must be free in a free community.* And as has already been pointed out, freedom is vital both in a genuine relationship to the Lord and within marriage. In addition, a free community requires *freedom of opinion, speech, and publishing.*

As an aside, I would also like to say that the economic concepts of both Wadström and Nordenskiöld have proved to be unworkable. The abolition of money or some easily transferable medium of exchange and basing everything instead on the exchange of raw materials makes no sense: it is entirely too cumbersome, and that was true even then. Nordenskiöld's concept of using alchemy to make gold available to all, as a way of eliminating poverty, is equally untenable, both chemically and socioeconomically.

All utopian communities, and really all societies, have had to deal with the problem of the imperfect transmission of values and in turn with the fading luster of these values to subsequent generations.

Freedom, too, while it neither can nor should be dispensed with, opens the door to unanticipated and/or unwanted change. Nonetheless, if the free community founded on the teachings of the New Jerusalem was actually to have provided a structure for living faith, for a life of true charity and humility for most of its residents, it would have prospered and thrived and could have become a beacon of light in the world. As many of the ingredients were there in the proposal, success or failure would have rested in the hands of those who chose to join. That a sufficient number did not join is, at least, somewhat telling.

The failure may have had more to do with the enormous difficulties and disasters that confronted the Sierra Leone and Bulama ventures in 1792 and 1795, respectively—including the death of August Nordenskiöld and another Swede, Jakob Strand—than it did with the Plan itself. Nonetheless, it seems evident that the time was not right.

Would such a plan work today, all other things being equal? My sociological assessment is that it would probably not. I would venture to say, for starters, that modern adventurers would find the Plan too hierarchical, too paternalistic, and insufficiently feminist. Some of the solid elements, such as possession of a common faith in the Lord and obedience to the laws of the Ten Commandments, also would not be welcome by many who would undertake the development of an entirely new free community. As I will point out in my final reflections, the emphasis on marriage as the foundation of civil society appears to be an equally problematic value in our current social climate.

Marriage and Civil Society in Our Time

In 2015, I taught a course called "The Sociology of Marriage and the Family." The last time I had taught it was in 2011. The field had shifted so much since then that I fundamentally had to reorganize my course. The focus had become much less on defining and explaining marriage and the family from a sociological point of view than it had on answering the following questions: "Does marriage as a social institution matter? Does family as a social institution matter? And if they do not matter, what are the implications for other social institutions, such as religion, politics, education, and economics?" Reading material from popular journals at that time included topics such as "Why Marry?", "The End of Men," and "The Changing American Family," among others. This material made it clear that marriage has been significantly weakened in contemporary American society. Recent trends included later marriage, more frequent cohabitation, high divorce rates, and more children born out of wedlock. The sociologist Andrew Cherlin points to what he has called the "deinstitutionalization of marriage," which involves the weakening of the social norms that govern the institution.[58]

Marriage in the past has been associated with economic well-being and stability, the health and well-being of children, and their successful socialization. The downward trend in marriage has already been associated with negative economic patterns for both divorced and single parents, as well as with the poor educational achievements and dropout rates of their children.

While there is much more that could be written about this, one might say that the current marriage crisis is reminiscent of the situation that Wadström encountered at the end of the eighteenth century— although the causes are quite different. Marriage today is an individual and personal choice based on love that centers on self-satisfaction. Marriages that lead to personal fulfillment and in which both spouses are happy and love each other are viewed as good. However, there appears to be a lot of conditionality in such agreements. Marriage as an institution requires personal submission to the institution, believing that it is good in and of itself. This is a quality that for many people today is as invisible as was the paper that was let down into the spiritual world.

While seeing marriage as essentially spiritual in our more spiritually attuned age might lead to a new appreciation of its value, the fact that it is a relationship whose success depends on the sacrifice of self-centeredness may postpone its embrace. People will need to see that true freedom requires discipline, and with discipline comes an appreciation of the great gifts that can come when the essence of love is understood to be "feeling the joy of someone else as joy within ourselves." [59]

Building a New Jerusalem in Africa in the 1790s

JONATHAN HOWARD, *architect, educated at University of Cambridge*

In 1792, a thousand refugees sailed across the Atlantic to build Freetown, showing the way for Americans at Monrovia and Frenchmen at Libreville. A hundred years later, this became a British protectorate, and in 1961, it became the Republic of Sierra Leone. The project was carried out by the Sierra Leone Company. Some members wanted to abolish the slave trade, and some wanted to emancipate slaves all around the world. They hoped to reduce the demand for slaves by starting competitive production in Africa. For this purpose, they recruited refugees from the American Revolutionary War, as either a philanthropic gesture or a profitable investment. From Britain and Sweden, they engaged a botanist, a geologist, and administrators, all of whom decided to build Freetown between the lion-like mountain and the river.

SOME OF YOU may have been on a camping holiday and gone canoeing or hiking. Toward the end of the day, you and your family had to find somewhere to put up your tent. Now imagine doing that for more than a thousand refugees who have just sailed across the Atlantic. In an impressive feat of navigation, you have arrived at the estuary of the Sierra Leone River. Thirty refugees have died on the way over. You have no map, and none of you have ever been there before. Admittedly, a few dozen of your countrymen are already there and are expecting you, but most of them only arrived from Europe a month previously.

That is what it was like to build Freetown in 1792. In spite of all the difficulties, Freetown survived and showed the way for Americans at Monrovia and Frenchmen at Libreville. Sixteen years later, Freetown became the crown colony of Sierra Leone. In 1896, the surrounding territory became a British protectorate; and in 1961, the crown colony and the protectorate together became today's Republic of Sierra Leone.

This essay is about the practical task of planning and building a New Jerusalem in Africa. I have never been confronted with such a challenge, but having spent eighteen years building in Africa, when I read late-eighteenth-century accounts of Freetown's first years, they sound very familiar to me.

Carl Bernhard Wadström

Carl Bernhard Wadström was one of seventeen Swedes who were in one way or another involved in the Freetown project.[1] He was never in Sierra Leone, but in *An Essay on Colonization*,[2] he tells the story of Freetown's first years. We don't know for sure where he got his information from. He would have read the reports of the Sierra Leone Company and talked to his countryman Daniel Wilhelm Padenheim,[3] who had just come back from two years of hard work on the site. Wadström had also met Philip Beaver,[4] who visited Freetown on his way home from the disastrous attempt to settle in Guiné Bissau. Wadström would also have met the Swedish botanist Adam Afzelius, who came back to England in 1796 after four years in Sierra Leone. Separate eyewitness accounts of having met with Wadström were later published by the Scottish physician Thomas Winterbottom[5] and, more scurrilously, by Anna Maria Falconbridge.[6]

In 1787, Wadström made a short visit to the island of Goree, off Dakar in Senegal, with two Swedish scientists, Anders Sparrman and Carl Axel Arrhenius.[7] Wadström could sketch well—a useful skill to have before the advent of photography. Most of the illustrations in eighteenth-century travel journals were made by engravers in Europe and were based only on verbal descriptions.

According to his published journal, they tried to continue as far as Sierra Leone, but they were unsuccessful; perhaps the Swedish king had simply not given them enough money. Wadström also wrote that his colleagues were primarily interested in natural science and that the Swedish king was primarily interested in gold, while his own main interest was colonization.[8] That the Swedish king was interested in gold per se may be an unfair portrayal of both his and his ministers' motives. Wadström may have meant that the king was only interested in Africa's economic possibilities. The king had certainly employed Wadström's colleague August Nordenskiöld as an alchemist, which suggests his interest in "gold."

Wadström was thirty-two years old when he came back to London from Senegal. He was interviewed about the slave trade by a parliamentary commission and then never went back to Sweden, instead choosing to stay in London and in Manchester—then a new industrial city with a lively Swedenborgian community. Wadström's *An Essay on Colonization* consists of two badly organized volumes. The copious appendices are reprints of more or less relevant pamphlets and letters. We cannot be sure of his contribution to the successful settlement in Sierra Leone, but we can imagine the energetic Swede—who had no private economic or political motives—scurrying between intellectuals, businessmen, and seasoned travelers. William Blake's poem, "And did those feet in ancient time," was first published in 1808,[9] but Wadström may have read it in manuscript format, as he did help "build the New Jerusalem," albeit in Sierra Leone's "green and pleasant land."

The Sierra Leone Company

For the Freetown project, there were several potential stakeholders. The abolitionist movement's objective was to abolish the trade in slaves, particularly from West and Southwest Africa across the Atlantic Ocean. Some but not all of those in the movement wanted to go further and emancipate slaves all around the world. The abolitionists hoped that the settlement project would reduce the demand for slaves on the transatlantic plantations by starting competitive production in Africa. They believed that slave labor was not as efficient as was "free" wage-earning labor and held that the export of slaves hindered the development of West Africa as a market for European goods. The abolitionists were not agronomists and so never seem to have analyzed whether competitive production in West Africa was sustainable.

They overestimated the fertility of the West African soil and underestimated the long experience of the transatlantic producers.

Without necessarily condemning slavery as inherently wrong, the abolitionists did claim that the slave trade was exceptionally cruel— even by late-eighteenth-century standards, when public flogging and capital punishment were part of daily life in Europe. For example, in a protest against the enclosures of common land, a broadsheet was published: *We hang the man and flog the woman / Who steals the goose from off the common, / But let the greater villain loose / Who steals the common from the goose.* This was not a protest against the unequal treatment of men and women but instead against the disparity between the cruelty toward slaves and the leniency toward owners. Note, too, that almost as many seamen as slaves died on the transatlantic voyage, yet there was no movement to protect seamen. The slave trade seems to have attracted sadistic traders and employers; perhaps slavery tends to make the relations between employer and employee inhuman.

The Sierra Leone Company was formed in London with capital contributed by private individuals; the government gave its official approval and logistical and financial support, but it was not originally a shareholder.[10] The company seems to have included two different types of stakeholder: those who hoped the venture would be a profitable investment and those who saw the company as a philanthropic organization. The former stakeholders were disappointed, as the company went bankrupt after seventeen years and was taken over as a crown colony. While there were at that time no non-governmental organizations (NGOs) such as Oxfam or Save the Children, the latter stakeholders were the only counterpart in control. Perhaps the modern debate on corporate social responsibility shows that this division between sustainable businesses and philanthropic NGOs still is unclear.

City of Refuge

The abolitionists hoped to reduce the transatlantic demand for slaves by starting British-owned competitive production in Africa. No one considered helping Africans to develop an export industry. The Europeans were not even sure of finding enough indigenous African labor. Did they consider Africans incapable of learning to become entrepreneurs or at least skilled workers in an agricultural export industry? If Africans were incapable of developing their own land, who else was going to do it? In response to this quandary, Thomas Peters, the self-appointed leader of the black Loyalists in Canada, arrived in London and met Granville Sharp, who must have regarded him as Moses did the manna and the quails in the Sinai desert. Here was the qualified labor that the project required. The first settlement in the Sierra Leone estuary, Granville Town, and the Bolama Island settlement only attracted Britain's feeblest citizens. Now, in response to Thomas Peters's visit, John Clarkson, a naval officer and brother of the leading abolitionist Thomas Clarkson, was dispatched to Nova Scotia to recruit settlers. He chose men with useful artisan experience; single women were not welcome. More than a thousand of them sailed from Halifax directly to Sierra Leone—a refugee elite who would build Freetown, the New Jerusalem.

The Loyalists had fought on the British side when the American colonists—the Patriots—rebelled in 1775. After eight years, the Patriots won and some five thousand Loyalists then fled to Canada's austere Maritime Provinces. Many of them were former black slaves who were recruited by the British with the promise of emancipation. In Canada, the black Loyalists felt discriminated against; they had fought for a freedom that they had not yet found. To survive, they organized themselves into Christian communities, such as the Countess of Huntingdon's Connection. [11] Their ambitions were modest: to be independent peasant freeholders or artisans—coincidentally, a Swedenborgian Utopia. [12] More than a thousand black refugees, often former seamen, had already made their way to London. There, a Committee for the Relief of the Black Poor was formed (rumor had it that London's white poor in search of relief began to blacken their faces). The black Loyalists in Canada and the black poor in England had reason to feel that Britain had been less than just to them. Black refugees on both sides of the Atlantic were subject to a special discrimination: the risk of being press-ganged back into slavery. As the 2013 film *12 Years a Slave* illustrates, even relatively well-to-do blacks could be kidnapped. [13]

Freetown was thus built by and for refugees. In 1794, it survived being plundered by a passing unit of the French Navy. This was no act of war; it was senseless destruction. Afzelius describes how his journal, scientific specimens, and garden were destroyed. At least the plunderers are not recorded as raping women or hacking off limbs, as happened two hundred years later in the Sierra Leone Civil War (1991–2002). In 1799, Freetown was reinforced with about five hundred Maroons—rebellious slaves from Jamaica. After 1807, Britons were no longer allowed to trade in slaves. Instead, the British Navy assumed the right to transport slaves found on board other nations' trading ships to Freetown, irrespective of where they had come from. These so-called *Recaptives,* together with the Maroons and the Nova Scotians, are the origin of the Krio ethnic group in today's Sierra Leone.

Idea and Reality of the Settlement

One of the first European proposals for a settlement, as opposed to a trading post, in Africa was made in Sweden in 1776 by Ulrik Norden-skiöld.[14] This was a purely economic proposal, based on agricultural production. Afterward, at a meeting convened by Wadström in Norrköping in 1779, the idea of a settlement as a Swedenborgian political experiment came up. And even later came the idea of a settlement that would discourage the slave trade. The Swedenborgian New Jerusalem would be a self-governing community, economically sustainable through the agricultural labor of freeholders. They do not seem to have felt a need for a central administration that would be responsible for infrastructure and defense. Nor were they interested in supplying the agriculturalists and marketing their produce. Thus, Freetown grew up with a British colonial administration and a Syrian or Lebanese merchant class.

The Swedenborgians did not appreciate the effort required to initiate and manage the New Jerusalem. Instead, it was carried out by the Sierra Leone Company, which saw itself as a benevolent estate owner and saw the Nova Scotians as tenants rather than as freeholders. At its inception, the Sierra Leone Company was expected to be economically sustainable; the settlement would produce an agricultural surplus that could be exported. In fact, the Freetowners depended on food sent out from England or acquired from local Africans in exchange for other goods.

Until 1794, the company did not allow the settlers to open shops or taverns; the "company store" had a monopoly, which must have been resented by the Nova Scotians, with their unhappy memories of the

American slave plantations. The Swedenborgian self-governing free-holders were dependent on the company for their livelihood; and by the turn of the century, less than a third of the households were those of farmers.

Building a New Jerusalem also appealed to scientists. Carolus Linnaeus's use of the term "economic botany" implied that scientific discovery could be very profitable. Irish physician Hans Sloane became a millionaire from West African cocoa. From the Royal Botanical Gardens at Kew, English naturalist Joseph Banks sent Captain William Bligh to fetch breadfruit from Tahiti. Breadfruit never became as profitable as did chocolate, but Wadström mentions it hopefully in *An Essay on Colonization*. Afzelius found a promising new sort of coffee bean.[15] Linnaeus taught his apostles to make a note of everything, as one can never be sure of what is important. Afzelius's journal has observations not only on botany but also on anthropology and climate. Perhaps intimidated by Linnaeus's other rule, to systematize everything, Afzelius never edited his journal; instead, it was done two hundred years later by Alexander Peter Kup.[16] Afzelius's mission description has survived,[17] but for the geologist August Nordenskiöld, we have no such document from the Sierra Leone Company. As indicated above, they probably wanted him to look for gold (diamonds were not discovered there until the twentieth century), but he died after a mission to establish trade contacts in the hinterland.

Although the directors of the Sierra Leone Company were all devout Christians, Christian missionary activity (including that of Swedenborgian missionaries) was a nineteenth-century development. Nor did the settlement projects attract relatively well-to-do adventurers, except Joshua Montefiore on Bolama Island.[18] While Cambridge University Press published *Romantic Colonization and British Anti-Slavery* as part of its series on Romanticism, the "romance" seems to have developed after the founding of Freetown, with a climax in the aristocratic settlement around Karen Blixen and Beryl Markham in early-twentieth-century Kenya. It began with Daniel Defoe (1660–1731), who published *Robinson Crusoe* (1719), which is based on the experiences of the Scottish seaman Alexander Selkirk (1676–1721), who lived for a few years on an island off the coast of Chile.

The first European attempt to settle—as opposed to opening a trading station—at the mouth of the Sierra Leone River was in 1787, the same year that Wadström visited Senegal, apparently unaware of Granville Sharp's initiative. While nearly all those who had settled in what they called Granville Town had either died or fled by 1792, the experience had shown that building a new community required a massive investment in human resources, material, and logistics. To mobilize these resources, the Sierra Leone Company was formed in London. No one in the late eighteenth century had any experience at building a new community "from scratch" in a faraway land. They did not consult Thomas Telford, who had designed the town of Ullapool in 1788 as part of a fishery project in northwestern Scotland.

A comparable project that was built in the last century is the municipality of Kitimat, which was planned in the 1950s by Clarence Stein for the Aluminum Company on the Pacific coast of Canada. Only Granville Sharp investigated what the Pilgrim Fathers had done in the previous century. As far as I know, none of them ever published a book about it; they emigrated on their own initiative and at their own risk. The Freetown promoters themselves had no intention of emigrating. Wadström, Nordenskiöld, and Sharp thought of a colony as consisting of self-governing peasant farmers, rather than as being a sustainable business venture.

Very few Britons had ever been in Africa. Surprisingly, not even the abolitionists wanted to go there. Indeed, all travel was dangerous, but were they afraid of "the fever"? In fact, alcohol killed more people than did malaria and yellow fever, and even for those who stayed in Europe, the life expectancy was short, particularly in the cities. Wadström may have used his prestige as an African traveler, his practical experience with mining and metalworking, and his enthusiasm for a Swedenborgian New Jerusalem as means to catalyze participation from different stakeholders. In his third book of the Kalahari trilogy,[19] Lasse Berg suggested that heterogeneous stakeholders may be an advantage for any project. But until Freetown became a crown colony, had it been a self-governing agricultural community or an estate run by the Sierra Leone Company?

When John Clarkson arrived in Sierra Leone, he expected to find in charge his "old friend" Henry Hew Dalrymple.[20] But Dalrymple had in dudgeon led a rival expedition to the island of Bolama, just off Bissau, and Clarkson found instead a letter asking him to take charge of the settlement. The Bolama project did not have the massive support that the Freetown project had, and so it failed miserably. Wadström had been involved in raising money for Bolama in Manchester, and in *An Essay on Colonization,* he pleads for making another attempt to settle the island. Subsequent historical research has not yet explained how it was that this rival expedition came to be and why they chose this particular island, but the island is often mentioned as appropriate for a European or American colony.[21] In the early twentieth century, Bolama was the center of Portuguese colonial administration, and its now-abandoned buildings are even more imposing than those on the island of Ibo, off the coast of Mozambique.

John Clarkson and his thousand Nova Scotians arrived about a month after did the administrators and scientists who were sent out by the Sierra Leone Company. Since the rainy season was about to begin, the planned New Jerusalem, which was to be called Freetown, had to be realized as quickly as possible. The English term *town planning* has two different meanings: 1) preparing an urban plan, or how a piece of real estate is going to be developed; or 2) community planning in its broadest sense, including economic planning and infrastructure, and the political power to carry it out. Both meanings were relevant in the case of Freetown.

Building Freetown

Anyone used to the Swedish tradition of holding laborious investigations would be surprised at the lack of planning documents associated with the Freetown project. There are three possible explanations for this situation: all the documents have since disappeared, all the planning was conducted orally, or those involved were prepared to risk their fortunes and their lives without knowing very much about the details of the project. Even the British state was able to give its support, in cash or by assigning ships from the Royal Navy, without requiring that subsequent reports and accounting measures be made.

The first step in the physical planning of Freetown was to choose a suitable area in a suitable part of the world. Wadström's *An Essay on*

Colonization gives the only succinct argument I have found for why the Sierra Leone estuary was considered the most appropriate site for a new settlement.

> The gentlemen, therefore, soon agreed that the chaos of jarring interests involved in the present politics, finances and commerce of Europe opposed a formidable obstacle to their design: and they were clearly of opinion *[sic]* that the only measure which promised any reasonable hopes of success would be the establishment of a new community, somewhere out of Europe, in the *original organization* of which such regulations might be adopted as would effectually exclude every political, financial and mercantile principle, which was not deemed consistent with the happiness of mankind. But the question was, to what part of the habitable globe they were to turn their views? Though many large tracts of Asia and America were unoccupied, few of them were unclaimed, and still fewer were within a convenient distance of Europe. To the western coast of Africa alone, these weighty objections did not apply. Abounding with tracts, neither occupied nor claimed by European powers, sufficiently near to Europe to afford an *infant* society the advantages of her fostering care, yet sufficiently remote to place a *mature* community beyond the reach of her influence, particularly, her commercial influence: in *these* respects, the Coast just mentioned appeared the best adapted for the proposed undertaking.[22]

During the two centuries following the Portuguese *descobrimentos,* the Europeans came to be reasonably well-informed about the world's oceans and their coasts, but they were much less informed about the inlands. Africa and Australia seemed to be more or less uninhabited, but even though Botany Bay in New South Wales was a possible site for a colony, it was much farther away than was West Africa. Eighteenth-century Freetown was not isolated; ships were often called in and the post to London only took about a month. London did not have much information about West Africa. The coast was reasonably well-mapped, but the hinterland was not mapped at all. There were seamen with experience from the coast, and there were six or seven published books on the matter, one of them by naturalist Henry Smeathman.[23] With his Swedish assistant Andreas Berlin, Smeathman had performed botanical research in Sierra Leone; and until he died in 1786, he campaigned in England for a settlement there. If he had instead performed his research in today's Monrovia or Conakry or Bissau, perhaps the settlers would have gone to one of those locations instead.

The Sierra Leone Company officers, who arrived only a month before the Nova Scotians did, had just enough time to decide that Freetown should be built on the relatively level strip between the mountain and the river. This area is still the center of the town, and when I came ashore from the ferry, I immediately recognized the eighteenth-century town plan. I had wondered why the first settlements were made on the narrow strip between the river and the lion-like mountain, thinking that perhaps the Africans had willingly ceded poor agricultural land. Then I read the architect R. J. Olu-Wright's 1968 article[24] in which he describes the nature of the terrain: near the south shore, the river runs more swiftly and is deep; the north shore has better agricultural land, but the river there is shallow, with treacherous sandbanks.

Sylvie Kandé has shown how the European concept of real estate was unfamiliar to West Africans.[25] The settlers made written agreements to occupy land, even though the African leaders could not read them and probably did not recognize the difference between a trading post and a settlement, a New Jerusalem. They certainly would not have understood how the Bolama proposers could try to finance their project in London and Manchester by selling lots on territory that had not yet even been visited, let alone purchased and surveyed.[26]

There were two surveying tasks. The first involved the town site, with its roads and its individual lots to be used for a home and garden for the settlers. Sites were also to be reserved for public buildings and for a wharf on the riverside. In the first days, there were already conflicts: Some settlers had built provisional shelters and did not want to abandon them; others had tried to lay claim to desirable land on the riverside. That the surveyor James Cocks was often drunk most likely contributed to the fact that the settlers who arrived from Nova Scotia had to wait for months until the town site was laid out in rectangular lots. When the Swedish quartermaster Daniel Padenheim arrived, he was at first not allowed to go ashore,[27] perhaps because Cocks did not want foreign interference.

An altogether different way of subdividing the site would have been to build a wall around the building lot and then to build rooms that were accessible from a central courtyard. With some Yoruba exceptions in Nigeria, West Africa did not have any such urban tradition until the nineteenth century. Indeed, it feels strange when eighteenth-century authors use the term *towns* to refer to African sites that we would call *villages*. Modern English, in fact, has a variety of terms that it uses to refer to these different levels of living environment: *town, village, country,* and *wilderness.*

The second task was to assign farming land. Not only had the Nova Scotians been promised a town lot on which they could have their home and garden, but they had also been promised farming land outside the town site. The land on the south shore, however, is not very suitable for agriculture. The Europeans consistently overestimated West Africa's fertility, as they were probably misled by the twelve-month growing season in which the year is divided between wet and dry, not warm and cold. Moreover, the measure of fertility in a rain forest is in the trees themselves. When they are cut down, the heavy rains wash away the topsoil, which never was very fertile in the first place. Agroforestry, of course, had not yet been invented.

Because of the mountains behind it, Freetown has more rain than the rest of Sierra Leone, and the rain falls heavily during four months. At the time, it would have eroded beaten earth roads that sloped down to the river. Today's central Freetown has deep channels on either side of the roadway, and they are sometimes covered with a concrete grid. I have not yet found any reference to how the settlers dealt with this problem, but I imagine they simply did not deal with it at all. Certainly, they must have found the long period of rain to be very uncomfortable. But at least they did not have to dig wells, as Freetown's streams with fresh water had long been known to seamen. The eyewitnesses say nothing about latrines or about the risk of polluting the streams. This is probably not because the subject was indelicate, but because they did not think it was important. Even in Stockholm and London, feces, along with other refuse, were collected in buckets and tipped into the river.

Health, Education, and Housing

The Sierra Leone Company sent out physicians and provided some medicine, but Europeans took more than a century to learn how to deal with tropical illnesses. (Even in Europe, healthcare was still primitive.) Afzelius collected and grew local medicinal plants, and the Euro-African slave trader Betsy Heard informed him about traditional African medicine,[28] which other Europeans showed no interest in.

Even though many of the settlers were illiterate, the company does not seem to have done much for adult education. Padenheim describes the library, which seemed to fulfill some basic needs:

> Jakob Strand, the third of our countrymen here, is secretary to the governor. He is considered hard-working and kind, has an academic background and is good at languages and music. A little house has been built for him; local timber has been sawn to appropriate dimensions and the walls and roof covered with European planks. Now it has been painted, it looks very nice. It has two rooms. One is his bedroom, the other his office, which is also our library. The company did not want our settlement to lack anything in the way of basic comfort or education and so they sent out an excellent little library, containing travelogues, encyclopaedias, most English authors, books on economics and so on. This was to begin with called the Public Library, where every settler had the right to satisfy his or her curiosity and educational needs, without restriction. But as the books thus became public property, there was a risk that everything might disappear. So Strand was appointed librarian and it was put in his care. It is still open for all and books can be borrowed one or two at a time, but the borrower is obliged to bring them back after a certain time.[29]

Education for children, however, was a priority, as Padenheim writes:

> Now in Freetown more than two hundred children go to school, forty of them local Africans. They begin the morning and the afternoon with song and prayer and are learning to read, write and calculate. On the north shore, about twenty Africans are making impressive progress; I have seen a sixteen-year-old African boy with a handwriting as elegant as the most well-trained European.[30]

Wadström's *An Essay on Colonization* reprints the Swedish architect Anders Johansen's curious drawing of a house built on a tree stump, his even more curious image of a German air-conditioning machine, and Wadström's own design for a hat with ventilation openings. They obviously could not imagine how, after their long voyage, the settlers' first need would be a provisional shelter for their families, particularly because the rainy season was only two months away.

In much of Africa, the amount of sand and clay in the soil is appropriate for making adobe building blocks, but on the Freetown peninsula, there is not enough clay. It is, however, clayey enough for the wattle and daub method, which is appropriate in places where there are plenty of rather crooked trees and branches. More or less straight poles are driven into the earth, and the space between them is intertwined with smaller branches and then filled with mud. A thatch roof does not require a geometrically exact structure; in fact, it is almost easier to roof a round house than it is to roof a rectangular one. Aminatta Forna has written that in Temne villages in the 1930s, rectangular houses were considered smarter and more up-to-date, but it was difficult to keep the dark corners clean.[31]

When they had time to build more permanent houses, the Freetowners did not turn to the local African building traditions but instead preferred European traditions with imported European building material. Termites do not seem to have been a problem, while in other parts of Africa, they eat anything made of wood. Until the late twentieth century, Sierra Leone was an important exporter of timber, but nothing was done to ensure new growth. Felling trees and sawing them up is hard work with hand tools. As recently as ten years ago in Angola, planks were sawn with two-man saws; the name *Sawpit* survives as a place name in Freetown. Once sawn, the planks should dry for at least half a year, otherwise they warp horribly. The company sent Freetown some prefabricated canvas-covered houses. Padenheim explains that the windows were hinged along the upper edge so that when they were opened, they acted as sunshades.[32] These windows were covered with canvas; glass was out of the question.

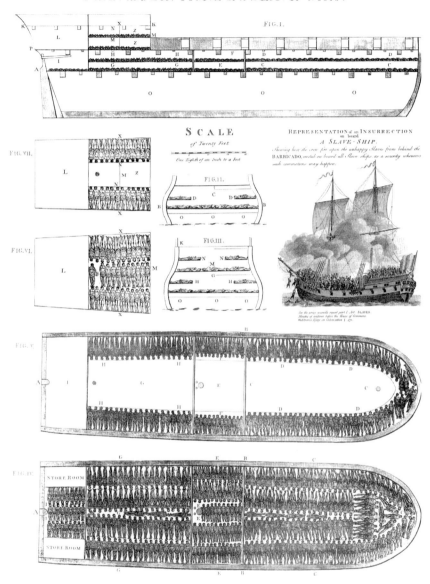

Plate 1. Plan and Sections of a Slave Ship, 1789, taken from Carl Bernhard Wadström, *An Essay on Colonization particularly applied to the Western coast of Africa, . . .*, 2 vols. London, 1794–95.

CIDARIS ERIT AFRICO.

Vide Nº 114, DELITIÆ SAPIENTIÆ de AMORE CONJUGIALI, ab Em. Swedenborg.

Plate 2. Engraving by Conrad Martin Metz after Louis Jean Desprez, *"Cidaris Erit Africo,"* published in the first number of the *New-Jerusalem Magazine,* London, 1790.

Plate 3. Carl Frederik von Breda, *Double portrait of Carl Bernhard Wadström (1746–1799) and Prince Peter Panah,* 1789, oil on canvas, Nordic Museum, Stockholm.

Plate 4. William Blake, "The Little Black Boy" (second plate), from *Songs of Innocence and of Experience,* copy Y, ca. 1825.

Plate 5. William Blake, "The Divine Image," from *Songs of Innocence and of Experience,* copy Y, ca. 1825.

Plate 6. A section of *A View of JOAL, on the Coast of Guinea in Affrica. Dedicated to the SOUND POLITICIANS of all the Trading Nations in Europe,* [drawn by] C. B. Wadström, del[ineator], Cath.e Prestell execut [Prestel, Maria Katharina, 1747–94 (engraver)], Aquatint, published by Wadström as the Acts Directs, No. 6, Poultry, London, [1789].

Plate 7. *A View taken near BAIN, on the Coast of Guinea in Affrica. Dedicated to the FEELING HEARTS in all Civilized Nations,* drawn by R[ichard] Westall [1765–1836] from sketches made on the spot by C. B. Wadström, Cath.e Prestell Sculp. [Prestel, Maria Katharina, 1747–94 (engraver)], Aquatint, published by Wadström as the Acts Directs, No. 6, Poultry, London, [1789].

Plate 8. *A View of the New SETTLEMENT in the River at SIERRA LEONA on the COAST of GUINEA in AFRICA, North Lat: 8º 29. Taken from the North Side,* created by Dutch engraver Cornelis Apostool [1762–1844], based on a sketch by C. B. W[adstrom] and printed on his order and at his expense, distributed for propaganda purposes, as were his other pictures from Africa, Aquatint, London, ca. 1790. This image appears across the front and back covers of the present volume.

Plate 9. Commemorative Carl Bernhard Wadström medal struck by the Swedish Academy in 1860, Lea Ahlborn engraver; portrait, *obverse; reverse,* a man seated by a palm tree, reading, broken shackles beneath, inscription: "My freedom is the result of your services." Photos courtesy of David Lindrooth.

The publication of the prints of *Plates* 6 and 7, above, was advertised by Wadström on page 67 of his book *Observations on the Slave Trade* (1789). 22 x 17 inches and sold at cost price of 15 shillings. These prints are discussed by E. W. Dahlgren on pages 18ff in his 1915 article "Carl Bernhard Wadström: Hans verksamhet för Slafhandelns Bekämpande och de samtida Kolonisationsplanerna i Västafrika." Courtesy of the British Library in London and the Royal Library in Stockholm.

So I have given some glimpses of the hard realities and practical sides of building the utopia outlined in far-reaching plans, theories, and visions. I consider myself a shameless Eurocentrist, as I am concerned with what the eighteenth-century Europeans thought about Africa and not with what the Africans of that period thought about the European projects. We have seen how these Europeans, faced with the unfamiliar task of building a new community in an unfamiliar climate, were not very interested in African building methods, African medicine, African hygiene, or African agriculture. So why are we bothering to think about what Wadström and his contemporaries did? At a conference in Freetown a few years ago, Cynthia Jarret-Thorpe, a former professional pilot, born in Sierra Leone, quoted the African proverb: "Even if you don't know where to go next, know at least where you have come from!" ≈

"The Little Black Boy": William Blake, Carl Bernhard Wadström, and Swedenborg's Africa

ROBERT W. RIX, *University of Copenhagen*

"THE LITTLE BLACK BOY" from *Songs of Innocence* (1789) is one of William Blake's best-known poems. It is usually seen as connected with the campaign for the abolition of the slave trade.[1] This campaign was running high at the time Blake etched the poem. In fact, only the year before, a writer in the *Morning Chronicle and London Advertiser* wrote: "I perceive by publick prints, there is an astonishing quantity of publick spirit flying about, like wild fire, from Johnny Groats's house, to the Land's End of England, and all for the freedom of the poor Slaves of Africa."[2] But beyond its link to the flurry of abolitionist sentiment at the time, critics have found it hard to agree on an interpretation of the poem. It is the aim of this essay to trace the vocabularies and the generic frameworks that Blake adopts so that we may open up the poem to new examination against the background of the discursive landscape in which it was written. And in doing so, I will argue that Blake makes specific reference to Emanuel Swedenborg's distinctive understanding of heaven and of Africans.

Such were the salient influences that Carl Bernhard Wadström and other Swedenborgians were promoting at the time that Blake wrote his poem. We have no evidence of any direct communication between Wadström and Blake, but they would have met each other when Blake attended (with his wife, Catherine) the first General Conference at the London New Jerusalem Church in April of 1789, the outcome of which was the publication of thirty-two theological resolutions that were unanimously approved. Among seventy-seven others, Blake signed that he was in attendance. Among those who signed on behalf of the conference participants, we find "Charles Berns Wadström, from Sweden."[3]

In 1789, Wadström was evidently interested in both Swedenborgianism and Africa (his *Observations on the Slave Trade* was published that very year). How he managed to combine these two pursuits will be elucidated in the following pages. I will argue that we need to pay attention to the Swedenborgian content of Blake's poem in order to decode its rather gnomic representation of Africans. It is not my claim, however, that Blake wrote a loyalist Swedenborgian piece. While he shared both Wadström's and other colonially-minded Swedenborgians' desire to provide a positive image of the African, he also distanced himself from their paternalistic and colonialist ambitions—as I will suggest in the conclusion of this essay.

The Symbolism of Blackness

Let us now engage in a close reading of "The Little Black Boy." Over two plates of Blake's self-invented "illuminated printing," the text reads as follows:

MY mother bore me in the southern wild,
And I am black, but O! my soul is white;
White as an angel is the English child:
But I am black as if bereav'd of light.

My mother taught me underneath a tree
And sitting down before the heat of day,
She took me on her lap and kissed me,
And pointing to the east began to say.

Look on the rising sun: there God does live
And gives his light, and gives his heat away.
And flowers and trees and beasts and men recieve [sic]
Comfort in morning joy in the noon day.

And we are put on earth a little space,
That we may learn to bear the beams of love,

And these black bodies and this sun-burnt face
Is but a cloud, and like a shady grove.

For when our souls have learn'd the heat to bear
The cloud will vanish we shall hear his voice.
Saying: come out from the grove my love & care,
And round my golden tent like lambs rejoice.

Thus did my mother say and kissed me,
And thus I say to little [sic] English boy;
When I from black and he from white cloud free,
And round the tent of God like lambs we joy:

Ill [sic] shade him from the heat till he can bear,
To lean in joy upon our fathers [sic] knee.
And then I'll stand and stroke his silver hair,
And be like him and he will then love me.
(E 9)[4]

A central concern in the poem is the question of complexion, which appears to go beyond any specific Swedenborgian references that Blake would have had direct access to in English translations,[5] but it is a question that ties in with the general turnabout in racial perception that formed the intellectual background for Wadström and his fellow abolitionists. Thus, I will very briefly discuss the discourse of racial complexion in the late eighteenth century.

Just as Wadström's politics concerning the equality of Africans and Europeans have been questioned, so too has Blake's poem been seen as Eurocentric.[6] One line of critical enquiry interprets the poem as showing that Blake did not believe in the equality of the races. Samuel Foster Damon's brief comments in 1924 are the first example of this interpretation.[7] Since then, Anne Mellor has understood the poem as showing that Blake "collaborates in a Western ideological production of the white body as the superior, more 'divine' body"; and Robert Earl Hood has concluded that Blake defends "the superiority of whites over blackness."[8] What is common to such readings is that they seem to confuse Blake, the author, with the first-person speaker of the lyric. Blake presents the speaker, a black boy, as part of a social system in which racist rhetoric is the norm. The African thinks that the English child's skin is as "white as an angel," but what carries more weight is his dawning realization that their souls are both equally "white."

By 1789, when Blake engraved and illuminated his poem, skin color had become a significant issue in abolitionist literature. In the writings of pro-slavery agitators, blackness had been seen as a mark of inferiority, but a number of abolitionist texts adopted a new understanding of color as simply a natural adjustment to climatic conditions rather than as a curse.[9] The main message in "The Little Black Boy" is that worldly differences will be overcome in heaven, as all people's souls are white. Blake's poem proceeds according to a paradigm that was already used by the seventeenth-century poet Richard Crashaw in "On the baptized Æthiopian" (a poem based on Acts 8): "Let it no longer be a forlorne hope / To wash an Æthiope: / He's washt, His gloomy skin a peacefull shade / For his white soule is made: / And now, I doubt not, the Eternall Dove, / A black-fac'd house will love."[10] For Crashaw, the reference to the Ethiopian is not an attack on racism but is instead an allegorical assurance that all worldly stains have no importance, as the Holy Ghost loves the beautiful soul inside of every human being. However, in the late eighteenth century, this allegorical sentiment was taken up in reference to the abolitionist cause. We find it developed at length, for example, in the former slave Ottobah Cugoano's landmark text, *Thoughts and Sentiments on the Evil and Wicked Traffic of the Slavery and Commerce of the Human Species* (1787), which Blake likely knew.[11] Throughout, the main plank of Cugoano's argument against slavery is that it runs contrary to moralistic reason, but when it comes to blackness, he swaps this argument for a Christian (partly mystical) interpretation. Initially, Cugoano invokes the maxim that skin color is irrelevant in the world beyond: "It does not alter the nature and quality of a man, whether he wears a black or a white coat, whether he puts it on or strips it off, he is still the same man."[12] The same metaphoric motif is developed by William Cowper in the frequently republished poem "The Negro's Complaint" (1788), where he seizes on the fact that a black man's complexion, which is a natural response to a hot climate, does not equate with his inner constitution: "Fleecy locks and black complexion / Cannot forfeit nature's claim; / Skins may differ, but affection / Dwells in white and black the same." [13] A similar idea is present in Mary Robinson's "The Negro Girl" (1800): "Then would they pity Slaves, and cry, with shame, / Whate'er their TINTS may be, their SOULS are still the same!" [14]

Like many other examples from *Songs of Innocence,* "The Little Black Boy" is centrally concerned with the theme of how religious virtues are received and practiced. What is most remarkable about this poem is that the African child is represented as someone who acts as a good steward for the English boy, offering to protect him "till he can bear, / To lean in joy upon our fathers knee" (*E* 9). The African child performs the virtuous act of charity as a matter of course, independent of any drilling from catechism or from some institutionally embedded church practices.

For Blake, true religion is received in the spirit, and men of all faiths can become one with the body of Jesus by performing acts of mercy and pity, without the crutches of Christian dogmatism. Such an idea is present in the *Innocence* poem "The Divine Image," where we find the testimonial that "Mercy Pity Peace and Love" are virtues available in equal measure among all humankind, whether one is "heathen, turk or jew" (*E* 13). In a commentary on this poem, Stewart Crehan contends that it is a response to eighteenth-century evangelicals, who in their missionary zeal were often more concerned with imposing civilization and Christian doctrine on the heathens than accepting the common humanity of different cultures. [15]

Is "The Little Black Boy" a response to evangelical missions among Africans? At the very least, Blake can be seen as inverting the usual conversion narrative offered by abolitionists, where a white benefactor teaches Christianity to the African. [16] Blake's topsy-turvy logic should be read against the mainstream axiom that Christians mission the heathens. For example, in *Short and Practical Discourses to Negroes, on the Plain and Obvious Principles of Religion and Morality* (1789), Richard Nisbet argues that his African congregation should be spared Christian knowledge that would overwhelm them, mentioning that he leaves out some parts of the Gospel until their "hearts are better prepared to hear of it." [17] Blake reverses this protection in his poem by letting the African boy "shade" the white boy from the Divine "till he can bear, / To lean in joy upon our fathers knee."

We should not forget that *Songs of Innocence* is intended to be poetry for children. By granting the heathen African child spiritual leadership over the English child in this way, Blake therefore also disrupts the nationalist, racial, and religious self-sufficiency that resonated in eighteenth-century children's poetry. The most famous example of this self-sufficiency can be seen in Isaac Watts's often republished *Divine and Moral Songs for the Use of Children* (first published in 1715). In "Praise for the Gospel," Watts's child speaker extols the fact that he "was born of *Christian* race" and not "a *Heathen*" who has never seen "the Book of God" or "Jesus and his Gospel known."[18] In Watts's "Praise for Birth and Education in a Christian Land," the child speaker thanks God for the fact that "I was born on British ground, / Where streams of heav'nly mercy flow, / And words of sweet salvation sound."[19]

The Spiritual Africans

For Blake, "innocence" is a mental state of intuitive religion that is associated with the uncorrupted child, but it is not reserved for the child. Blake and the Swedenborgians may have seen Africans in a similar way, as the latter persistently emphasized the Africans' primitive but noble purity. For the Swedenborgians, this view was part of a socio-discursive critique directed at what they saw as the wayward complexity and obscurity of Church doctrines. In the *New-Jerusalem Magazine* (1790), an abolitionist-oriented publication with which Wadström was deeply involved, Africans are described as "comparatively like children, who . . . learn more easily to walk in the path of virtue" and are better prepared for receiving divine knowledge internally than is the European "man of maturity," who is "corrupted" and "has already shut his interior against heaven." For this reason, "the lot of the men of the Old Church is . . . infinitely worse than that of the Heathens."[20]

The Swedenborgian ideas of the specially gifted Africans find parallels in other literature. Since the Middle Ages, the claim had regularly been made that Africa had become a refuge for the Lost Ten Tribes.[21] The former slave Olaudah Equiano hinted at this idea in *The Interesting Narrative* (1789), in which he describes a "strong analogy" that appears "to prevail in the manners and customs of my countrymen and those of the Jews, before they reached the Land of Promise, and particularly the patriarchs while they were yet in that pastoral state which is described in Genesis."[22] One of the similarities between the Africans and Jews is monotheism, which Equiano refers to as the African belief in "one Creator of all things."[23] Other analogies are found in the practice of circumcision, offerings, and feasts according to the Mosaic laws. Furthermore, the customs of the biblical patriarchs are invoked as a suggestive comparison to African manners: "Like the Israelites in their primitive state, our government was conducted by our chiefs or judges, our wise men and elders; and the head of a family with us enjoyed a similar authority over his household with that which is ascribed to Abraham and the other patriarchs."[24]

Some of these ideas may feed into Blake's poem, but its concrete constellation of metaphors points to a Swedenborgian context. I am not the first to point to Swedenborg in connection with "The Little Black Boy." Morton Paley comments briefly on it in his magisterial essay on Blake and Swedenborg; Stewart Crehan mentions it in just one short line; and more recently, Camilla Townsend, Anne Rubenstein, and Deirdre Coleman have all given it passing notice.[25] Kathleen Raine remains the critic who gives most attention to the poem's Swedenborgian metaphors; she does not at all, however, consider the contemporary abolitionist exertions in the Swedenborgian milieu with which Blake came into contact.[26] In the following pages, I will identify two interrelated motifs from Swedenborg's writing: the first relates to the doctrine of "the two suns," which Blake can be seen as implementing as a guiding conceit in the poem; and the second concerns Swedenborg's insistence that Africans are a uniquely spiritual people.

One important Swedenborgian idea is the representation of God as a spiritual sun. This is explained at length in *Divine Love and Divine Wisdom* (§§83–172), which Blake owned and annotated. Swedenborg writes that in "the spiritual World there is equally Heat and Light, as in the natural World; but the Heat there is spiritual, and in like Manner the Light, and spiritual Heat is the Good of Charity, and spiritual Light is the Truth of Faith" (§84).[27] The idea of a spiritual sun is a pivotal idea for Swedenborg, and it appears in much of his writings. The founders of the New Church in London also considered to be central the teaching of the existence of the two suns that provide for life (both material and divine), and they made reference to it in section XIII of the circular letter Blake signed when he attended the meeting in the New Jerusalem Church.[28]

Swedenborg explains that the spiritual sun is really just another way of describing Christ: "The Sun of heaven is the Lord, the light of it is Divine Truth, and the heat of it Divine Love, proceeding from the Lord as a Sun"—because, in the spiritual world, "the Lord appears in heaven as a Sun."[29] Nonetheless, he is not the sun; but "Divine Love and Divine Wisdom, in their proximate Emanation from Him, and round about Him, appear as a Sun before the Angels," that is to say "Himself in the Sun is A MAN, our Lord Jesus Christ," as Swedenborg explains in *True Christian Religion*.[30] Blake visualizes this in the illustration of the poem's second plate. In some copies, Christ is depicted with a radiant halo (L, T, V, Z, and AA), and visible beams emanate from his head in copy Y. (See *Plate* 4.)

When the black boy's mother imparts to him that the "cloud will vanish" as one approaches the Lord, it corresponds to Swedenborg's use of cloud as a metaphor for the errors of understanding that prevent man from receiving the heat and light of the spiritual sun. As Swedenborg writes: "Evils and falses are as so many black clouds, which, by their interposition between the Sun and the human eye, intercept it's [sic] lovely light and cheering influences," and the conversion to the Lord is an influx of God's "Heat and Light of Heaven" flowing into "the Interiors of the Body, in Consequence whereof there is an Elevation, as it were out of a Cloud and into the higher Air."[31]

I shall now examine the mystical wisdom that Swedenborg provides about some Africans, those who he claims possess an unusual spiritual insight, along with Blake's use of this wisdom as a template for his representation of the little black boy in heaven. In *Heaven and Hell*, Swedenborg tells us that some Africans in the interior of the continent show the "readiest disposition to receive all the good things and truths" of the spiritual world (§326). In *True Christian Religion*, Swedenborg describes the various nations of people in heaven and evaluates them according to how capable they are of receiving the heat and light of the spiritual sun. In §§835–40, Swedenborg details how "the Africans excel the other Gentiles in the Strength and Clearness of interior Discernment" (§837) and therefore have a superior understanding of God. The Africans' higher spiritual knowledge was vividly discussed in the milieu of Swedenborgians. *New-Jerusalem Magazine*, for example, printed a full-page illustration (in January 1790) of two Africans in "the World of Spirits." The illustration is described in detail, making reference to the passage in Swedenborg's *Conjugial Love* to which it relates (§114). It is a collection of "Angelic Spirits, selected from among the learned of the different kingdoms of Europe" who are in a competition to deliver their thoughts "on *the true origin, virtue, and power, of Conjug[i]al Love.*" The prize is a golden miter. It turns out that the Christians have no proper idea of "Conjugial Love," which was an important (albeit controversial) Swedenborgian concept. But, the Africans, who had stayed in the background for the competition, stepped forward and delivered a speech that communicates the truth on the subject; despite the fact that they had no scriptural knowledge, their intuitive wisdom earned them the miter. The engraved image is inscribed with the triumphant *"Cidaris erit Africo"* ("Africa will have the miter"). (See *Plate 2.*) This is used as an example of the Africans' intuitive understanding of divine truths.[32] There is no competition in Blake's "The Little Black Boy," but the same mild shock tactics are used: that the African boy understands the Divine more clearly and pertinently than does the English boy.

In this connection, it is probably no coincidence that Blake sets "The Little Black Boy" in "the southern wild." This description of Africa resonates with contemporary discussions of the continent as uncivilized and backward because of its hot climate and lack of properly organized agriculture.[33] But, for Blake, the uncultivated, pastoral landscapes—like the "valleys wild" of the "Introduction" to *Songs of Innocence* (E 7)— are privileged loci for harmony, care, and divine vision. The African communities, with their strong social bonds, were occasionally represented as antediluvian in abolitionist literature. Wadström, for example, writes that "the amiable simplicity of manners which reigns in the villages remote from the slave-trade" makes European visitors "imagine themselves carried into a new world, governed by the purest maxims of patriarchal innocence."[34] Such pronouncements share something in common with Blake's *The Four Zoas,* in which the millennialist emancipation of all "Slaves from every Earth in the wide Universe" is celebrated with "a New Song drowning confusion in its happy notes." *Confusion* is Blake's term for religious mystification, which will one day be overcome and its demise celebrated as a song composed by "an African Black," who knows the new paradise better than others since it is like a return to his "sweet native land" (Night the Ninth–134.30, 31, 34, 35; *E* 403).

The question is to what extent does the mother in "The Little Black Boy" keep open to heaven her boy's interior understanding? Some critics have raised doubts about the helpfulness of the instruction the mother provides. In an article discussing Blake's poem, Michael J. C. Echeruo, for example, questions whether the mother's seemingly pantheistic learning has any value, as he finds it difficult to correlate with Blake's idea of embodied theology.[35] This chimes with earlier readings of the mother's instruction as either limiting or oppressive,[36] so this is obviously an important issue that must be solved in the interpretation of the poem. In this respect, Swedenborgian symbolism may offer us some help. Blake would have read in *Divine Love and Divine Wisdom* that the sun in our natural world is not only a reflection of the divine presence in the spiritual world, but it also receives its energy from the divine light in the spiritual world.[37] So, by observing the way that the heat and light of the natural sun benefit our world, we can begin to understand how love and wisdom work in the world of the spirit.[38] In Swedenborg's conversation with Africans in the spiritual world, they explained to him that by observing how the natural sun provides for everything on earth—from the lowest plant to the highest creature—one may form an idea of God as the "Sun of the Universe," and thereby "clearly see and acknowledge his Omnipresence, Omniscience, and Omnipotence" (*True Christian Religion* §837). If we allow that the black mother in Blake's poem, like Swedenborg's Africans, expresses a version of Swedenborg's teaching of nature as one of divine "correspondences," then she is facilitating the boy's acceptance of God's divine love and charity. Blake is frequently seen as a poet who rejects nature, but in several places in his writing, he solicits a reading of the natural universe as a series of interpretable signs. For example, around 1788, Blake commented in his annotations to Johann Caspar Lavater's *Aphorisms on Man:* "every thing on earth is the word of God & in its essence is God" (*E* 599).

It has been suggested that the scene of the mother instructing the child is a borrowing of a *topos* in the literature published by African writers at the time.[39] Such a *topos* may have acted as an inspiration for Blake, but the lesson Blake's African mother provides for her child—that "we are put on earth a little space" to prepare for a higher world—follows a structure known from other examples of eighteenth-century children's poetry, notably Anna Laetitia Barbauld's popular 1781 collection *Hymns in Prose for Children*. In Barbauld's Hymn XII, the adult speaker instructs the young child to use the pleasure of sense to prepare for an even higher splendor in eternal heaven. The idea is that the child should absorb the glory of the natural universe in order to prime the child for the eternal beauty to be experienced in heaven: "we are to be here but for a little while, and there for ever."[40]

If we then turn to the black boy's vision, Swedenborgian readers could not help but recall Swedenborg's account of how "Little Children" in heaven are taken care of "under the immediate guardianship and protection of the Lord."[41] All children (heathen as Christian) are taught through "beautiful similitudes and instructive emblems, adequate to their genius and capacity." One lesson they must learn is the key Swedenborgian tenet that the Lord unites his divinity with his humanity.[42]

In the illustration on the second plate of Blake's poem, the African sees someone he calls "our father," whom we recognize as a conventional representation of Christ. The black boy understands him to be like a simple shepherd who takes care of his lambs, and his abode is a "golden tent" (a "tent" being an image from the Bible often used to indicate the simplicity of faith).[43] The image of the Divine as a human, caring father is important to Blake, just as it was to Swedenborg. The latter claimed that a proclivity for understanding the Divine as embodied in human form was particularly strong with Africans. In analyzing "The Little Black Boy," this claim requires our attention.

The Divine Human

We may here briefly examine Swedenborg's account of the conversation he had with Africans in the spiritual world. Swedenborg commends the Africans for having "no other Idea of God than as of a Divine Man," and for their understanding that God, whose love is "like most pure Fire," cannot enter into man "unless its Rays be veiled" in the form of the body of man.[44] The notion that God became embodied as the "Divine Human" was one of the main tenets of Swedenborg's Christ-centered mysticism. The heathen Africans would not know of Jesus, of course, but Swedenborg claims they had a correlating idea of the Divine embodied in human form. Thus, the Africans that Swedenborg converses with in the spiritual world show great astonishment when they learn that there are Christians who worship God "as of a Substance like Æther."[45]

African religion is taken up elsewhere in Swedenborg's writings. In *Heaven and Hell,* Swedenborg further holds that it is fundamental to the African creed that "God is visible in a human form."[46] In Blake's copy of *Divine Love and Divine Wisdom,* Swedenborg also states that humankind in the distant past had "no other Idea of God than that of a Man," and today there are still "Gentiles, particularly the Africans . . . [who] entertain an Idea of God as of a Man, and say that no one can have any other Idea of God." Therefore, Africans reject the error that God is abstract, a teaching that had infested the Christian Churches.[47] Blake annotated this passage: "to think of holiness distinct from man is impossible to the affections" (*E* 603).

What Swedenborg lauded in the (envisioned) African penchant for spirituality is precisely what he found missing in European Christianity: humans should conceive of God as a man, for it is not possible to think of, love, and be conjoined with something indefinite. In *True Christian Religion,* he concludes his treatment of the subject by rejoicing in the claim that the Africans' conception of the Divine is now spreading its influence across the African continent. This is good because it is a belief that is free from the mistaken tenets of European Christianity, which demand obedience to the abstract theology "taught by Ecclesiastics."[48]

Blake's African child clearly perceives the "father" in human form, as do Swedenborg's Africans. This is evident from the casual intimacy inherent in the black boy's reference to "our father," on whose knee one may readily "lean in joy." This strikes a notable contrast to the presumably English child-speaker in "The Tyger," who can only guess at the existence of an ineffable divinity in "distant deeps or skies" (*E* 24). The illustration on the second plate of "The Little Black Boy" shows how the African child guides the white boy to an up-close-and-personal meeting with Christ (the divine human). That the English boy is learning to pray to the divine human seems to be indicated by his posture, which replicates the praying figures at the top of "The Divine Image." (See *Plate 5*.)

That Blake shared Swedenborg's antagonism toward abstract religion is discernible in *The Book of Ahania*, where the figure Fuzon questions the worship of a god who is only a "Demon of smoke" and an "abstract non-entity" (2.10, 11; E 84). Similarly, in the "Preludium" to the revolutionary poem *America a Prophecy*, the spirit of revolution becomes reified in the figure of Orc. Significantly, the shadowy daughter of Urthona recognizes him as "the image of God who dwells in darkness of Africa" (2.8; E 52). Like Christ who became flesh to provide hope and salvation for humankind, Orc's revolutionary power to dispel tyranny and renew human communities derives from his embodiment in human form. This is not a far cry from the political effects anticipated in the Swedenborgian tract *Plan for a Free Community at Sierra Leona*. It is here held that insofar as the belief in the "One Visible God in a Human Form" was adopted in the proposed colony, one would never need a "despotic Monarch" to hold the community together, since everyone would take care of one another. [49]

Blake and the Swedenborgian Abolitionists

Can we then conclude that with "The Little Black Boy," Blake has written a Swedenborgian poem? Well, the question has no simple answer. I have argued that Blake was inspired by Swedenborg's symbols and ideas, presenting the Africans as preserving a privileged perception intuitively tuned into the Divine. Nonetheless, when we look at the writings published by contemporary Swedenborgians, Blake's reversed scene of instruction on the second plate (where the African boy seems to guide the English boy) is clearly at odds with their view on missionary activity. Wadström's abolitionist tracts and the prints directly concerned with Swedenborgian matters adhere to a mainstream evangelical model, which called for missioning among the Africans. In fact, an overview of the printed matter published by Swedenborgians during the late 1780s and early 1790s will reveal that Swedenborg's ideas of the spiritual Africans were invoked primarily to justify the proselytizing of the

Swedenborgian gospel, not to argue for the preservation or protection of their "innocence."[50] In *Observations on the Slave Trade,* for example, Wadström argued for the colonization of Africa by first shrugging off all warnings that this "would be introducing among the simple and inno-cent people the corrupted manners of the Europeans." On the contrary, he explicitly argued for the benefit of securing the Africans' "Cultiva-tion," as this may take place through colonization. In this connection, Wadström stretched and expanded the commonplace metaphor of Afri-cans as "children" to its absolute limit; they must be brought to maturity through the careful guidance and religious instruction provided by civi-lized Westerners, who can act as their "religious fathers."[51]

In this respect, Wadström and the Swedenborgians fit into a larger historical framework. As historians have noted, the beginning of Brit-ish abolitionism coincided almost exactly with the revived activities of the British missionary movement.[52] The physical emancipation of Africans from the chains of slavery was intrinsically connected with the spiritual deliverance of their souls. This is no more clearly seen than in the conclusion to John Wesley's much-read tract *Thoughts upon Slavery* (1774): "O burst thou all their chains in sunder; more espe-cially the chains of their sins: Thou, Saviour of all, make them free, that they may be free indeed!"[53] Robert Hindmarsh expresses a sim-ilar idea: "the Reason why Europeans are not made Slaves is because they are in Possession of the Word; which cannot but keep Slavery at a Distance." From this it follows that "were the Africans in Possession of the Word, it would be equally impossible for them to become Subjects of Slavery," as the "covetous European" would not dare to treat them as harshly as they do at present.[54]

If we hold on to these words and then move to Blake's poem, we realize that it contains an element of controversy. Alan Richardson has summarized "The Little Black Boy" as a vision in which the African boy exerts "a self-affirming discourse of his own," without the need for traditional church doctrines. In this way, Blake can be seen as level-ing a critique at "the colonialist discourse informing antislavery poems and tracts," since these often made it a moral requirement for blacks to be educated and Christianized.[55] Although Richardson does not mention it, this reading ties in with the religious relativism that Blake had articulated the year before in the short tract *All Religions are One* (1788). Here, Blake celebrates the diversity of religions. "As all men are alike (tho' infinitely various) So all Religions & as all similars have one source," Blake writes. This source is the "true Man," which is the inner divine (*E 2*).

But what are we to make of "The Little Black Boy"? The African child is more than just an equal; he helps the English boy to overcome his restricted vision. As was the case with the concept of the noble savage in European tradition, Blake's African becomes a vessel to criticize the abuses at home—in this case, perhaps, the English system of religious education, which is addressed elsewhere in the *Songs*.

Given the Swedenborgian context of Blake's poem, it will be useful to see the religious independence of African innocence as at least partly a response to the Swedenborgians' missionary ambitions. We may pick a pertinent example from Joseph Proud's collection of Swedenborgian hymns (1790). The fifty-fourth hymn, "On the New Church in the interior parts of Africa," contains a call to the Swedenborgians to proselytize in Africa:

> JERUSALEM from heav'n descends,
> And far and wide her light extends;
> Now Afric's sable sons rejoice,
> And shout to hear the Saviour's voice.
>
> The idol gods behold they fall,
> And truth celestial conquers all;
> Darkness gives place to sacred light,
> And heav'n is open'd to their sight.
>
> The showers revive the thirsty land,
> The barren deserts fruitful stand;
> The thorny wastes rich plenty yield,
> And golden harvests grace the field.
>
> The vallies rise they laugh and sing,
> The hills their thankful tribute bring;
> And now the sable barb'rous race,
> Exulting praise the God of grace.

Ye happy negroes we conspire,
Join your glad notes and raise them higher;
May Europe's songs with Afric's rise,
And Praise united reach the skies. [56]

Proud presents a vision of Africa no longer subjugated by slave traders but conquered by "truth celestial." Africa is in "darkness" but will be
illuminated by Jerusalem's "sacred light," and the blacks will have their
eyes opened to Christianity. The prospective result of the missionary
work is that Africa will turn from a "barren" land to one that is spiritually "fruitful"—a symbolism that follows the prophecy of Isaiah 35:1.
The hymn concludes with a vision of Europeans and Africans united in
their praise of God. This parallels what we find in Blake's poem, but it
is predicated on the expectation that the "barb'rous race" of heathens
will be converted to Christianity. Only then can the "sable sons rejoice, /
And shout to hear the Saviour's voice." In contrast, Blake does away with
the need for European missionaries; it is the black boy's African mother
who teaches him to "hear" the divine "voice" that calls him to "rejoice."

In terms of actual plans for a Swedenborgian mission to Africa, we
may turn to Wadström. Blake most likely knew that this leading Swedenborgian was instructing the royal African prince Peter Panah in Swedenborg's teachings. Wadström had bought Panah's freedom in May
1788, and the African was subsequently baptized into the New Jerusalem Church on Christmas Day of the same year. To commemorate
Wadström's patronage, a portrait was painted in which the Swedish gentleman teaches Panah Christianity through the vehicle of Swedenborg's
Divine Providence. [57]

We learn from other sources that the purpose of the Swedenborgian instruction was for Panah to return to Africa to disseminate "the
rudiments of the everlasting Gospel" among his people. [58] The portrait, which uses an artificial African setting with a hut and a palm tree,
was painted by the Swedish painter Carl Frederik von Breda, who lived
and worked in London from 1787 to 1796. Under the title *Portrait of a
Swedish Gentleman instructing a Negro Prince,* it was exhibited in 1789
at the Royal Academy in London, which is where Blake may have seen
it. [59] (See *Plate* 3.) For all intents and purposes, the scene of instruction

on the second plate of "The Little Black Boy" is a compositional parallel to the title page of *Songs of Innocence,* where two children stand before a nurse or mother who is holding an open book in her lap that the two children are reading. But, perhaps with von Breda's image in mind, Blake's illustration of the black boy placing his hand on the white boy's back bears a similarity to Wadström resting his charitable hand on Panah's shoulder. The presence of the dawning morning light and the blue and yellow hues used in several of Blake's hand-colored plates may also suggest a connection. In any case, beholding the two scenarios together is instructive, as it spells out Blake's attempt at color-reversing the standard scene of instruction in evangelical literature and representations.

In Blake's "The Little Black Boy," the Africans show a spiritual self-sufficiency maintained through a close kinship-bound community, and they can be seen as emblematizing the concept of "innocence" on a cultural level. With respect to this representation of Africans, Blake may be hostage to a sentimental (if not ultimately patronizing) make-believe of Western liberalism, but "The Little Black Boy" problematizes evangelical attempts to colonize "innocence." In handing over the agency of spiritual guidance to the African, Blake is promoting an idealist and wholly utopian defense of "innocence" that was out of touch with progressive evangelicalism—and that may have served as a retort to it. If Blake had provided us with a poetic counterpart in *Songs of Experience,* we might have seen this turn into a direct criticism. ≈

Swedenborg and Modernity

INGA SANNER, *Professor of the History of Ideas, Stockholm University*

AN IMPORTANT SOURCE of inspiration for Carl Bernhard Wadström (1746–99) was the Swedish scientist and mystic Emanuel Swedenborg (1688–1772).[1] Wadström was by no means alone in this regard, but he was definitely among the earliest and most ardent followers of Swedenborg. From the late eighteenth century up until today, thinkers have continued to be highly inspired by Swedenborg. Surprisingly, references to Swedenborg surface in thinkers whose ideas are not immediately connected with the worldview of an old, pre-modern mystic.[2] From utopians to feminists to proponents of free love, examples from several divergent streams of thought may be found! How are we to understand this?

The question to be answered, or at least reflected upon, is how one could grasp the connection between Swedenborg and "modern" thinkers, or those who are active in a later period that is sometimes labeled *modernity*. Of course, one must take into consideration the fact that *modern* and *modernity* are extremely complex terms and are difficult to use in this context. Without ambitions of producing any clear definitions, here they are simply used to denote a certain period in Western history—namely, that from the end of the eighteenth century up to the middle of the twentieth century.

Hence, the following more specific question may now be raised: What was it in Swedenborg's worldview that made him relevant to thinkers who lived in a later part of history, starting at the end of the eighteenth century, when Wadström was active?

Christianity and Modernity

In an attempt to answer this question, we have to start by reminding ourselves of the history of Christianity. Swedenborg was indeed a Christian
thinker, but in his own particular way. His way of interpreting Christianity was in many respects in line with ideas that became prominent in
more modern times.

It is not possible to understand the emergence of Western modernity without considering certain changes within the Christian tradition,
two of which are particularly worth mentioning here: 1) the general
ambition to make Christianity more "down to earth" and 2) the conceptions of humanity, which were crucial in adapting Christianity to modern ideas. Swedenborg played an important role in both these senses.

Firstly, let's consider the tendency to make Christianity more "down
to earth." During the eighteenth and nineteenth centuries, many philosophers emphasized that Christianity was not mainly about heavenly
things but rather that it was about the real, existing world, with concrete
relevance for living people. As science and empirical methods became
more influential by the second half of the nineteenth century, this "down
to earth" attitude became increasingly important. Swedenborg was one
of many thinkers who paved the way for this development by saying that
science and religion were not in opposition to one another. On the contrary, Swedenborg emphasized, they were in perfect harmony with each
other: investigating earthly matters was actually a way of getting closer
to God! This attitude made it possible to combine a belief in science
with a religious position.[3]

Of course, Swedenborg was not unique in proposing such a view,
and this particular aspect of his worldview is not even the main reason
for his popularity among modern thinkers. Even more significant to the
impact that he had are his ideas about the spiritual world, which constitute a strong and very particular characteristic of his theology.

The spiritual world is a realm, or perhaps more accurately a state or
even a state of being, that every person has to enter after death before
arriving in heaven or in hell. As a matter of fact, it is during a person's
stay in this middle world when it will be decided whether she or he
will go to heaven or to hell. Swedenborg's descriptions of the spiritual
world are very detailed, as he has much to say about what is going on in

that part of existence.[4] At the same time, his descriptions of the spiritual world are very concrete and tangible. Generally, he describes landscapes with mountains, valleys, trees, and people. These people perform all kinds of activities that they used to indulge in when they were alive—carrying out their daily chores, working, eating, meeting friends, marrying, making love, and so forth.[5]

The Swedish scholar Ronny Ambjörnsson, who is one of the co-authors of this book, has observed that Swedenborg's realism in describing the spiritual world made his visions more concrete and therefore quite easy to transfer to the ordinary world. Swedenborg's visions were used as points of departure for developing utopian ideas. Accordingly, his descriptions of the spiritual world were used as blueprints for visions of future societies. Wadström was an early example of someone creating such standards.[6]

The Spiritual World

Swedenborg's concrete description of the spiritual world helps us understand why his ideas became attractive to later scholars, but this is not the only significant feature. What it is that *happens* to those persons in the spiritual world is of utmost importance! A way of understanding Swedenborg's relevance to posterity is to take his more general conceptions of humanity into consideration, one of which can be seen in relation to his criticism of the Christian idea of original sin—that every person is sinful by birth and therefore by nature. In opposition to a more traditional Christian view, Swedenborg emphasized that it is possible for human beings to strive for perfection—even if they would never reach this goal. When Swedenborg discusses this possibility of a person's development, his concept of love plays an important role.

Swedenborg believes that there are two kinds of love that are active in a person—love for oneself (egoism) and true love—and that there is normally a struggle between these two kinds of love. In order to attain moral fulfillment, true love has to win this internal struggle, thereby becoming internally dominant. If true love becomes dominant, the person will go to heaven; otherwise, she or he has darker prospects.[7]

This process takes place within the spiritual world, but in order to understand what is happening there, we have to consider another important part of Swedenborg's worldview: the difference between the outer and the inner aspects of a person. The outer aspects are those shown in social life, when relating to other people. These aspects are expressions of how we want to appear to other people. Normally, we want to look better than we really are. This means that the outer aspects are the artificial and even false parts of one's personality, since they do not reflect our true selves. In ordinary life, we are able to hide our true feelings and motivations, but this is no longer possible when we enter into the spiritual world. There, our true personality, or true self, will become visible and prominent—whether we want it to be or not. This is described by Swedenborg in an almost physical way: the outer self fades away while the inner self emerges.[8] This process profoundly affects people, as their thoughts and feelings become visible and impossible to hide. Whether you like somebody or not, your feelings are shown by your expression.

Another consequence of the fading away of one's outer self is that the person in question becomes more sensitive than she or he had been before the transformation took place. This means that they will be able to perceive other people's inner lives and experience the world as a whole in a more direct manner than ever before.[9] Communication between people becomes much easier and more direct; words are no longer necessary to create understanding, since private thoughts and feelings become public. It is worth mentioning that Swedenborg took great interest in both music and mathematics, and he regarded them as examples of wordless and ideal languages.

It is also worth noting that there is a dimension of Swedenborg's ideas that comes close to an early type of cultural criticism. Swedenborg was very critical toward certain aspects of contemporary social life, which he considered full of hypocrisy and false pretense. For example, he pointed out how learned people used their knowledge for superficial showing-off rather than for furthering true wisdom. Such perversions were supposed to disappear in the spiritual world, since all false pretensions would appear lofty in the open air.

Let us now return, though, to our discussion of what it is that makes Swedenborg's conception of humanity so modern.

Modern Man

As mentioned above, one very important element of Swedenborg's thought is the idea of moral perfection as a possibility for human beings. This was a prominent idea in the nineteenth century, at a time when words like *sympathy* and *altruism* played key roles in the different radical visions that were had about the improvement of humanity, including visions of a new society. This idea even gained ground among Christian thinkers during that time. [10]

And as we have already established, another important aspect of Swedenborg was the idea of the realization of the true personality, or the true self. Even though he did not use the word *authentic,* this term would be suitable to describe his ideas about the realization of one's inner and true personality. During the nineteenth century, and right up to our time, ideas about self-realization have been abundant and they have often been accompanied by the distinction between artificial outer aspects of human personality, which are formed by social conventions, and a true inner self. [11]

In the nineteenth century, many different visions of an ideal humanity were formulated. In these visions, we find elements that are similar to ideas articulated by Swedenborg—some of them inspired by him directly and some indirectly via other thinkers. Ideas about humans being capable of perfect communication were common at this time, and several attempts were made to create a perfect and universal language with the aim of unifying humanity. The most well-known example of these efforts was the creation of Esperanto in 1887. Telepathy, which was perceived as a kind of direct communication that would presumably evolve in the future, is another example. Such attempts at evolved communication can be regarded as visions of humanity as a united whole, dreams that remained vivid throughout the nineteenth century. [12]

Ideas concerning a more sensitive human being were common as well. Some of these visions contained rather speculative ideas about a future in which human beings would develop new senses that would permit them to perceive the world, in general, and other persons, in particular, in a more direct and empathetic way. *Compassion* and *sensitivity* were key words used in these descriptions.

The importance of self-knowledge as a means to realizing one's true personality is yet another element in Swedenborg's worldview that is in line with the ideas of the nineteenth century. As Swedenborg describes it, when one's inner self becomes visible in the spiritual world, that person gains a perfect memory. They remember everything that happened in their life, and, in order to work for self-improvement, they have to go through every part of their memory once again, which can be quite a painful experience. If one has the courage to do this and has the strength to regret everything that went wrong, the process toward perfection may start. Reading the book of one's life is thus a way to ennoble one's personality—looking back as a way to build one's future. This indeed was a widespread idea among theosophists and psychologists in the nineteenth and twentieth centuries—understanding the past as a way to become a better person! These kinds of ideas can be found among spiritualists as well as among forerunners of psychoanalysis. [13]

Love and Personality

There is one last area that must be addressed in our quest to better understand Swedenborg's relevance to later thinkers. This will take us back to the concept of love, but this time love between a man and a woman (Swedenborg's only concern is heterosexual relations). Although being rather controversial during his lifetime (and among many thinkers thereafter as well), Swedenborg's theories of love became highly influential during later periods.

According to Swedenborg, true marriage must be founded in true love, not in social conventions or expectations. To him, the ideal marriage is based on personal commitment, and a necessary condition for realizing this is the possibility for a man and a woman to learn to know one another before marriage. Therefore, Swedenborg argued in favor of long engagements, where both parties would have the opportunity to discover whether their personalities would fit one another. He also eagerly emphasized that love contains both physical and psychological dimensions and that they have to be in harmony with one another. [14]

What was really radical in his thinking on this subject was the idea that lovers became husband and wife in the spiritual world, even if they had not been married before death. From a divine perspective, a man and a woman whose personalities were in harmony with one another were considered a married couple. This was a way, although an indirect one, of saying that divorce is sometimes necessary in order to create loving relations. Of course, one has to add that according to Swedenborg, long engagements were the best way to avoid divorce.[15]

Furthermore, the ideal love between a man and a woman was of utmost importance since, according to Swedenborg, love is a way to realize one's true personality. In a love-based relationship, both parties gradually realize who they are and can find the inner parts of their personalities. Obviously, these kinds of ideas resemble modern views about love as a means of self-realization.

One might add that Swedenborg assigns man and woman completely different characteristics, and, as a consequence of this, they have separate roles in the process of self-realization. Women are seen as superior when it comes to morality, while rationality is the male characteristic par excellence. This way of distinguishing the sexes became prevalent during the nineteenth century. Connected to this view was the belief that men would be capable of learning from women in moral matters so that they would be able to restrain their allegedly much stronger sexual instincts.[16]

Swedenborg's view of sexuality as a natural and important part of love has been appreciated by several later theorists. These intellectuals have emphasized the combination of spiritual and bodily aspects as a necessary condition for a relation characterized by true love. Swedenborg did not view this as being in opposition to Christian views; on the contrary, he emphasized that spiritual as well as bodily matters were part of God's creation.

⤳

Let us now summarize these brief reflections on Swedenborg's influence on modern thought. First, Swedenborg is modern since his description of the spiritual world is concrete and therefore rather easy to transfer to the ordinary world. Second, he is modern since he believed in the possibility of striving for perfection for all human beings. Third, his vision of the ideal person contains concepts such as moral fulfillment, authenticity, perfect communication, sensibility, self-knowledge, and self-realization—all of them key concepts in modern times. Finally, Swedenborg is modern since he regards love as a way of self-realization and as a way to express one's personality in relation to another person's. Self-realization is seen as a process that one is unable to handle by oneself; instead, it has to be performed together with a person one loves.

One More Remark

In addition to these conclusions, one might ask if conceiving of Swedenborg as a modern thinker is more a matter of observing similarities between ideas of certain kinds than it is of describing various types of influence. In both cases, it is tempting to suggest that in taking the risk of being anachronistic, Swedenborg, and probably Wadström as well, were "ahead of their time."

Swedenborg and Wadström both passed away during the latter half of the eighteenth century. According to some historians, the decades just before the year 1800 are regarded as the time of birth of "modernity" proper, due to the substantial changes that were taking place in Western society at that time. The German historian Reinhart Koselleck has labeled this period as the *Sattelzeit,* or "saddle period," arguing that it was during this period that several important concepts underwent significant changes of meaning. From the French Revolution onward, the word *revolution,* for example, suggested a sense of a future state of being rather than, in the older sense of the word, referring to something revolving back to where it came from. [17]

Swedenborg's ideas are easy to connect with dreams of a better future, and this is probably the main reason why his ideas are so useful to modern academics and writers. When it comes to the fate of the individual or even to social life as a whole, dreams of a different and better future are important components. During the nineteenth century, dreams of an ideal society were prominent alongside the dreams of an ideal humanity. Even though these radical dreams faded out in the twentieth century, the visions of self-realization as a means of creating an ideal person were still vivid and strong. Swedenborg's thought encompassed a wide range of ideas about such betterments and such ways toward universal progress; and accordingly, it has since then been possible to pick up the parts of his worldview that were most suited for each actual situation. [18] ≈

A World Apart: The American Antislavery Issue

JAMES F. LAWRENCE, *The Graduate Theological Union and Pacific School of Religion at Berkeley, California*

CARL BERNHARD WADSTRÖM'S reception history in the United States among American Swedenborgians on the slavery question presents a crucible case study of sorts. The US context witnessed the vilest experience of slavery for modern Europeans and Euro-Americans since the enslavement and owning of human beings happened on the domestic soil of white people. It involved a much deeper complicity in the social institution for the benefit of a much larger percentage of the white populations than was true in the European situations, where slavery was largely confined to faraway colonies and to the general economy as part of its international trade. In the American slavery context, the enormity of economic self-interest and its profound integration into the cultural fabric was on another order of enmeshment than was true for European countries with the slave trade. In addition, the rapid growth of the Swedenborgian movement in early America in the half-century leading up to the Civil War was such that the American context represented the largest number of Swedenborgians living in any one country. How did Swedenborgian thought perform in retrospect? And how was Wadström's work received and used in Antebellum America by the growing Swedenborgian population there? Was there a susceptibility to similar ideas?

American religion historians generally agree that antislavery activity in the United States falls into three distinct periods, or phases.

Spurred primarily by Enlightenment-era rhetoric in the American Revolution on human rights, the first phase arose in the middle of the eighteenth century, crested in the late 1780s, and became quiescent by 1810. A renewed phase could be seen as beginning in 1831, as this watershed year was driven principally by fresh religious vision from the Second Great Awakening, which advocated for both personal and social perfection. This new wave also captured the imagination of many black slaves within their own religious structures. Finally, the outbreak of civil war jolted huge numbers of the quiet middle in the North into antislavery commitments.[1] Religious discourse took a leadership position only in the second of these three phases, with political liberals having a more prominent position in the first and third.[2]

The sources of original American antislavery discourse—engaged by both Enlightenment political philosophers and social conscience religionists—owed their impetus to imported European texts and thinkers. And it is through these sources that the dominant traditions in early American Christianity had advantages over Swedenborgianism, because Swedenborg's reception did not take hold in Europe until the 1780s, and it did not even congeal there until the first phase of American antislavery activity had concluded. That is, with only a few exceptions, all Swedenborgian activity in the New World was homegrown. It did not have the benefit of a living tradition from Europe that included antislavery rhetoric as did Baptists, Congregationalists, Presbyterians, and Wesleyans, who together comprised eighty percent of religious Americans until well after the turn of the century. Though there were individual readers of Swedenborg certainly as early as 1784, American Swedenborgianism enjoyed only the tiniest of boosts from European emigration, and only the faintest trace of engagement with English Swedenborgian discourse on the slavery question can be found within voluminous extant publications. Generally speaking, American Swedenborgians overwhelmingly were cultured domestic converts seeking intellectual escape from Calvinism.[3]

The middle wave of antislavery fervor stemming from religious discourse on the question in America involved a "perfectionist" spirituality that was at odds with Swedenborgian theology. A Calvinist episode emerging especially among Baptists and Methodists, this vision foresaw holiness and "second blessing" sanctification creating such a radical restoration of persons that society as a whole could become perfect. These revivalists held that the new nation would not receive the full divine blessing until a complete sanctification of national life was achieved. There was no place for human slavery in such a vision. The British scholar of American religious history, Richard Carwardine of Oxford, estimates that by the 1850s, more than ten million people, or forty percent of the American population, had close sympathies with perfectionist spirituality and with the high emotional revival style that pushed such full sanctification fervor of evangelical Christianity.[4] Yet, due to a fundamentally different understanding of eschatology, the new religious movement of Swedenborgianism distanced itself from that dominant religious meta-narrative in the culture.

Swedenborg's first theological work came off the presses in England in 1749 with the first of eight volumes of his magnum opus, *Arcana Coelestia,* so the earliest conceivable date of his influence in American discourse would be 1750. Despite the importance in retrospect of Wadström's visionary project of African emancipation and African spirituality and spiritual potential, and despite Wadström's rootedness in Swedenborgian theosophy with regard to these social and political projects, his work and thinking seem not to have made the voyage across the Atlantic to the US debate on slavery. There are no known references either in early American Swedenborgianism or at any time before the Civil War by American Swedenborgians regarding Wadström's life, the Sierra Leone project, or his spiritual abolitionist reasoning from Swedenborg's writings. The earliest American reference to Wadström's work appears a full half-century after the Civil War in a 1911 article by Carl Theophilus Odhner on the larger subject of "The Early History of the New Church in Sweden."[5]

Furthermore, a thorough investigation of the twenty thousand-item research collection for the North American Swedenborgian Church in the nineteenth century,[6] which includes a comprehensive collection of pamphlets, tracts, and serial periodicals, uncovers only fifteen significant voices speaking in extant discourse on the slavery question from Swedenborgian incipiency in the American states until the end of the Civil War—and of these, only eleven are polished published pieces, as the remaining four are shorter comments in letters to the editor or personal correspondence. Of these fifteen voices, one is pro-slavery, another accuses Swedenborgianism as a whole of being pro-slavery, and most consider American Swedenborgianism to be generally mute on the slavery question. In addition to printed discourse, there is also printed evidence of at least two Swedenborgians with documented leadership positions in the American Anti-Slavery Society and of a few individuals known as active in the Underground Railroad. [7]

Nonetheless, an early American follower stands out. A wealthy Virginian who at one time owned 445 slaves is one of three figures (along with Wadström and Lydia Maria Child) commonly cited on American Swedenborgian websites as evidence for an early progressive American Swedenborgian abolitionist history. Colonel Robert Carter (1728–1804) experienced a passionate Christian conversion into the Baptist tradition in 1778 during the First Great Awakening. Not long thereafter, he built a Baptist chapel in Virginia because Baptist church buildings were very scarce due to Baptists being at that time a persecuted sect in that state. Carter began reading Swedenborg in 1790, had many communications with Swedenborgians in Baltimore and Philadelphia, and was active in procuring and disseminating Swedenborg's writings. On August 1, 1791, he took the legal steps to emancipate all of his slaves, resulting in *the largest manumission by a single individual in the history of United States slavery before the Civil War.* The few secular historians who have looked closely at Carter's life remain unsure about his motivations for releasing his slaves. Marguerite Beck Block surmises that since the Baptists were more abolitionist than were the Swedenborgians, it is probably true that the first antislavery seeds sown occurred through his connection to the Baptist church, but the timing of his manumission with his embrace of Swedenborgianism is surely intriguing. [8]

Though Carter went on to become active in early organized Swedenborgianism for another three decades, with a considerable legacy of personal papers and formal church writings, there is no subsequent commentary on the matter. The only extant comment, in fact, is on the actual legal document of manumission itself in its prefatory sentence: "I have for some time past been convinced that to retain them in Slavery is contrary to the true Principles of Religion and Justice, and that therefore it was my duty to manumit them."[9] This straightforward and sole surviving comment alludes to both Enlightenment rhetoric and Christian humanitarianism, but it clearly indicates a longstanding conviction that predates his engagement with Swedenborgian thought.

The Second Great Awakening and the Antislavery Movement, 1800–60

A remarkable quiescence throughout religious America served as an interlude during the first three decades of the nineteenth century, but it kicked up again in a fury in the late 1820s with the advent of the Second Great Awakening. Antebellum religion historian Douglas Strong argues that the primary religious impulse driving the new upsurge of antislavery agitation was a perfectionist spirituality rooted in holiness theories that espoused the possibility of a "second blessing" in sanctification such that a person could become *wholly* restored. There were some who extended the perfectionist vision to society itself: the new nation would not receive the full divine blessing until an all-embracing sanctification of national life was achieved. An imminent Last Judgment and Second Coming was believed to be at hand during the Second Great Awakening, but that *eschaton* could not occur until such holiness by believers was achieved. Swedenborgians professed the distinctive eschatology of the Last Judgment having transpired throughout the year 1757 with a consequent need for society to conform to the New Church worldview. Therefore, they believed perfectionist spirituality not only to be wrongheaded but also futile, and the American Swedenborgian longstanding passivity is partly explained as a protest against such a "superficial" perspective of the fundamental spiritual problem and its solution.

As this second great phase ensued, the abolitionist cause did not gain the foreground in any American denomination other than that of the Friends. Since abolitionist activity was slow to arouse the church in large numbers, it left that institutional structure and became more independent. Thus, while the emotional tenor of evangelical Christianity was high, and social improvement programs such as temperance were very popular, the social extension of holiness that would involve the abolition of slavery did not gain ground but remained a minority position in the churches—both those in the South *and* the North. Indeed, according to John McKivigan—perhaps the leading religious culture historian on the slavery question in the Antebellum United States—few specialist scholars today believe that the sectional splits that sundered the two largest religious groups in the 1840s—Baptists and Methodists—into North and South had anything to do with an intensifying antislavery passion in the North, but rather that they were caused by internal governance affairs that mirrored national governance tensions. It took almost until the outbreak of the war before sharp and tough antislavery discourse became actually dominant in the northern wings of these denominations, and the very same is true of the Swedenborgian Church as testified to by the records in the archives.

Reading groups and religious societies centered on Swedenborg's reformation of Christian thought were taking hold in the newly independent United States of America throughout the last decade of the eighteenth century and the first decades of the nineteenth century.[10] By 1817, there were enough groups and churches to spur a national convention in Philadelphia that drew representatives from seventeen organized groups (the practice of a national annual convention has been consistently observed to the present day), and by the commencement of the Civil War in 1861, there were sixty-four legally incorporated churches with approximately 2,500 members, though the readership of Swedenborg in America by mid-century vastly surpassed that number as Swedenborg's name recognition was widespread.[11] Only one Swedenborgian church, in Abingdon, Virginia, was built south of the Mason-Dixon Line before the war. Despite the fact that numerous Swedenborgian individuals and families appear in the record in various states of the South, and several missionary circuit-riding Swedenborgian ministers made trips to various parts of the South, there were no ordained ministers working in the South full-time before the war.[12]

During this second era of antislavery discourse in American history, there is no extant discourse in Swedenborgian circles before 1850, and the only traces of Swedenborgian thought applied to slavery are comments regarding this very silence and suspicions that the church in general was not antislavery. The earliest documentation on the matter in current scholarship arises from the opinions about Swedenborgianism in general, and about the kingpin Boston Swedenborgian church specifically, as revealed through the correspondence of the prominent American abolitionist Lydia Maria Child (1802–80). Child had become active for a time in the Boston church, whose pastor was one of the most prominent and powerful Swedenborgian clergymen in the Antebellum period, Rev. Thomas Worcester. Along with Wadström and Carter, Child is one of three heroic figures claimed on contemporary websites as being part of a progressive American Swedenborgian history on slavery, and some even suggest that she was influenced by her Swedenborgian spirituality to become abolitionist. The fact, however, is nearly the opposite. In recalling her activity there in the late 1820s, she writes in personal correspondence to prominent abolitionist Gerrit Smith, who had once subscribed to the Swedenborgian publication *Intellectual Repository:*

> The [Boston Swedenborgian] church and pastor were so bitterly pro-slavery, and so intensely bigoted [sic], that I doubted whether such a church could have come down from heaven.[13]

All of Child's biographers have held that she left the Swedenborgian congregation due to the church's reaction to her 1833 book, *An Appeal in Favor of the Class of Americans Called Africans,* but Tisa Anders now argues that Child had already left the church in 1828. The immediate cause of Child's separation from the Swedenborgian Church had been her pastor's refusal to perform the marriage rites for mixed marriages— that is, between Swedenborgians and non-Swedenborgians! Instead, her Unitarian minister brother, Convers Francis, Jr., performed their wedding ceremony. Child never went back to the New Church, though she laments a number of times in correspondence in later years that she was still drawn to Swedenborg's ideas and spiritual vision, and she tended to congregate with spiritualist movements after the Civil War.[14]

The Opening Salvo

Starting in 1850, a trio of antislavery Swedenborgian clergy who knew each other well broke the silence. Though Richard DeCharms[15] (1796–1864), Solyman Brown (1790–1876), and George Bush (1796–1859) disagreed on other matters concerning the often intellectually tempestuous new denomination, they were all decidedly antislavery. A specialist in nineteenth-century Swedenborgian history, Scott Trego Swank, identifies these three as among the most controversial Swedenborgians of the century. [16] In addition, one pro-slavery voice, William Henry Holcombe (1825–93), recently converted and newly acquainted with Bush, also came into print.

DeCharms was first out in print against slavery via a holiday sermon address that was expanded into a tract. [17] In addition to controversial stands, DeCharms also had an overbearing, contentious personality that undermined his ability to be a leader in the denomination, but his voice was widely disseminated. Originally a printer, he routinely took strong published stands on such contemporary Swedenborgian controversies as spiritualism, homeopathy, and anti-clericalism. His sixty-three-page antislavery tract, in which he identifies himself on the title page as "An Ordaining Minister of the New Jerusalem," presents a rousing excoriation of American slavery, drawing upon numerous practical and philosophical opinions to buttress his fundamental argument that forced bondage is an evil wholly at odds with true Christianity. Yet from a political and social perspective, he does not espouse immediate abolition and prefers colonization instead, which would also be Brown's position and the most popular position among the minority of antislavery Antebellum Swedenborgians.

Though similar to Wadström's own visionary plan for a colony for freed slaves and a haven against the slave trade, the concept of free colonies for black people had been active in America since 1816 with the formation of the American Colonization Society (ACS, with the complete legal name of The Society for the Colonization of Free People of Color of America), and given that there is no extant reference to Wadström in Swedenborgian discourse until the twentieth century, it is more than likely that American Swedenborgians were drawing upon the American discourse of colonization as one response to the social tensions created by the institution of slavery in the United States.

The idea of freedom as an irreducible condition of human regeneration, which itself is deemed in Swedenborgian thought as God's only true purpose in creation, became the lynchpin in American Swedenborgian antislavery reasoning. Later in 1850, DeCharms wrote to his friend, the prominent New York University Oriental languages professor—formerly Presbyterian and recently turned Swedenborgian—George Bush, who was about to come out in print himself and who would become the best-known antislavery American Swedenborgian:

> It is impossible that your abhorrence of the southern system of servitude can be stronger than mine. That southerners should regard <u>human</u> beings with <u>immortal souls</u> as <u>property</u> on a level with cows, horses, and asses, is an abomination indeed! But for their sakes, I wished to put African slavery in the best light that they might see it to be an evil permitted for good, and have all the generous impulses of their own noble nature stimulated into free and rational activity in cooperation with the Divine Providence for its removal. [18]

Curiously, however, despite this strong opening salvo, DeCharms does not have another published word on the subject until 1862, a full year after the war commenced. He did, however, remain prolific by publishing and editing a three-year (1854–56) Swedenborgian serial periodical called *The New Churchman* and issuing several more tracts on topics he deemed important.

Solyman Brown, an eclectically accomplished Swedenborgian convert who was a well-published poet, a historically significant New York dentist, [19] and a licensed Swedenborgian minister (despite his anticlerical intellectual persuasions), followed on DeCharms's remarks with a vigorous denunciation of slavery. [20] Though the pamphlet is undated and often misdated in biographical sketches with a year as late as 1859, Bush's own periodical provides notice of its publication in 1851. [21] Relying especially on the idea of the supremacy of liberty, but also employing the idiosyncratic Swedenborgian theme of the "celestial" attributes of black Africans, Brown's sermon and tract is fiercely antislavery. It is worth noting that Wadström's emphasis on the celestial nature of black Africans as an argument against slavery was overall much less used by American Swedenborgians than it was by English Swedenborgians, and it was also employed for pro-slavery positions. Swedenborg's depictions of the spiritual innocence of black Africans quite readily could be construed to support the common Southern argument that black people were too childlike to fend for themselves on their own in society—the innocence Swedenborg describes seems like the innocence of young children. As with DeCharms, Brown appears to have gone quiet on the topic, at least in print.

An Orchestrated Conversation

The one who worked hardest to create a public Swedenborgian conversation on slavery was George Bush (1796–1859)—great-granduncle of George Herbert Walker Bush (1924–2018), and great, great-granduncle of George Walker Bush, the 41st and 43rd presidents of the United States, respectively. George I, as he is sometimes dubbed, in addition to being a highly regarded professor of Oriental languages and Semitic thought at New York University, was also a prominent public intellectual popular for his public lectures. A foremost American scholar on Semitic cultures, he produced several well-received commentaries on the Old Testament as well as the first book-length American biography of Mohammed, founding prophet of Islam. The formerly well-connected and influential ordained Presbyterian clergyman created a sensation when he converted to the Swedenborgian Church, and he was arguably the most significant mainline intellectual of the nineteenth century to become Swedenborgian.

Avidly antislavery, Bush felt by the late 1840s that the general silence in the Swedenborgian Church on slavery could not be excused, and he began correspondence with several Swedenborgians on both sides of the question as he planned for a published running dialog to air the issues. His resulting two-year series of articles represents the only systematic Swedenborgian conversation on the slavery question in Antebellum America. Entitled "Aphorisms on Abolition and Slavery," the series spanned 1852–53 in *The New Church Repository and Monthly Review,* the publication he founded and edited, and was re-published in its entirety by Bush in 1855, including additional information about the origins of the conversation.[22] Before his Swedenborgian conversion, Bush had edited an antislavery paper in the 1830s with Gerrit Smith, who was also the Liberty Party candidate for the American presidency in 1848, and he confided to Smith before starting the series that he wanted to test the prevalent silence in the New Church to see if Swedenborgianism was a de facto haven for pro-slavery sympathizers.[23]

Bush had been attempting to raise consciousness and dialog on the slavery question in private correspondence for some time, and after the series began appearing, he attempted to elicit replies to and conversations with the fourteen aphorisms—theological antislavery principles he claimed were originally mailed to him by an individual who is never identified. [24] Clearly a number of energetic responses came in, both pro and con. The Aphorisms series takes the form of a running dialog with viewpoints that are never precisely quoted, and the identities of his correspondents are not published. Bush functions as moderator but does not play a neutral role, as his antislavery views are obvious and he editorializes liberally, but he takes special pains to be fair and courteous. Some readers were enthralled to have the subject raised, such as a farmer in the West Indies and an abolitionist in the North, neither of whom had joined the Swedenborgian Church—though they adhered to its theology—due to its silence on the slavery question. Others were horrified that the difficult subject was being broached at all, feeling that it was not appropriate to air it out in public discourse. Bush lost many subscribers due to the series, though he claims in the 1855 republication that most came back.

The Aphorisms series likely succeeded in revealing a relatively accurate portrait of American Swedenborgianism's position on slavery at that time. A spectrum that could be replicated in most American Christian denominations is seen: *immediatist* abolitionism; *gradualist* antislavery dismantling; colonization (exporting!) of black people to a free society somewhere else; a *temporary* pro-slavery position based on a confidence that a just divine providence was working toward some good end; and a *wholesale* pro-slavery position based on the perspective that slavery was a useful social institution for the betterment of both races.

Other Antislavery Activity

Though there is no other published antislavery Swedenborgian discourse in extant sermons, tracts, pamphlets, or articles during the 1840s and 50s, and though there is considerable evidence that Swedenborgians as a whole were passive on the slavery question, there also is evidence of numerous activist Swedenborgian laypersons. At least some

Swedenborgians participated in the Underground Railroad, the secretive system of routes and safe houses designed to smuggle bonded slaves from the South to freedom in the North.

Hiram Colburn, a Boston shoe merchant active in Thomas Worcester's Beacon Hill church, spearheaded his large extended family's conversion to Swedenborgianism and turned their household into an Underground Railroad waystation during the 1840s and 50s.[25] The prominent Chicago attorney and close colleague of Abraham Lincoln, Jonathan Young Scammon, was a noted antislavery voice in the Chicago New Church Temple; and the physician Charles Volney Dyer and his wife, Louisa, also of that congregation and friends of Lincoln, were prominent Chicago abolitionists as early as the mid-1830s. Dr. Dyer served as a Stationmaster on the Underground Railroad. After the war, Lincoln appointed Dyer to the Mixed Court for the Suppression of the African Slave Trade. Established in 1862 through a treaty with Great Britain, this court served as a medium for hearing cases regarding searches and seizures of vessels on the high seas suspected of carrying slaves for the purpose of the slave trade.[26]

There were also at least two Swedenborgians who played prominent leadership roles in the American Anti-Slavery Society. William Cooper Howells (1807–94), the father of the eminent American literary lion William Dean Howells, was a career Ohio newspaper publisher and editor, including a stint as co-editor of the *Ohio State Journal,* in which he vigorously penned pieces in support of John Brown, the radical abolitionist in Kansas. Howells also served as manager and possibly as founder of the Ohio branch of the American Anti-Slavery Society. Due to his Quaker upbringing, he had been antislavery before his Swedenborgian conversion in 1834, but never living close enough to a Swedenborgian church to attend regularly, his relations to organized Swedenborgianism appear cordial but distant. Yet, Swedenborgianism was a faith commitment that would sustain him for his remaining six decades, as he was vocal about his spiritual persuasions and kept a large lithographic picture of Swedenborg in the family parlor room, as attested to by his son's fond memories.[27] His fusion of Swedenborgian thought and antislavery politics centered in his interpretation of Swedenborg's doctrine of love as an obvious paean to selflessness and egalitarianism.[28]

William Bolles (1800–67), proprietor of W. & J. Bolles, a publishing and bookselling firm in New London, Connecticut, was, according to the nation's most prominent abolitionist, William Lloyd Garrison, both a Swedenborgian layperson and a radical abolitionist.[29] He withdrew from the Baptist church he was attending in 1838 when he learned that the minister and most members were strongly pro-slavery and would not tolerate dissent on the matter in the church,[30] and he proceeded to publish two antislavery newspapers, *The Ultimatum* (1838) and *The Slave's Cry* (1844). It is of interest, however, that despite both the fact that he was a publisher and Garrison's testimony of him as a Swedenborgian, there is no record or mention of him anywhere in the annals and archives of the Swedenborgian Church.

Breaking Point and the American Civil War, 1861–65

The outbreak of hostilities in April 1861, though not entirely unexpected, jolted a great many fence-sitting Christian leaders from perches of passivity. Though this pattern included Northern Swedenborgians, the increased volume of conversation was still surprisingly faint compared to most mainline denominations. By this time, Bush had died, DeCharms was in poor health and estranged from the church, and Brown had ceased to be a voice, though Holcombe in the South would step up his pro-slavery appeals in writings that encompassed the most elaborate racial-spiritual theories that would ever issue from an American Swedenborgian. Yet in this third phase, the first visible conversation since Bush's strategized discussion ended in 1853 emerged as a few new Northern Swedenborgian voices sounded for the antislavery cause, even if at times the pro-Union rhetoric exceeded the antislavery rhetoric in emphasis.

The Swedenborgian bias against speaking of social controversies in church is well illustrated by William Hayden's (1816–93) early tract. He had been the first editor of the denomination's national weekly, and he was minister of the Swedenborgian church in Portland, Maine, when the war broke out. He delivered a Sunday evening public lecture in Portland's City Hall that reveals its genesis as a church sermon, with an opening comment regarding the rarity of broaching social issues in a Swedenborgian church:

In the extraordinary character of this event [war] will be found my apology, if apology is needed, for departing, for once, from an otherwise uniform course of avoiding the discussion of such topics in the pulpit, and for a single hour regarding the subject from a moral point of view. [31]

The general silence on the slavery question in the pages of the chief church periodical circulating among the national membership was glaring to some. One year after commencement of the war, Urbana University president and pastor of Cincinnati's first New Church temple, Chauncey Giles (1813–93), wrote to a fellow antislavery pastor in Chicago, J. R. Hibbard (1815–94):

I do not think a weekly journal of the Church should be so strictly ecclesiastical or abstractly spiritual that it cannot notice current events. On the contrary, it seems to me to be one of its special duties. I would have it comment on events and books in the light of spiritual truth. . . . The *Messenger* has kept itself almost criminally aloof from a word of sympathy or any expression of interest in this terrible crisis of our national life. I think it ought to have done all it could to sustain the members of the Church in this trying hour. Spiritual things are clothed with natural in this world. I have no belief in the method of teaching truth that begins and ends with the generalities that we must shun evils and do good. What evils shall we shun, what good shall we do? Here are themes for discourses and illustration in endless variety. I must do good to the neighbor, but the country is more the neighbor than the individual, and cannot I express a word of sympathy for her when she is in the clutches of demons and is struggling for her very existence? [32]

Slow Conversions

Thomas Worcester (1795–1878), the same minister Child had declared to be pro-slavery when she knew him in the late 1820s, was now president of the national church and had been for a long while the most powerful man in the denomination. According to the memorial biography penned by his best friend, the noted philosopher Sampson Reed, Worcester had always thought slavery to be an evil but that it had been permitted by providence for some "wise and beneficent end," and that he was "waiting the indications of Providence as to the time and means of its removal." [33] This, if true, would fit Worcester in the extreme gradualist camp of the antislavery spectrum. Worcester believed in following the laws of society and so resisted actions that would contravene laws; but with the outbreak of hostilities, Reed further surmises, Worcester then regarded actual war as the indication of providence that slavery should be removed, and he gave a major address on the matter six months after the war commenced. Quite notably, the tract primarily focuses on the necessity of keeping the Union intact and still does not emphasize the evils of slavery. [34] He subsequently elaborated his message in his "Presidential Address" the following summer at the denomination's forty-third annual convention held in Boston, June 5–12, 1862—reported to have enjoyed the largest gathering in the denomination's forty-five-year history. [35] Tellingly, the talk's reputation had Worcester coming out full force for the Northern cause, yet for some, such as the newly vigorous antislavery minister Benjamin F. Barrett (1808–92), the address was irresponsibly tame. Writing in *The Crisis,* a Midwestern free-spirit Swedenborgian publication, Barrett dubs Worcester's presidential address as "humdrum," "indirect," "obscure," and "inappropriate" considering the gravity of the subject, and he concludes that "Jeff Davis and his rebel confederates, had they been present on the occasion, might not only have listened to the announcement of such a subject with perfect composure, but might have followed it with a loud Amen." [36]

Chauncey Giles's slow conversion resulted in a far fiercer emotional stance than Worcester's. The Cincinnati pastor had been one of many key Swedenborgian leaders who avoided the slavery question until the war and who could be described as soft pro-slavery until after the war commenced. In fact, Giles confided to Holcombe in personal correspondence in January 1861 with war looming that he was not antislavery and did not vote for Lincoln. [37] Yet, as his letter to Hibbard a year into the war reveals, he came to deeply regret both his own slowness to the cause as well as his church's. In 1863, he "published by request" what stands forth today as the single most lacerating antislavery publication written by an American Swedenborgian. [38] The twenty-four-page pamphlet is an elaboration of a public speech Giles delivered on April 30,

1863, to honor the national fast called for by US President Lincoln in Proclamation 97, "Appointing a Day of National Humiliation, Fasting, and Prayer." In tough, uncompromising language, Giles excoriates the treatment of black Africans by citizens of a country supposedly founded upon egalitarian ideals:

> Both in principle and in all its effects, Slavery is directly hostile to the principles of a free government. Fire and water, cold and heat, light and darkness, are not more squarely antagonistic to each other than true republicanism and slavery; and it is a remarkable fact in the history of human progress, that these two principles so hostile to each other should have been planted side by side in the same nation. [39]
>
> The great evil of slavery is not that one man is enriched by another, and served by him. Every one is compelled to serve others, either voluntarily or involuntarily. . . . The great sin of slavery as it now and ever will exist until man becomes regenerated is, that it keeps the slave forever a child. It strikes at the manhood in human nature; it puts muscle above brain; it arrests man in the first step of his progress, and insists upon keeping him there, that he may be made a better tool of service. It does not allow him to go beyond and become a man, for that would interfere with his forced labor. [40]

The final several pages are devoted to the ideal and goal of a well-educated and empowered black African-American "nationality" that would become a vital part of the American life, and only then would white America be on the road to atonement for its sins. Like Worcester before him and as will Holcombe in his conversion experience, Giles draws upon Isaiah 58:6–12 in his concluding paragraph as a supremely relevant biblical passage:

> Let us make this day a time of repentance and sincere sorrow for our sins, and the beginning of a perpetual fast, such as the Lord hath chosen and will prosper,—a fast in which the people as one man labor "to loose the bonds of wickedness, to undo the heavy burdens, and to let the oppressed go free, and to break every yoke. Then shall our light break forth as the morning and our health shall

spring forth speedily, and they that shall be of this people" shall build the old waste places; we shall raise up the foundation of many generations, and we shall "be called the repairer of the breach, the restorer of paths to dwell in."[41]

Rare Protests and a Late Church Resolution

Five additional voices appear in the 1860s, four clearly antislavery but two pointing to the continuing muted voice of the church. It is telling that *The Crisis,* edited by the radical spiritualist clergyperson Henry Weller (d. 1868), did not include a single mention of the slavery issue until the eve of war. In an editorial published on January 1, 1861, Weller argues the distinctive New Church theme that the evil of slavery is one of many surface features of a world ensnarled in spiritual ignorance. It is futile to work from political or governmental strategies when the real power for social change can only come from a spiritual transformation. Swedenborgians do better, Weller advises, giving all their effort to the reformation of Christian thought that began with the Last Judgment a century earlier but whose effects are still in infancy.[42] All evils are a form of bondage. He remarks on the overthrow of serfdom in Russia and goes on to say,

> On our own affairs we will not speculate—sufficient to the day will be the evil thereof; and a time will probably be soon upon us in which every true lover of his kind will be called out, in some way or other, to the battle-field. As yet we feel that the *whole question* between South and North is not understood in its full bearing, and we are waiting for a fuller knowledge; but whenever a clear path opens to us, we shall not hesitate to take up spiritual weapons for the right, on whichever side of the line it may lie.[43]

This same doctrinal reasoning is also evident in an official communication made from the floor of the denomination's convention in the summer of 1862. That summer, the General Convention of the United States sent an epistle signed by the national ordaining minister to the General Conference in England, J. P. Stuart (1810–82), in response to a letter from the British General Conference expressing sympathy and concern regarding the outbreak of the American Civil

War.[44] Stuart, who was one of the most prominent figures of the then-nascent Academy movement that would result ultimately in a theologically purist denominational schism in 1890, responds with two characteristic New Church interpretations of the situation: 1) slavery is not the deep cause of the conflict (though not specifically identified as such, this comment is consistent with the Last Judgment hypothesis that posits theological darkness as the deep cause, with such moral evils as slavery as one of numerous surface effects); and 2) providence is in charge of the process.

J. R. Hibbard was another Academy-sympathizing, theologically conservative clergyman to come out during the war against slavery. He had known Abraham Lincoln personally since the 1840s, when Hibbard was the regional circuit minister covering the newly growing Swedenborgian congregation in Springfield, Illinois. It was there where the future emancipation president maintained his law practice, and he knew many of the local Swedenborgians.[45] Hibbard published a tract in 1862 that had originally been delivered as a sermon at the one-year anniversary marker of the commencement of the Civil War. Starting with a biblical text from Revelation 21:5, "And he that sat upon the throne, said: Behold, I make all things new," Hibbard interprets the war in light of the Swedenborgian doctrine of "hereditary evil."[46] This doctrine postulates that specific negative traits and tendencies from familial and cultural influences are present with every person and every society, offering context for the work of spiritual regeneration. Declaring that the process of reformation is the same for a nation as it is for an individual, the clergyman extends the doctrine by featuring another Swedenborgian idea— that the "natural man" comes from the mother and the "spiritual man" comes from the father. This being so, the birth of the American nation is just as much a heavenly creation as is a new human life, and there is hereditary evil from the nation's "English mother"; and that evil is the dross that is being burned off in the present conflict!

A quite distinguished Swedenborgian author who enters the published discourse is Theophilus Parsons (1797–1882), a Harvard University law school professor and active intellectual leader[47] in Worcester's Boston church. In 1863, he issued a forceful tract condemning slavery that received considerable attention.[48] Couched as a legal analysis, he traces slavery's pre-American history and argues that the evil of slavery is built into the United States Constitution itself. Its growth and entrenchment in the American socio-economic fabric is but an organic outcome of the errors and spiritual short-sightedness of earlier generations. Ultimately, he lays the fundamental blame at the door of human selfishness, which must be confronted by all contemporary Americans. Though Parsons's tract unfolds with the argot of a political analysis of the history of the Union, its effect is ultimately a religious vision of saving the Union through its development of moral integrity.

Finally, Benjamin F. Barrett, the one who had belittled Worcester's 1861 conversion address, was another radical Swedenborgian cleric who contributed to the published record during the war. In 1864, deep into the war, Barrett issued two important items. One was a tract, also "published by request," that began as a sermon justifying the horrible carnage of the war on two principles: 1) that no human life is actually ever lost (a reference to Swedenborg's signature teachings on the afterlife); and 2) that the great cause of the war against slavery demanded every effort to extinguish it. [49] Here Barrett broaches the primary idea with which Swedenborgians were most prominently associated in the broader culture: the spiritualist phenomenon then sweeping America, with its emphasis on contact with the spiritual world, immortality, and immediate survival of physical death. Swedenborgians are absent in contemporary scholarship of religion and slavery in Antebellum America, but they are quite visible with respect to the death and carnage of the Civil War. [50]

Barrett concludes that to permit the Confederate states to build a society with slavery as its economic cornerstone would be "a cowardly surrender to the empire of Satan." [51] The feisty cleric, who would after the war sever ties with the denomination and become an independent Swedenborgian editor and publisher, also penned a damning indictment of the church late in the fall of 1864 over its glacial approach to the slavery issue. After giving a fulsome history of the complex wrangling and delays over resolutions on the floor of the annual Swedenborgian Church conventions, with the delegates defeating a resolution condemning slavery as late in the war as the summer of 1863, Barrett rebukes the church for waiting until the summer of 1864 to declare opposition to slavery:

Now a true church—one that dwells nearest to the Lord and the wisest of angels—certainly ought to be gifted with more than ordinary insight into things in general. It ought to be quick to see and prompt to its duty at all times. It ought to take the lead in every just and holy cause. It ought to be the first to proffer its sympathy— its "moral and spiritual support" to the country in a season of "great trial and peril." Is it too much to say that a true church will be ever foremost in its proffer of aid and sympathy in a holy cause? Yet here is the General Convention, claiming the pre-eminence over all other churches—claiming to be "the specific New Church," and to receive influx from the highest and best of the angels, lagging full three years behind all the other churches in declaring its loyalty, or in proffering its sympathy with the government at a time of great national peril. [52]

Conclusions

Three useful conclusions can be drawn from this study of Swedenborgian discourse in the context of the slavery controversy in Antebellum America. First, Charles Bernhard Wadström's influence never made it to the New World. The Swedenborgian movement in America was a new Christian denomination comprised almost entirely of contemporary converts from indigenous efforts, and the earliest American Swedenborgians did not benefit from an existing channel of discourse with the incipient English Swedenborgian movement. Wadström's thought, writings, and stories had no visible penetration into pre-Civil War American Swedenborgian movements. The inspiration from the English and French colonial context of Wadström, therefore, found no landing point on the American shores to shape Swedenborgian thought in the New World context.

Second, American Swedenborgians reasoned differently than did Wadström when searching Swedenborg's teachings for pertinence to the slavery conflict. Swedenborg was not a social reformer theologian in the modern sense and did not address specific social issues in his extensive theological corpus. This includes the institution of slavery, even though it was prominent in the London where he spent thirteen years working on his spiritual books. The English capital was home for a large number of black people in various forms of servitude connected to the slave trade in which England had been so deeply enmeshed. About ten million slaves were merchandized in eighteenth-century England, and London was by far the busiest port city through which such commerce passed. Placards still selling sub-Saharan Africans were common and publicly visible in Swedenborg's London, and abolitionism against this practice was hotter in Swedenborg's London than it was anywhere else in Europe.[53] Yet there is no direct line of theological application in his writings to guide devotees on the slavery issue. As a result, a post-modern retrospective identifies Swedenborgians in England, South America, and North America as shaping a variety of arguments from Swedenborg's abstract theology influenced by local context.

Enlightenment ideals of liberty, tolerance, and egalitarianism appealed in England and France, where self-interest in the slave trade was much further removed from daily living for a vast majority of Europeans, thereby making this context ripe for arguments of liberty from Swedenborg's writings. In the American context, however, where the institution of slavery dominated the economy and also was interwoven in the social fabric much more extensively, the removal of such a colossal social institution seemed a suspicious diversion from the primary work of heralding the New Jerusalem theological revolution that they believed needed their whole attention. Spiritual abstractions about the Last Judgment, hereditary evil, spiritual freedom, divine providence, and racial theories gave support for passivity and postponement of action. Their commitment to divine providence as they understood it in Swedenborg's thought made most American Swedenborgians confident that matters were firmly under control. And since their understanding of a redeemed world—the heavenly Jerusalem descending to earth through the Last Judgment—evoked a profound and pervasive change of theological vision for the masses, they had no confidence in mere political victories achieved through the current uninformed spiritual theology.

Third and finally, then, the rumor of a courageous and visionary antislavery Swedenborgianism in Antebellum America is a myth with no backing. The figures commonly touted as exemplars of a progressive American Swedenborgian antislavery voice—Wadström, Carter, and

Child—under scrutiny all fail to manifest as specifically Swedenborgian antislavery voices in the American controversy. The accurate Swedenborgian record that can be discerned in tracts, pamphlets, articles, sermons, personal correspondence, and reports portrays a conservative religious movement in relation to the slavery question during all three American antislavery phases, spanning the late Enlightenment through the end of the Civil War. The preponderance of New Church people clustered in soft versions of both pro- and antislavery perspectives that resulted in a widespread passivity and a cultural backseat in the conversation. A few strong antislavery Swedenborgians are visible before the war, and a few more appear after the war began. Some worked in antislavery societies and in the Underground Railroad, but the evidence suggests they were a small minority. A few published antislavery appeals, but except for Bush, DeCharms, and Brown, they were late compared to major American Christian denominations. Swedenborgians must be placed well behind the curve for religious antislavery work and testimony in the American context. ⁓

A Story without End—Summary and Final Reflections

Anders Hallengren, *Stockholm University*

Twelve million bonded black Africans were transported from Africa to the Americas—packed on British, French, Dutch, Portuguese, and Spanish merchantmen and cargo vessels—during the centuries of transatlantic slave trade. The growing wealth of North America and the Caribbean and South American colonists, landowners, planters, and shareholders was built on chattel slavery, forced labor, indentured servitude, and serfdom.[1]

As Neil Kent observes in his introductory overview, this was by no means a uniquely Western phenomenon. As enslavement in its various forms has counterparts worldwide and has been a fundamental element of many growing economies to this day, the success of the abolishment of slave trade can certainly be questioned.

Mark Florman's essay, "It Happens Here," represents the research work done by the Centre for Social Justice, which claims that tens of thousands of people living in the United Kingdom today are either enslaved or traded as chattel. This dark business that has now eventually come to light in the UK is part of a much bigger network of crime that now accounts for more than thirty million slaves around the world. The statistics corroborate the estimate made by the UN's Office of the High Commissioner for Human Rights (OHCHR) in Geneva. The UN's International Labour Organization (ILO) is specific in their monitoring of the work market, regularly updating their information on forced

179

labor, modern slavery, and human trafficking. This global business is as profitable as it is evil.

- Approximately twenty-five million people worldwide are victims of forced labor, with women and girls being disproportionately affected (accounting for 99 percent in the sex industry and 58 percent in other sectors).

- Approximately sixteen million victims are exploited by private individuals or by enterprises, 4.8 million of whom are victims of forced sexual exploitation.

- Approximately four million victims are exploited by a state or government.

- Domestic work, agriculture, construction, manufacturing, and entertainment are among the most affected sectors.[2]

Much remains unrecorded, though, and hidden statistics gradually surface. According to a recent estimate presented to the UN Assembly in the fall of 2017 by Alliance 8.7, more than forty million people around the world were victims of modern slavery in 2016, including not only the nearly twenty-five million in forced labor but also 15.4 million in forced marriage! The ILO has also released a companion child labor estimate, which confirms that about 152 million children were subject to such mistreatment.[3]

How is it possible that modern slavery can go on? It forms a dark net beyond our grasp and detection. How can it be stopped? We must bring it to light, making it known to as many people as possible, and take the necessary legal and political actions. These things, finally, are now taking place.

It is a lack of knowledge, insight, and experience that allows for this exploitation of fellow human beings to go on without the appropriate reaction and necessary response. Due to arbitrariness and a dearth of enlightenment with regard to equal freedom for all races, Swedes and other Europeans partook in the slave trade. And this behavior persisted until new ideas and realities slowly emerged in the common conscious-ness, as Thomasson and Rönnbäck showed in their chapters.

Religion is not of much help settling the issue, since slavery has been ecumenical, so to speak, and human progress in the history of religion is assuredly equivocal. It is true that a belief in a God who sees everything you do may have an impact on your behavior, as children's doings are affected by their knowledge of someone watching them; but the action of the faithful completely depends on what conscience and church doctrines prescribe or allow. The same applies to laws and law enforcement. What is the probability of being caught red-handed and prosecuted when governments and authorities shut their eyes to injustice or pretend that there is no injustice at all? Crimes continue without punishment.

According to the fourteenth Dalai Lama, compassion is what is needed, as the only hope for humanity is empathy—the channel of understanding and love for our neighbor. This channel can only be opened by means of experience and awareness. Knowledge in this broad sense is required for heartfelt charity (*caritas*).

As we have seen from Ambjörnsson, Williams-Hogan, Howard, and Rix, Carl Bernhard Wadström's final great awakening took place when he was struck by the cruelties of the slave trade, which he saw with his own eyes on his long trip to West Africa and gleaned from reliable observations made by others. Wadström became a witness and in turn a staunch abolitionist, making plans for creating humane civil societies in Africa that were free from slavery and the slave trade and for founding a prospering utopian city of refuge.

Wadström's ensuing visions and plans, as well as his arguments, were partly built on his belief in Swedenborgian values and ideas. As evidenced by James F. Lawrence, though, Swedenborg's nineteenth-century post-Doomsday New World followers, who apparently trusted destiny and the works of divine providence in the new era, were (with a few great exceptions) largely confident onlookers, anticipating amendments to come by divine force. These Swedenborgians were avoiding worldly and political matters, as many other Christian churches did, when slavery was the issue in the Antebellum un-United States of America, where eloquent, fundamentalist, pro-slavery agitators in the South used quotations from the Bible as swords against reformers.

Obviously, Swedenborgianism was as little a sufficient condition as it was a necessary one for someone to become an abolitionist, but it was manifestly compatible with an abolitionist standpoint, as our example shows. We might regard Wadström as an anomaly, but that is neither true nor the whole story. Many antislavery-minded people and activists (such as the formidable freedom fighter Ralph Waldo Emerson and other Transcendentalists) did not want to join any abolitionist movements, which were sometimes considered to be revolutionary, violent, or sectarian. Moreover, and as pointed out by Inga Sanner, Swedenborg's impact encompasses reform movements and transformational thought of various kinds up to our times.

We know that leading Swedenborgians were at the forefront of the liberation of the serfs and land reform in Russia during 1861, as well as were involved in the democratic Decembrist revolt (*Vosstanie dekabristov*) in 1825.[4] In some Caribbean societies, Swedenborgian ideas had played a crucial role in bringing radical reform and in contributing to the rising status of people of African descent.[5]

Furthermore, most Swedenborgians today are black Africans, the majority of whom live in Western and Southern Africa. In fact, there are numerous active churches and congregations in Togo, Ghana, Côte d'Ivoire (Ivory Coast), Kenya, the Republic of South Africa, Nigeria, and the kingdom of Lesotho.[6]

The background is historical, and the grounds are theological. How did all this happen, and what was it in particular that people took note of and were inspired by in Swedenborg? The theological grounds for attraction, conversion, and reform can be summarized under the following main points:

- the emphases on freedom as an inalienable human quality, free will as the foundation of morality, and responsibility for oneself, since without free choice, there are no morals or ethics;

- that all human beings are equal before God and that there is no predestination, punishment, or "Day of Doom": our fate is all up to us;

- the emphasis on goodness, or love for our neighbor, and the supreme importance of behavior: action is more significant than belief, as love is primary and faith secondary;

- that the neighbor is society, country, and the human race in its entirety;

- the teaching of the profound spirituality possessed by Africans; and

- a doctrine of spirit that connected with African primal religion and readily appealed to its people.

Edward Wilmot Blyden, the well-informed Liberian envoy to England, made the following statement in his speech at the annual meeting of the Swedenborg Society in London in 1892:

[Liberia] may be regarded, and in no remote sense, as a result of the teachings of Swedenborg and of the example and labours of his followers. . . . Swedenborgians have a sort of claim upon Liberia, and right to feel interested in her prosperity and success; as the only aboriginal prince ever brought away from her territory for training in England was brought away by a follower of Swedenborg, and the most exhaustive account of the region of country now occupied by the republic, given a hundred years ago, was by Dr. Wadstrom, that eminent Swedenborgian who lived among and toiled for the people of Mesurado, long before Liberia was settled. Providence, in permitting Liberia to be founded there, seemed to be following up and putting a seal upon those self-denying members of the New Jerusalem Church.[7]

Inspired to do so by his fellow countryman Rev. John P. Knox,[8] Blyden joined the free black emigrants in the region that is the present Sierra Leone and Liberia, and he became a prominent figure in the colony set up for freedmen by the American Colonization Society. A citizen of the former Danish West Indies who was educated in the United States, Blyden was a learned and prolific writer.[9] He had become professor of Latin and Greek at Liberia College in 1861, later serving both as its president and as an ambassador to England and France.

Blyden called attention to the prominent Swedenborgian scientist James John Garth Wilkinson's tract *The African and the True Christian Religion*,[10] repeatedly commending its value for those who have no access to Swedenborg's works. He considered Swedenborg and the Swedenborgians to be among the fathers of this nation, and he is himself today remembered as the father of Pan-Africanism.

Rule of law and proclamations neither suffice nor permit us to rest in oblivious satisfaction. Neil Kent maintains that slavery considerably declined in medieval Christian Europe, as it had increasingly been deemed immoral. Indeed, in the city of Florence, ruled by the *Arti Maggiori,* slavery was abolished in the year 1289, according to the published Chronology of the Guilds. Nevertheless, a Florentine exile, the fourteenth-century traveler Francesco Petrarch, with Genova and Marco Polo's Venice as his homeports, observed that the Mediterranean merchant ships carried more slaves than grain.[11] As we have seen, there have been many great words offered in the cause of condemning slavery. And there is still time to set "examples"—for anyone, of whatever faith! ⌇

Appendix A: Wadström's Witness Report to the Houses of Parliament

> "How are the expenses of this plan to be defrayed, and by whom?
> —As I have no regard to any particular interest, but human-
> ity at large is my point of interest, I leave such to Providence."
>
> CARL BERNHARD WADSTRÖM (1790)

CARL BERNHARD WADSTRÖM'S COMPLETE WITNESS REPORT to the Houses of Parliament in 1790. From the House of Lords Minutes in the Parliamentary Archives, London, UK. Published by permission of the Houses of Parliament. Copyright ©Parliamentary Archives. Full text of the detailed firsthand account that changed history both in Europe and Africa where the business of the "King of Sin"[1] et al. was revealed, and showed why Wadström came close to being captured and sold himself. For anyone who wants to know the state of affairs in Senegal in the 1780s, this testimony is still an indispensable source of knowledge.

Mercurii, 28° die Aprilis 1790.
CHARLES BERNS WADSTROM,[2] Esquire, called in.

Mr. Wadstrom expressed his wish rather to answer in French, on account of his imperfect knowledge of the English language; but that he was ready notwithstanding to give the information he has possessed of in English to the best of his power.

Whereupon the Committee agreed to receive his information in English, and he was examined as follows:

Of what country are you a native?
—Of Sweden.

Of what profession are you?
—I am in the service of the king of Sweden, chief director of the assay office of gold and silver.

Do you still retain that situation?
—Yes.

Were you ever in Africa?
—Yes.

In what year?
—In the years 1787 and 1788.

What was the occasion of your going there?
—The king of Sweden being a great lover of natural history, of antiquities, and other curious subjects relating to discoveries, had engaged Dr. Sparrman,[3] who having been in Africa was already well acquainted with it, and made me an offer to accompany Dr. Sparrman and other Swedish learned gentlemen, to set out for Africa, in order to explore the country for the aforementioned purposes.

Was any particular department allotted to you in that expedition?
—That part which concerned mineralogy, antiquities, and in general what regards the state of man in that country.

Did you proceed from Sweden to Africa directly?
—We went first to France, with recommendations to the French Court, to receive further recommendations to the Coast. The letters containing such recommendations I should wish, with the permission of the Committee, to produce.

And the Witness being desired to produce the said letters, the same were delivered in, and copies thereof are as follow: viz.,

"À Versailles, le 29 Juillet, 1787.
"Monsieur,
"J'ai reçu la nouvelle lettre que
"vous m'avez fait l'honneur de m'écrire
"le 16 de ce mois à l'occasion de Mrs
"Sparmann, Arrhénius, et Wadstrom, qui
"se proposent de voyager en Afrique. Ce
"n'est en effet qu'avec des marchandises
"que l'on parvient à traiter avec les habitants
"de ce continent ; mais comme ils
"pourraient éprouver des difficultés à cet
"égard sur la partie des côtes entre le Cap
"Blanc et le Cap Verd, dont la traite
"est réservée à la Compagnie du Sénégal,
"j'ai écrit, conformément à vous désirs, à
"cette compagnie pour les faire lever ; je ne doute
"pas qu'elle ne se prête, autant qu'il dépendra d'elle,
"à procurer aux Srs Sparmann, Arrhénius, et Wadstrom,
"toutes les facilités nécessaires pour le succès
"de leur voyage."

"J'ai l'honneur d'être avec un très Sincère attachement,
"Monsieur,
          "Votre très humble et
              "très obéissant Serviteur,
"Le Maréchal [Marquis] de Castries."[4] [Charles Eugène Gabriel de la Croix de Castries, *Maréchal de France & ministre de la Marine*]

"M. le Bon de Staël d'Holstein." [= The addressee Baron Erik Magnus Staël von Holstein, Paris, the Ambassador of Sweden to France.]

❧

"Paris, le 12 Août 1787.

    "Monsieur l'Ambassadeur,
"La Compagnie s'était empressée d'offrir ses services
    "les plus étendus à M. M. de Sparrman, Arrhenius,
    "et Wadstrom. Les ordres qu'elle a reçus depuis,
    "à ce sujet, de M. le Mal de Castries, et la recommandation
    "que vous lui avez fait l'honneur de lui
    "adresser, sont autant la récompense de son zèle que
    "des motifs de devoir et d'encouragement. Elle a
    "êu plusieurs conférences avec ces savants sur les
    "moyens de rendre leur voyage de l'intérieur de
    "l'Affrique aussi sûr et le moins pénible qu'il sera
    "possible. Ils trouveront dans les comptoirs et
    "auprès des agents de la compagnie les renseignements,
    "les secours, les ressources que la colonie peut comporter ;
    "et en attendant ils seront traités avec
    "beaucoup de distinction dans le navire qui va les
    "transporter au Sénégal.
"La compagnie se félicite infiniment d'avoir une
"pareille occasion de témoigner à votre excellence
"combien elle désire de lui être agréable.
    "Je suis avec respect,
        "Monsieur l'ambassadeur,
            "Votre très humble et très
                "obéissant serviteur.
            "Par procuration de la compe du
            "Sénégal,
                "Fraisse Adr Deur.[5] [= *Administra-*
teur-Directeur de la compagnie du Sénégal]
"M. le Baron de Staël-Holstein."

                        ~

"J'ai l'honneur de vous envoyer, Monsieur, la réponse
    "de Mr de Fraisse, par laquelle vous verrez qu'il n'y

"aura plus de difficultés pour votre passage et que
"celles qui ont été élevées provenaient d'un malentendu.
"Je n'ai que le temps de vous renouveler
"ainsi qu'à vos compatriotes l'assurance des
"vœux que je fais pour le succès de votre voyage.
"Voudrez-vous bien, Monsieur, leur en faire part,
"et agréer celle des sentiments que je vous ai
"voués.
"Le Bon Staël de Holstein. [6]

"Paris le 24. Août." [1787]
"M. C. B. Wadstrom." [*Addressee*]

[*With these encouraging words, the Swedish ambassador addresses his compatriot in French, providing him with the official travel documents, including a passport for him and his fellow-travelers signed by King Louis XVI of France.*]

❧

What part of the continent of Africa have you visited?
—From Senegal down the coast almost to Gambia.

To what European power did Senegal, Goree, &c. then belong?
—That part of the coast belonged then to the French.

How long were you ever ashore on the Continent at one time?
—I was, at different times, several days, and once or twice about a week or eight days.

Were you up any of the Rivers;
—Yes, I was up the river [at] Joal. [7]

Did you understand the language of the natives?
—But very little; however, it was very easy for me to converse with the natives, who generally speak French, English, and even Dutch, which languages I speak; I mean that most eminent Negroes on the shore speak those languages.

Did you make it your business to converse with them, and to obtain from them all the information they were capable of giving you?

—Yes; by means of one of those three languages I always found people who could interpret what I wished to know.

Is it from memory only that you are about to state to the Committee what you saw and heard in Africa, or have you any journal written at the time, and on the spot?

—I have, in all my travels, constantly kept a daily journal in such a manner as the time would permit (which journal I could produce if the Committee should wish to see it, although it is in a very rough state) in which I have introduced rough draughts of objects that have come under my observation; this journal I have now in my pocket.

Had you any opportunity of knowing how Slaves are obtained on that part of the Continent which lies between Senegal and Gambia?

—I think perfectly well; partly from my own experience, and partly from good information.

What judgment then did you form of the ways in which Slaves are obtained?

—Three ways particularly came to my knowledge, by which Slaves were obtained on that part of the Coast where I was. The first is what they call General Pillage, which is executed by order from the King, when Slaving vessels are on the Coast; the second, by Robbery by individuals; and thirdly, by Stratagem or Deceit, which is executed both by the Kings and individuals.

In what manner is the great pillage usually executed?

—It is executed by order of the King, by means of his military, who go out on horseback, armed with guns, pistols, sabres, and bows and arrows, and sometimes with long lances; they set out generally in the evening, and seize upon such Negroes as are unprepared.

Did you ever see them actually sent out on such expeditions?

—During my stay at Joal, for about a week, there were scarcely any day that such excursions were not executed by order of the King.

What was the occasion of your visit to Joal?

—The French Governor at Goree[8] used to send every year presents to the Black Kings, to keep up the commerce; and I with my fellow-traveller were permitted to follow one of these embassies that was sent to the King of Barbessin at Joal.

Did you put down in your journal an account of the expeditions which you have mentioned to have been set on foot for the purpose of getting Slaves?

—It would have been too tedious to have set down every one, they being of such a similar nature; but I have set down a sufficient number to have a compleat knowledge of these proceedings.

Were these parties sent out by order of the king?

—Yes; always.

Do you know how the king was prevailed on to send them?

—When such presents are sent, it is become a custom that the king always, to shew his gratitude, gives Slaves to those who conduct these embassies.

Did the king appear willing and disposed thus to harass his subjects?

—No; he was excited by the French officer and the Mulattoes[9] that accompanied the embassy, by means of a constant intoxication, to send out the above mentioned parties for pillage.

Was it agreed amongst these merchants that this mode should be taken of prevailing on the King to consent to their purposes?

—Yes; it was generally every morning upon consultation so agreed.

Were you ever present when the king expressed any unwillingness thus to harass his people?

—Always when he was sober; and I had an opportunity of hearing his sentiments at a time when he was sober, which were very sensible—for by recurring to my journal before-mentioned, I recollect a conversation between the king and the embassy to the following effect: The king said, he thought it hard that he should be obliged to continually distress his subjects; he complained that the inhabitants of Goree [10] were continually coming to Joal under pretence of trade; that they took occasion to present him with various articles; articles trifling and insignificant in themselves, and which he neither liked nor wished for; and that they then came upon him with long accounts, with the debts said to be due, and with pretensions without end; and he was sorry to say concerning the Governor of Goree, that the Governor living among these people was always on the spot to hear their tales; that he listened too readily to their complaints; that he thought little of the sufferings of the Negroes; and that he must certainly have been imposed upon to suffer his name to be used upon such occasions.

Was this conversation of the king's interpreted on the spot?

—Yes; I took down, word by word, the interpretation of the Mulattoes, and that at different days, when he held the same language; and I reckon those speeches among the most curious anecdotes of my journal, with regard to the sensibility of the natives.

Did the king after this order the pillage to be executed?

—Yes.

What is the name of the country to which Joal belongs?

—The name of the country is Sin, and the name of the king, in their language, is Bur, which is the reason that the king is called Bursin, or Barbessin, which is a corruption of the term.

Do you believe that the king of Sin pillages in other parts of his dominions?

—Undoubtedly—because the Mulatto merchants from Goree go up to the kings of the country, when they are in want of Slaves, and excite the kings to such pillages, which has been told me by the Mulattoes themselves (who do not make any secret of it) as well as by the French officers.

What is the name of the country between Sin and the River Gambia?

—Sallum—and the king is called Bursallum.

Do you know if the king of Sallum also practices the pillage?

—Although I have not been with him, I know that he practises the same manner of getting Slaves—of this I was convinced by being present at Goree when a sloop arrived from Sallum, containing twenty-seven Slaves, of whom all, except four, were women and children taken by pillage, which was told me by the captain himself.

Did the captain inform you that it was a common way of procuring Slaves in that country?

—Not only this captain, but also the Mulattoes and merchants of Goree in general assured me, that it was an usual way by the kings all over that part of the coast.

What is the name of the country between Sin and the river Senegal, and to whom does it belong?

—That is properly divided into two kingdoms, but since the French, two years ago, dethroned the king of Tin, this kingdom, together with Cayor, belong now to the king of Damel.[11]

Does the king of Damel also exercise the Pillage on his subjects, when there is a demand for slaves?

—The merchants and Mulattoes of Goree assured me that was the case; and although I had not such occasion, as at Joal, to see how the Slaves were brought in, and how the parties for pillage were going out, I was plainly convinced of the same practice prevailing in his dominions.

You have mentioned robbery by individuals as one way of obtaining Slaves; what do you mean by those terms?

—I mean by those terms, when individuals seize upon one another, and bring their prey to the Goree merchants to be sold; of which I have known several instances, during my stay at Goree.

Can you specify any instances of this sort?

—I saw in the Captiveries,[12] or places where the Slaves are kept, a woman taken in that way from Rufisque,[13] on the Continent, from her children and husband, which was explained to me by a Mulatto that conducted me; I saw very often Negroes brought in from the continent, who were taken in that way; I had a particular opportunity to make me acquainted with the mode of taking Slaves, by a young slave himself, who belonged to one of the French officers, and who was himself taken in this way, in the interior part above Cape Rouge;[14] I could state several instances, but it perhaps would be too tedious.

Did this boy describe to you the mode of his being taken?

—He told me that he was taken by robbery from his parents, and that such robberies happen very often in his country.

Do you particularly remember that this woman of Rufisque before-mentioned was separated from her children?

—Yes—I took the instance down in my journal from the Mulatto, who told me it himself, and shewed me the woman.

Would not the children also have been articles of merchandize if brought down?

—Certainly; and so they are when they are not too far off in the country; in which case they cannot support the fatigues of walking down to the shore.

In short, without particularizing more influences, is the Committee to understand that this was a common practice?

—During my stay at that part of the Coast it was a general way of procuring single Slaves. —I mean to make a distinction between pillages, by which they can take several at once, being armed accordingly, and robberies, which are a surprise upon individuals.

Did you hear of any people in particular on the Coast who were spoken of as being noted stealers of men?

—Yes—I was myself very near being in danger from such a one, whose name was Ganna, at Dacard;[15] having agreed to travel with him to Senegal, when the great Maraboo[16] of the village hinted to me to take care of that man, as he was known to be a thief of the above denomination, and employed by the Mulattoes and Slave merchants at Goree to procure them Slaves in the afore-mentioned manner; the Maraboo told me that he could easily take me to the king of Damel, who was then in misunderstanding with the French, by which means I should have been exposed to have gone into captivity; that I might be redeemed at a great ransom to be sent back to Goree; this was afterwards, at my return to Goree, confirmed by several of the inhabitants, who congratulated me upon my escape.

You have mentioned stratagem and deceit as a way by which Slaves are obtained; can you relate any instances to explain and confirm this assertion?

—I saw one Negro brought into Goree from Dacard, bought by a French merchant during his stay at Dacard that very same day; this negro was visiting that village from a neighbouring one, and coming under the eye of this French merchant, who took a fancy to him, and hinted to some of the inhabitants his desire of getting him, he became a captive by the consent of the whole village, who had agreed with the merchant about the prize of the merchandize; consequently he was delivered to the merchant by surprise, leaving his wife behind, who kindly desired to follow her husband; but the merchant, not having merchandize enough, obtained only the husband, who was exceedingly distressed, and I saw him in his irons at Goree the day of his arrival. — Another instance of the same kind was as follows: The king of Sallum sent for a woman from without his kingdom to come and sell him some millet; but upon her arrival seized on her and her millet, and sold her to a French officer at Goree, who was then there, and with whom afterwards I saw this woman every day during my stay at Goree.

Did the young man of Rufisque, whom you have just now stated to have been separated from his wife, appear to be disconsolate from that circumstance?

—I endeavoured from curiosity to talk to him, and to encourage him; but he was lying on the ground in a very distressed manner, in chains, fastened as is usual with the fresh Slaves that are brought in.

You have hitherto spoken of the manner of making Slaves in the country between Gambia and Senegal ;[17] do you know if any Slaves are furnished from the neighbourhood of the last-mentioned river, or brought down it?

—All the Slaves sold at Senegal are brought down the river, except those that are taken in the neighbourhood of Senegal, by the robbery of the Moors.

Were you ever yourself on the river Senegal?

—Yes.

In what particular part?

—At the Island of St. Louis, and also on the Continent.

Do you know in what way the Slaves are obtained that come from the neighbourhood of that river?

—They are all taken by the Moors, by seizing on them, sometimes in large parties, which they call Petty Wars, encouraged by the Senegal company, and other merchants depending on the company.

What is the nature of this encouragement?

—It is generally by articles of merchandize given to the Moorish kings; partly to engage the Moors to deliver to them as many Negroes as possible, and partly to prevent the gum arabic from being carried down to the English at Portandick.[18]

Whence did you obtain information on this head, and on the mode in which these Slaves are obtained?

—I obtained the information of these particulars from the inhabitants and officers of Senegal; and with regard to the mode, I also obtained it from the Moors themselves, and that even in the presence of the director of the company.

Is this bounty paid regularly every year, or is it only occasional?

—It is regularly every year, as well to the Moors as to the other nations of the Coast, as mentioned above, for keeping up the commerce; but the year when I was at Senegal, the Moors received a particular bounty, in order to procure the Company a sufficient number of Slaves, they being engaged according to their charter to deliver every year 400 Slaves to the Colony of Cayenne; and the Company having been disappointed of their annual provision of Slaves from Galam, [19] by means of King Dalmanny's having stopped the trade in his dominions.

And the Witness was directed to withdraw.

Jovis, 29° die Aprilis 1790.

CHARLES BERNS WADSTROM called in, and further examined.

Can you relate any particulars respecting this stoppage of the trade by King Dalmanny; from what motives he stopped it, &c.?

—The King Dalmanny being brought up as a Grand Maraboo himself, and elected King over that nation, which was the first instance in that nation of the same person being Grand Maraboo and King, and, in consequence, having had a better education, would not suffer any strong liquors to be used; and being attentive to the cultivation of the country, had entirely prohibited the Slave trade throughout the whole Kingdom, so as not even to suffer the passage of Slaves through his dominions, which include both sides of the River Senegal; he consequently stopped the whole commerce with Galam for that year, by which commerce the Company reckoned upon receiving 800 Slaves (which they had already bought up at Galam) and for which purpose there were lying at the mouth of the River Senegal several vessels to transport them.

Did the Senegal Company, on this interruption of the trade, endeavour to prevail on King Dalmanny to depart from his resolution?

—Certainly; the Company sent a deputation, with a number of valuable presents to King Dalmanny, which he immediately returned, wishing not to have any more such offers made to him; and I had myself an opportunity to be present with the Director of the Company when these presents were brought back; and they were shewn to me by the Director himself, who seemed very sorry that such a heavy expence should arise from the detention of the vessels in the River for so long a time without a cargo.

What steps then did the Senegal Company take to procure their complement of Slaves, when they could not get them from the usual sources of supply?

—They had recourse to their usual way on similar occasions; to excite and bribe the Moors by gratuities, and to supply them with necessary arms, gunpowder, and ammunition, to seize on king Dalmanny's subjects, and to bring them in to the Company as Slaves.

Did the Moors, being thus bribed and supplied with arms, begin their incursions?

—On the 12th of January, when I came to Senegal, the Moors had already begun their incursions, and had delivered 50 Negroes to the Company, who were taken in the dominions of King Dalmanny, and whom King Dalmanny sent down to the Directors of the Company to ransom. —When the messengers from King Dalmanny arrived, the 50 Slaves were already dispatched to Cayenne; by which means the Director was of opinion that the accommodation which might have taken place by the ransom of these Slaves was prevented.

Were any more afterwards brought in by the Moors?

—There were some brought in every day.

In what condition were they brought in? Can you describe the circumstances of their Situation?

—The greater part were very much wounded by sabres and balls.

Into what place were they put on their arrival at the factory?

—In the Slave Hole of the company.

Did you ever visit them there?

—The Director himself conducted me thither with Doctor Sparrman, with whom he consulted for medical assistance to be administered to them.

What then appeared to you to be their situation?

—Their situation was very pitiful—I found a great part of them, and particularly one, who was lying in his blood, which flowed from a wound from a ball in his shoulder.

Did you ever hear of the persons who have employed themselves in seizing others for Slaves being themselves taken and sold in their turn?

—I can mention the following instance: —A Negro was seized by a Moor, brought in and sold to the company, and was shipped on board immediately—but some few days after, the Moor who seized him was himself taken by a Negro, and brought into Senegal, and sold—he was put on board the same vessel with the first Negro, which caused a great disorder for some days. —The company used seldom to buy Moors [20] as Slaves for many reasons; but being under necessity to fulfil their agreement according to their charter with government, they did not lose any opportunity of providing as many Slaves as possible, of whatsoever quality.

From whom did you hear this, and have you any note of it in your journal?

—I heard it from the Director [21] himself, and I put it immediately down in my journal.

Do you believe that the Europeans are ever guilty of stealing, or treacherously carrying off the natives of Africa?

—While as I was at Goree, I was informed by Captain Wignie, from Rochelle, who was just arrived from trading in the River Gambia, that there were three English vessels cut off by the Negroes, a little before his departure from Gambia, in the month of August or September (I think September). This circumstance he mentioned in the following manner: —One of the Captains having compleated his assortment of Slaves, was ready to set sail, and received on board several of the Free Negroes to take leave, and who were treated with liquors—but a favourable wind made him take resolution to sail off with the whole—the wind, however, shifted, and drove him back to the same part of the shore; where, not only he was seized and killed, with all his crew, but also two other English vessels at the same time, by the animosity that this transaction caused in the inhabitants. —I have, during my stay in London, by accident fallen in with the insurer of two of these vessels, who stated to me the fact as being true. —One vessel was called Good Intent, I think, of Liverpool, Captain Gardner; the other, I think, was the Fanny, commanded by Captain Mather, and was from London. —I have reported this fully to the Privy Council. As I was informed, both of these Captains were killed, together with great part of the crew—the remainder came to Albreda, the French settlement in the river Gambia, and were taken care of.

Did you hear that other instances of a similar sort had happened at former times?

—I have heard that such instances happened often on the Coast, particularly by the Dutch and the English—but cannot state any particular instance.

From whom had you this information?

—That is the general opinion; which the French officers told me.

Is it your opinion that the Europeans are guilty of any fraudulent practices in the course of trade?

—I have been very often an ocular witness to the payment of the merchants to the Negroes, and have found how the traders avail themselves of the ignorance of the Negroes in calculation; how they produce false measures; as for instance, bottles that contain but half of the contents of the samples, and mixing water with their brandy after bargain has been made; there are so many methods in almost every article, by which they can deceive the Negroes without their perceiving it, that it would be tedious to enumerate them.

What opinion have you formed of the capacity of the Negroes?
—I consider their understanding as not being fully improved, but is as capable of being in all respects brought to the highest perfection, as those of any white civilized nation.

What opinion did you form of their temper and dispositions?
—They are very honest and hospitable; and I had not the least fear in passing often days and nights quite alone with them; and they shewed me all civility and kindness, without my ever being deceived by them.

Are the natural and social affections as strong in them, as in the inhabitants of other countries?
—According to all my observations on this sort of people, I am quite convinced that in regard to the affections they have them in a much stronger and higher degree than any of the Europeans that I have had the opportunity to examine; and as for social life, I am clearly convinced by my own experience, and by good information from many persons, that, at least in that part where I have been, there is not the least doubt, but they are capable of being soon brought into such a state of society as we enjoy in Europe, when proper opportunity is afforded them.

Have they any manufactures amongst them?
—I have been surprised to see with what industry they manufacture their cottons, their indigo, and other dyeing articles, as well as several sorts of manufacture in wood; they make soap; they tan leather, and work it exceedingly well, and even with good taste; they make vessels of clay, such as Pots, Pipes, &c.; they work bar iron (which is an article of commerce from Europe) into several articles, as for instance, lances, instruments for tillage, poniards, &c.; they work in gold very

ingeniously, and so well, that I have never seen better made articles of that kind in Europe; a great number of articles for ornaments of gold, silver, brass, leather, &c.

Do the natives dye their own clothes?
    —Yes; they dye in blue, yellow, brown, and brownish orange colour.

From what drug is this blue produced?
    —From Indigo; which grows abundantly all over the country, and even so plentiful, that it often spoils their ground for millet and rice plantations; this Indigo is prepared by pounding it in large wood mortars; they put a little hot water over it, and make a paste of certain consistency, which is afterwards dried in the sun; this Indigo is, according to the account of officers and merchants, who have been in America and the West Indies, in all respects equal to the best Carolina Indigo; I have brought samples with me of the productions of the country, and also of these productions manufactured, which I have here in London to produce, in case it should be required.

Whence are the yellow and brown dyes you have mentioned produced?
    —They are produced from vegetables and seeds, which were taken particular note of by Doctor Sparrman, as being within his department; and I have in my collection a kind of beans used for colouring, and which is also a great object of commerce with the Moors, who carry them, even over land, to Morocco, upon their Camels.

Is their cloth neatly manufactured?
    —Their cloth and their leather they manufacture with uncommon neatness; and I have samples with me to shew in case it should be desired.

Can you particularize any of their leather manufactures?
    —They manufacture saddles, pistol cases, sheaths for sabres, bags, sandals, and various sorts of decorations; such as gris-gris (an amulet or superstitious ornament) and various other kinds.

How do they forge their iron?

—They forge their iron with great dexterity upon anvils of wood (which is remarkably hard and heavy) when they have no opportunity to get stone for that purpose.

What articles do they work in gold?

—All sorts of ornaments, such as ear-rings of great variety in point of fashion, rings, bracelets, and other decorations.

Are there much of the brown and orange dyes, of which you have before spoken, used in that part of Africa you have visited?

—The whole army of the king of Damel are dressed in clothes of these colours.

By whom are the canoes made which are used in these countries?

—The canoes are generally made by the Negroes near the shore; but the trees for these canoes are cut and transported from a great distance from the shore; even so far, that it requires several weeks to transport them down; the trees are brought down by the inland Negroes.

In what manner are the trees brought down, and why do they go for them so far?

—They are brought down by a great number of Negroes at once, who draw them with ropes upon pieces of wood that they put under them, and the trees are not hollowed out before they come to the coast, to prevent them from breaking in pieces; it is generally a whole village that undertake such a business, and bring such a large tree to a neighbouring village, and so on till it comes to the shore; they receive in return, part in European merchandize, and part of fish and salt, which latter article is prepared from the salt water by the negroes near the shore; they go so far for them, because wood of a close texture for this purpose is very seldom found near the shore.

Of what materials are the ropes you have mentioned made?

—They are particularly of a kind of aloe, which grows abundantly on the Coast, and which properly prepared are extraordinarily strong, and of which I also have samples with me.

How do they carry back, into the interior country the European goods, fish, and salt, which they receive in exchange for these trees?

—Partly on camels, and partly upon their heads; they carry astonishing weights upon their heads.

From the whole of your observations and experience, have the Negroes a spirit of commerce in them, and have they industry in proportion to the extent of the market which is open to them for sale of their commodities?

—Certainly they have an extraordinary genius for commerce; and their industry is in all regards proportionate to their demands.

Do you believe that if they had an extensive market opened to them for sale of their native produce, and if they could no otherwise get our manufactures that by the disposal of this produce, their indolence would be such as to prevent their supplying the market?

—Not otherways than by introducing some degree of civilization; which would be very easy in case the Slave Trade was not the only means of commerce.

Do you mean to say, that if the Slave Trade was abolished, they would extend their cultivation and manufacture?

—Yes; particularly if some good European people had enterprising spirit enough to settle among them in another way than is the case at present. —Hitherto no other sort of settlement has been made but by people whose only desire has been to make a fortune in a short time, and then to leave the coast.

How does the continuance of the Slave Trade obstruct the progress of industry and civilization in Africa?

—Because, according to what I have found, that Trade takes up solely the minds of the natives, who are continually excited by the merchants to engage in that business; and on the other hand have no encouragement or inducement to improve their country, and cultivate the productions.

Are there any Slaves kept by the natives on that part of the continent of Africa you have visited?

—At Goree and Senegal there are; but on the Continent there are scarcely any.

How are those, which there are, generally treated?

—They are treated very well among themselves, and they never part with their own Slaves if they have any, because it would be dangerous for themselves if they parted with them, on account of the fear of insurrection among the other Slaves. —This rule is observed generally very strictly, even with the French Officers at Goree and Senegal.

How is the island of Goree supplied with vegetables, and other provisions?

—From the continent, by Free Negroes, who come in eight or ten canoes almost every morning loaded with such provisions.

Is rice cultivated in any quantity in this country for sale?

—Rice is not cultivated at Senegal and down the shore to Sallum in any quantity, but south of Sallum down to Gambia, and particularly at the River Caramansa, there is a great abundance of rice, which I often have had the opportunity to be informed of, by seeing many boats or small vessels loaded entirely with rice, not only to supply the inhabitants of Goree and Senegal, but also for supplying vessels there—I have got examples of that rice.

What is the quality of that rice?

—The French Officers at Goree reckon the rice from Caramansa to be of the best quality.

What is its colour?

—It is brownish; of the colour of corn nearly in the exterior part or husk, but the rice separated from the husk is very white—I have samples to produce if required.

Were many curious drugs discovered by Dr. Sparrman, to whom you said the botanical part of this commission was entrusted?

—Among about 2,000 or nearer 3,000 specimens of plants which he brought with him to the cabinet of natural history, of the Royal Academy at Stockholm; I heard him often declare that he could find, if not the whole, at least a great part of the whole Materia Medica, and drugs for various manufacturing uses in this part of the world.

Does the Slave Trade render it dangerous for the Natives to travel about from one part of the country to another, except in parties, or well armed?

—Certainly; and I consider it is the chief hindrance to the improvement of the cultivation; in so far as the Negroes never venture to go out into the fields unless very well armed.

And then the Witness was directed to withdraw.

Veneris, 30° die Aprilis 1790.

CHARLES BERNS WADSTROM, Esquire, called in, and further examined.

Do the natives of Africa print their cotton cloths?

—Yes; with several sorts of wooden stamps or prints, in which they cut out figures according to their taste—I have got patterns of these clothes so printed.

In what manner were the troops of the king of Sin armed, which went out on the pillaging expeditions?

—They were not so regularly armed and cloathed as the troops of the king of Damel—but they had generally a large gun, bow and arrows, lances, and sometimes pistols.

When did you first arrive in Africa, and in what part?

    —I believe it was in the middle of October 1787, but I could tell that from my journal. —We arrived first at Senegal; but could not come on shore because of the current, which carried us down to Goree.

When did you take your final departure from Africa?

    —The 19th of January 1788.

Did Dr. Sparrman, and your other companion, leave it at the same time?

    —Yes.

How far did you go into the interior parts of Africa, and what places in particular did you visit there?

    —The farthest I went, as I believe, did not exceed six English miles from the shore, or about two or three French leagues—I was at Joal—that was the place where I was farthest in the country. —During my stay at Joal, I went with my companion traveller in the neighbourhood, and to several villages on the shore—I was at Dacard—at Bain—at Rufisque—at Cape Rouge, and some other places between those places and Joal—where we were on shore, I visited the interior part as far as we could for one or two days, according as our time permitted—at Dacard and Bain I was quite alone for several days at once, and went about five or six miles up in the country with the Negroes residing on the shore—at Senegal we were for about a week, and went sometimes on the continent.

Where did you reside at the other times, when you were not on the continent?

    —At Goree and Senegal.

How many days in the whole do you think you passed on shore upon the continent?

    —I think I can reckon about three weeks all together.

Is the evidence you have given the Committee the result of your observation on the Spot, or have you obtained any part of it by the information of others since you left Africa?

—It is all the result of my observations and information on the spot,
except as the names of the vessels and their commanders which were cut
off in Africa, which particulars I obtained since I came to this country;
every thing else relating to that transaction I heard, as before mentioned
by me, in Africa.

Is kidnapping or stealing of men allowed by the laws, or punished as a
crime, when discovered, in the parts you have been speaking of?

—It is not allowed by the laws; but I have not heard any single
instance that such a thing has been punished, as it is generally executed
in a manner that it can scarcely come to the knowledge of the kings.

From your information and belief as to the government of that country, do you think, if the Commission of such a fact should come to the
knowledge of the kings, it would not be punished by them?

—Yes, I believe it would, particularly if some European traders were
present when an examination of such a supposed offence was going on.
I was present at Joal when a captive was brought in for some crime; but
the king, although excited by the Mulattoes from Goree to condemn
him, in hopes that they might have the purchase of him when convicted,
acquitted the prisoner.

Are there any of the Negroes upon the continent of Africa, within the
limits you have mentioned as having visited, born Slaves?

—There are, particularly at Sallum, but fewer higher up the
Coast—the farther up you come to the Coast, the fewer—and on the
continent, opposite Goree, there are but very few.

Are not the wealth and consequence of the great men in that country
generally estimated in proportion to the number of their Slaves?

—No—at Sallum[22] the king, and the greater people are generally esteemed for their wealth, in proportion to the silver, and European merchandize that they have—but higher up the Coast they are

esteemed rich, according to the quantity of millet that they can produce, and of cattle that they have—and also of camels and horses.

How do the kings, and great men at Sallum, procure their silver and European merchandize?

—The silver, which consist particularly in Dutch and Spanish dollars,[23] is in this country the principal trading commerce, without which they cannot do any trade with the king of Sallum; by consequence the Mulattoes and Merchants at Goree are obliged always to provide great quantities of them for the trade, as well as other merchandizes.

Do not the kings and great men receive that silver and merchandize in return for Slaves sold by them?

—Yes.

As Slaves then are what the kings and great men give in exchange for silver and European merchandize, must it not be the interest of such men to protect their Slaves from the depredations of others?

—The king of Sallum generally executes what they call kidnapping here upon his neighbours; but higher up the Coast, this kidnapping is executed by order of the kings, even upon their own subjects.

What number of Slaves are annually supplied to the Slave ships from Joal?

—I was informed by the Mulattoes of Goree, that the yearly quantity was near 1,200, but I have reason to believe it was not so much.

What number are supplied annually from Senegal?

—I was informed that the yearly quantity of Slaves, when the Trade is open with Galam, amounts to above 1,000; but I have reason to believe, that it has exceeded this number in the time of the preceding kings of Dalmanny.

In what parts of the country are the manufactures in gold, and other articles you have mentioned, principally carried on?

—At Senegal, and the whole Continent down to Goree, the Negroes are remarkably skilful in working gold and iron; but in regard to the perfection of spinning and weaving cotton cloths, the inhabitants of Sallum are known for an extraordinary ability, which I think depends, for the greatest part, on the goodness of the cotton, which becomes better and better lower down on the Coast, and of which I have samples brought with me from the principal parts where I have been on the Coast, even manufactured into thread and clothes.

Are not those articles, and particularly those manufactured in gold, principally the work of the Moors, and not of the Negroes?

—No—I have taken sketches or drawings of different manufacturing implements, which I have taken from the Negroes, and have only had opportunity to see one Moor, who was established at Senegal, work in gold. —I have however reason to believe, that among them the art of working in gold is derived from the Moors; but that the Negroes are become so skilful in working gold in what is called fillagree, [24] that they are equal to any European goldsmith in that branch.

You have said "that the Negroes work ornaments in gold so well, that you never seen better made articles, of that kind, in Europe;" Is the Committee to understand that that is your serious opinion of them?

—Yes, in regard to fillagrees, and even other articles; I have seen buckles that could not have been better made by any European goldsmith, except the chapes, and tongues and anchors; and there are scarcely any officers at Goree and Senegal that do not bring to Europe some samples of such manufacture.

Did you make any discoveries in Africa in mineralogy, and in the antiquities of the country?

—I have brought with me a collection of minerals, from that part of the coast where I have been, which chiefly consists of specimens of volcanic productions; and I think that nobody has given yet such a faithful description of the mineral productions of that part of the coast as I flatter myself I can give; at least I have not yet heard from any author that there have been such considerable volcanic productions described as I found almost wherever I have been on the coast.

Did you go far into the country, on the continent, in search of minerals?

—Yes, as far as I have before mentioned.

When you quitted Africa, did you go from thence directly to Sweden?

—No; I returned to Havre.[25]

When did you arrive in Sweden?

—I have not been in Sweden since.[26]

Have you made any report to the king of Sweden[27] of the result of your researches, respecting the subjects which were particularly allotted to your attention by him when you first went to Africa?

—Not yet as fully as I wish and hope to do.

Is the substance of your report to the king of Sweden as full and particular as the evidence you have given to the Committee, respecting these matters?

—No—but I can take upon me to answer, that my monarch will be extremely well pleased that I could have been evidence in a cause that so much regards humanity at large, before a nation so respectable and humane as the English nation.

Did Dr. Sparrman and the other gentleman you mentioned return directly to Sweden as soon as they could?

—Dr. Sparrman went first to Paris from Havre, and then here to England, where he remained for some time with me, and afterwards returned to Sweden; but the other gentleman,[28] as captain in the Swedish artillery, returned immediately from Havre to Sweden.

When did you make the report you speak of to the king of Sweden?

—Such reports, without mentioning the particulars, have been made several times to such persons as have had constant opportunities of reporting them to the king.

When did you make the first report?

—I cannot remember exactly the time.

When did you come to this country, after your return from Africa?
—In March 1788.

Is it your intention to return to Sweden soon?
—My intention is, as has been for these two years past, rather to pass my time in such a peaceable country as England is at present, than to return to my own country, particularly as I have been favoured with permission from the monarch to be absent.

Is it your intention to visit Africa again?
—If I could be of any use in such an undertaking I should not have the least objection.

Have you ever signified such a wish and disposition to any person in this country?
—It is well known, as I have taken the liberty of mentioning this before the Privy Council when I first had the honour to appear before them.

Have you any plan in agitation for that purpose at present?
—I have; and I suppose when that is investigated without prejudice, it will be found to be framed upon principles interesting to humanity at large, and this nation in particular.

Are you going in consequence of any mission from your sovereign?
—No.

How are the expenses of this plan to be defrayed, and by whom?
—As I have no regard to any particular interest, but humanity at large is my point of interest, I leave such to Providence.

Are the expenses of your voyage, and the plan you mentioned, to be defrayed by yourself, or by whom?
—I refer to the answer immediately foregoing.

What part of Africa are you going to, and how soon do you mean to set out?

—I have not any particular place nor time in view; but as I have said before, if I can be of any use to the cause of humanity at large, I have no objection to any place, nor to any time, when such a thing can be executed.

Do the Maraboos deal in Slaves?

—On some parts of the Coast they do, but generally not.

How do the Maraboos live, and how are they maintained?

—They live as the other Negroes; they support themselves.

Do they ever command in the army?

—No, not that I know of.

Is it the custom of the French to excite wars to obtain Slaves?

—Not only to excite petty wars or pillages, which are considered to be the same, but also private stealing of them.

Is it the custom of the English?

—I cannot answer that; the coast where I have been being entirely occupied by the French; but I have heard that the Dutch and English frequently use that method.

Are not the sabres and other instruments which you have spoken of in your evidence manufactured by the Moors?

—Not at all; all the sabres as far as I know, are an article of European trade all over the coast; and, except working in gold, the Moors are not at all known for any industry, except seizing on Negroes, and collecting gum arabic.

Do the subjects of the kings, in the parts of Africa that you have visited, pay taxes?

—I found during my stay at Joal, that the king had a certain interest in the trade, but no particular taxes; king Damel I was told had some taxes from his subjects, but so irregular, that there was no regular system of taxation in force.

Where taxes are much in arrear, do the kings send parties out to enforce the payment?
— I did not hear any one instance of that.

When payment for taxes are made to the kings, are they generally made in Slaves, or if not, how are they made?
— I have found where I have been that the general taxes which kings Damel and Barbessin receive from their subjects, consist in millet and cattle, which they sell to the French settlements at Goree in great quantities.

Do you understand that a great part of the trade in Slaves is carried on by the princes of the country?
— At Sallum it is almost entirely; at Sin, the king has the principal commerce; but being a good-natured man, he suffers his subjects to carry on the trade; but king Damel has no such prerogative in the trade.

Do any of these princes receive a duty per head, either from their subjects or from the European merchants or captains, upon the Slaves sold?
— I do not know.

Did you ever hear of poison being taken out by the French Guinea ships,[29] or the purpose for which it was taken?
— I heard it from two captains of French vessels, and one French merchant at Goree; and it was mentioned to me in a manner that I neither wondered at it, nor had the least doubt of it; because they shewed me the necessity of it. When in their passage they are taken by calm, short provisions, or contagious sickness; such an instance was mentioned by Captain Le Loup,[30] when the commander of a vessel from Brest[31] was obliged on their passage of two or three months to poison the Negroes; and that out of a cargo of 500 Negroes, there only remained 20 when they arrived at the Cape.

When in answer to this question, "How are the expences of this plan to be defrayed, and by whom?" you said, "As I have no regard to any particular interest, but humanity at large is my point in view, I leave such to Providence." Did you mean any thing more than that the plan is as yet incomplete; and that you trust that, under the guidance of Providence, it will be brought to an issue favourable to the interest of humanity?

And the question being objected to,

The Witness was desired to explain his meaning in the answer referred to? [32]

—I do not know how these expences may be paid; but trust that Providence will open means by which they may be paid, and the plan put into execution, when once the time comes.

Had not the English been used to trade on that part of the Coast which you have visited, previous to its being occupied by the French?

—Yes; and that is the reason why the Negroes speak such good English.

Did you ever hear that the several methods of obtaining Slaves, which you have stated in your evidence, were practices newly introduced?

—No, it had been an ancient custom ever since that port had been settled, as far as I know.

And the Witness was directed to withdraw.

Appendix B: Swedes Associated with Settlement Projects in Africa

JONATHAN HOWARD, *architect, educated at University of Cambridge*

> *"As then the inhumanity of this trade must be universally admitted and lamented, people would do well to consider, that it does not often fall to the lot of individuals to have an opportunity of performing so important, a moral and religious duty, as that of endeavouring to put an end to a practice, which may, without exaggeration, be called one of the greatest evils of this day* existing upon the earth."
>
> From "Description of a Slave Ship" in
> *An Essay on Colonization* (1794–95)

Adam Afzelius (1750–1837), botanist, traveled to Sierra Leone, together with August Nordenskiöld, Jakob Strand, and Daniel Wilhelm Padenheim.

Carl Axel Arrhenius (1757–1824), chemist, accompanied Wadström to Senegal.

Andreas Berlin (1746–73) was sent by Linnaeus to assist Henry Smeathman's botanical research in Sierra Leone, and he died there.

King Gustav III (1746–92) was interested in Ulrik Nordenskiöld's 1776 colony proposal and in August Nordenskiöld's ideas about colonization and alchemy. Gustav supported Wadström's 1787 Senegal visit, but he had already in 1780 acquired the West Indian island of Saint Barthélemy, a Swedish colony until 1878.

Anders Johansén [Andrew Johansen] (1758–1822), architect, published a book about Bolama Island, *A Geographical and Historical Account of the Island of Bulama, with Observations on its Climate, Productions &c, and an Account of the Formation and Progress of the Bulam Association and of the Colony Itself, to which are Added a Variety of Authentic Documents and a Description Map of the Island and Adjoining Continent* (1794).

Christian Johans[s]én (1746–1813), Anders's brother, was a prominent Swedenborgian artist, writer, and translator; he was also one of the contributors to *Magazine for Philanthropists* (1787).

Johan Henric Kellgren (1751–95), famous poet and critic, in 1784 published "A proposal for the founding of colonies in India and on the African coast." He notoriously ridiculed Swedenborg and his followers.

Carolus Linnaeus (1707–78) sent out seventeen so-called apostles of economic botany; eight of them died on their missions.

August Nordenskiöld (1754–92) worked in London with the Swedenborgian community and was sent as a geologist to Sierra Leone by the Sierra Leone Company; he died there.

Carl Fredrik Nordenskiöld (1756–1828) was a prominent Swedenborgian journalist, publisher, and author who translated Thomas Paine's *Rights of Man* and several writings by Swedenborg.

Ulrik [Ulric] Nordenskiöld (1750–1810) published a book entitled *Dissertation on the Benefit for Sweden of Trade in the [West] Indies and in Africa* (1776).

Daniel Wilhelm Padenheim (1750–1821) was quartermaster in Free-town from 1792 to 1795, and he published a book in 1801 about his experiences there.

Anders Sparrman (1748–1820), botanist, also accompanied Wadström to Senegal.

Jakob Strand, Secretary to the Council at Sierra Leone and frequently praised by Wadström, died from the tropical hardships at his post on the 30th of October 1794, as respectfully reported by the governor (*An Essay on Colonization,* Part 2, §722), and he "left [no] widow and orphans to deplore his death" (Ibid., §721); birthdate undetermined. His journal of 1792 is preserved in the British Library, London.

Emanuel Swedenborg (1688–1772) was not directly involved in any project, but his utopian ideas inspired two Johansén brothers, three Nordenskiöld brothers, and to a lesser extent Anders Sparrman. Coincidentally, the Nova Scotians' ambition to be "free" peasants was a very Swedenborgian utopian concept.

Thomas Thorild (1759–1808), Swedish poet, was in London at the same time as were Wadström and the Nordenskiölds.

Carl Bernhard Wadström (1746–99) was in Senegal from 1787 to 1788.

*En∂note*s

Prospects and Retrospect

1. This speech was made by the former Lord Mayor of London at the *Carl Bernhard Wadström Conference 2015* in Egyptian Hall on June 2, 2015.

On Human Bondage

1. *Britain's Forgotten Slave Owners,* I–II, BBC Two documentary film by David Olusoga, 2015.

It Happens Here

1. Visit www.ilo.org/global/topics/forced-labour/lang--en/index.htm.
2. Visit https://www.gov.uk/government/uploads/system/uploads/attachment_ data/file/383764/Modern_Slavery_Strategy_FINAL_DEC2015.pdf.
3. See the "Independent Anti-Slavery Commissioner: Strategic Plan 2015–2017" at http://www.antislaverycommissioner.co.uk/media/1075/iasc_strategic-plan_2015.pdf.
4. Sections 57, 58, and 59 of the Sexual Offences Act 2003 criminalize trafficking into, within, and out of the UK for sexual exploitation; section 4 of the Asylum and Immigration (Treatment of Claimants, etc.) Act 2004 criminalizes human trafficking into, within, and out of the UK for non-sexual exploitation; and section 71 of the Coroners and Justice Act 2009 criminalizes holding a person in slavery or servitude or requiring a person to perform forced or compulsory labor.
5. See page 51 of the *First Annual Report of the Inter-Departmental Ministerial Group on Human Trafficking* at https://www.gov.uk/government/uploads/system/ uploads/attachment_data/file/118116/human-trafficking-report.pdf.
6. Results of CSJ Freedom of Information request, August 2012.
7. See page 4 of "UKHTC: A Baseline Assessment on the Nature and Scale of Human Trafficking in 2011" at cdn.basw.co.uk/upload/basw_33454-4.pdf.
8. See page 3 of "The Trade in Human Beings: Human Trafficking in the UK, Sixth Report of Session 2008–09, Volume 1" at https://publications.parliament. uk/pa/cm200809/cmselect/cmhaff/23/23i.pdf.

9. See Robert Booth, "Children lost from care in human trafficking cases, says Council," in *The Guardian,* October 18, 2011, https://www.theguardian.com/law/2011/oct/18/children-lost-human-trafficking.

10. Anonymous child-safeguarding practitioner, in evidence to the CSJ.

11. See George Arbuthnott, "The slaves in your weekly shop," in *The Sunday Times Magazine,* October 6, 2013, https://www.thetimes.co.uk/article/the-slaves-in-your-weekly-shop-swhpxlhxp2s.

12. CSJ/YouGov polling, November 2012.

Knowledge, Silence, and Denial

1. *Läsning i blandade ämnen* 1 (1797), 91: "Se här åter et vigtigt ämne, väl i allmänhet mindre nära beslägtadt med vårt lands fördelar; men som visserligen ej derföre skall sakna philosophens och mennisko-vännens varma deltagande."

2. For Wadström's and Sparrman's contributions to the British debate, see Klas Rönnbäck's article, "Enlightenment, Scientific Exploration, and Abolitionism: Anders Sparrman's and Carl Bernhard Wadström's Colonial Encounters in Senegal, 1787–88, and the British Abolitionist Movement," on pages 63–85 of the present volume.

3. For a bibliography and insightful discussion on how these episodes are treated in Swedish historiography, see Gunlög Fur's chapter, "Colonialism and Swedish History: Unthinkable Connections?", in *Scandinavian Colonialism and the Rise of Modernity: Small Time Agents in a Global Arena,* eds. Magdalena Naum & Jonas M. Nordin (New York: Springer, 2013), 17–36.

4. Carl Sprinchorn, "Sjuttonhundratalets planer och förslag till svensk kolonisation i främmande världsdelar," in *Historisk tidskrift* (1923): 109–62.

5. Jonas Ahlskog, "The Political Economy of Colonisation: Carl Bernhard Wadström's Case for Abolition and Civilisation," in *Sjuttonhundratal: Nordic Yearbook for Eighteenth-Century Studies* 7 (2010): 146–67.

6. [Carl Magnus Könsberg], *Kort anwisning på in- och utrikes handelswahror . . .* (Norrköping, 1768), 41: "Detta Africanske folkslaget upköpa Fransoser, Engelsmän, Holländare, Portugiser och Danskar på Guineiska kusten. . . . Brukas af Europerne wid deras Bergswärk och plantager uti America."

7. Utrednings Förslag för en Colonie bestående af 80 Personer, vol. 1, Saint Barthélemysamlingen, Swedish National Archives [Riksarkivet], Stockholm: "Såsom Climatet icke tillåter at Europaer nyttias vid svåra arbeten, och deras ringa antal i begynnelsen icke förslår til annat än bewakning och tilsyn, ty är uphandling af Negerslafvar en nödvändighet til et antal af 250 st åtminstone."; Holger Weiss, "Ett utkast i fel mapp? Några randanmärkningar rörande svenska kolonialplaner i Västafrika under 1700-talets senare hälft," in *Svärdet, ordet och pennan. Kring människa, makt och rum i nordisk historia. Festskrift till Nils Erik Villstrand den 24 maj 2012,* eds. Christer Kujava & Ann-Catrin Östman (Åbo, 2012), 561–83.

8. [Ulric Nordenskiöld], *Afhandling om nyttan för Sverige af handel och nybyggen i Indierna och på Africa* (Stockholm, 1776).

9. Anders Sparrman, *Tal om Den tilväxt och nytta, som Vetenskaperna i allmänhet, särdeles Natural-Historien, redan vunnit och ytterligare kunna vinna, genom undersökningar i Söder-hafvet* (Stockholm, 1778), 17: "Är ännu af Flaggmän osedd, samt en til fina Hamnar och Naturalier aldeles okänd del af vår glob ... Den önskade jag i synnerhet skulle, till Sveriges heder ... på alla chartor teknas med namn af Svenska Länder och Svenska Mæcenater!"

10. [Johan Henric Kellgren], "Förslag, Til Nybyggens anläggande i Indien, och på Africanska Kusten," in *Nya Handelsbibliotheket* (Stockholm, 1784): 65–80.

11. *Anmärkningar rörande slaf-handeln på kusten af Guinea; upsatte af Carl Bernhard Wadström* ... (Norrköping, 1791).

12. Carl Bernhard Wadström, *An essay on colonization, particularly applied to the western coast of Africa, with some free thoughts on cultivation and commerce* ... (London, 1794–95; n.p. at the end of the work).

13. Sture Waller, "Det svenska förvärvet av St Barthélemy. Huvuddragen av de svensk-franska förhandlingarna och parternas syften," in *Historisk tidskrift* 73 (1953): 231–55.

14. I have tried to survey newspapers and periodical publications, but the investigation is by necessity restricted to the reading of a few titles from selected years. Books on the press of this period have been of great assistance: J. Viktor Johansson, *Extra Posten 1792–1795. Studier i 1790-talets svenska press- och litteraturhistoria* (Gothenburg, 1936); Harald Elovson, *Amerika i svensk litteratur. En studie i komparativ litteraturhistoria* (Lund, 1930); Magnus Nyman, *Upplysningens spegel. Götheborgs allehanda om Frankrike och världen, 1774–1789* (Stockholm, 1994); Åke Holmberg, *Världen bortom västerlandet. Svensk syn på fjärran länder och folk från 1700-talet till första världskriget* (Gothenburg, 1988).

15. *Stockholms Posten*, 17 Nov. 1781: "Ännu finnas länder på jorden at uptäcka. ... Ännu finnas rikedomar att röfwa, Landskaper at plundra, hufwud at döpa, halsar at strypa, blod at utgjuta."

16. *Upfostrings-Sälskapets Tidningar*, 10 Oct. 1782: "Spaniorer, Engelsmän, Holländare och Fransoser kalla sig Christna, och hålla ännu många tusend Menniskor uti detta grufliga tilstånd fångna, samt handla därmed såsom med oskäliga djur."

17. *Dagligt Allehanda*, 16 Nov. 1786: "Det är en skam för den uplysta werlden, at slafhandel ännu drifwes äfwen utaf de folkslag, hwilka bekänna sig til Christendomen. Detta bruk hindrar wettenskaper, slögder och folkökningen."

18. *Tryck-Friheten den Wälsignade*, 15 Jan. 1784: "Ändå ges i denna stund intet land, där menskligheten är wärre förnedrad än i America, just i Herr Franklins Fädernesland. En mensklighetens wän måste wara antingen utan ögon eller och rysa för et land, där, twärt emot Landets Religion, som förklarar alla människor för Bröder, man får i hwar plantage, se sju til åttahundrade människor sänkta i träldom, ja rent af räknade til Djur-Riket."

19. *Götheborgs Allehanda*, 12 Mar. 1780; *Hwad Nytt? Hwad Nytt?*, 1 May 1778.

20. "Uppträden ur Mänsklighetens historia. Drag af caractér hos en Slaf," in *Telegraphen*, 28 Mar. 1798.

21. Richard Bell, "Slave Suicide, Abolition and the Problem of Resistance," in *Slavery & Abolition* 33:4 (2012): 525–49.

22. *Medborgaren,* 27 May 1789: "ja, det är handeln ... genom hwilken wi kunna föda Porcellaines arbetaren i China, och den modfäldte slafwen wid socker planteringen i Westindien."

23. Pehr Kalm, *En resa till norra America* ... (Stockholm, 1751–63), 2:477f.

24. Anders Sparrman, *Resa till Goda Hopps-udden, södra pol-kretsen och omkring jordklotet, samt till hottentott- och caffer-landen, åren 1772–76* ... (Stockholm, 1783–1818); Gunnar Broberg, David Dunér, and Roland Moberg, eds., *Anders Sparrman. Linnean, världsresenär, fattigläkare* (Uppsala, 2012).

25. Carl Peter Thunberg, *Resa uti Europa, Africa, Asia, förrättad åren 1770–1779* (Stockholm, 1788–93); Marie-Christine Skuncke, *Carl Peter Thunberg: botanist and physician. Career-building across the oceans in the eighteenth century* (Uppsala, 2014).

26. Thomas Clarkson, *An essay on the slavery and commerce of the human species, particularly the African* ... (London, 1788), 46; in the Swedish edition: *Afhandling om slafveriet och slafhandeln, särdeles rörande negrerne, så väl i Africa, som West-Indien* ... (Stockholm, 1796), 59.

27. Jacob Wallenberg, *Min son på galejan, eller En ostindisk resa* ... (Stockholm, 1781), 98: "Sku vi, som slafvar, dras till någon okänd ö? Från hembygd, flicka, wän? Nej, låt oss helre dö!"

28. Olof Swartz, *Inträdes-Tal Innehållande Anmärkningar om Vestindien* (Stockholm, 1790), 17: "En dag aflifvades en Neger vid Cavaillon på St. Domingo, som hade mördat sin Herre. Tummarne afhöggos, och han krokades under hjulet, utan at fälla en enda tår. Man hörde honom endast säga: Då jag mördade min Herre, var det illa för Honom: nu måste jag dö för hans skull, det är illa för mig."

29. Jöran Fredriksson Silfverhjelm, *Samlingar för hjertat och snillet* (Stockholm, 1789), 54: "Om en Neger ihjälslår en af de hvita, det må vara för hvad orsak som hälst, så brännes han lefvande; men om en hvit dödar sin slaf, så försonas denne ogerning genom en ganska obetydelig plikt, och som man sällan utfodrar."

30. Margareta Björkman, *Läsarnas nöje. Kommersiella lånbibliotek i Stockholm 1783–1809* (Uppsala, 1992).

31. [Eric Ulric Nordforss], *Bukoléon. Blandad läsning för olärde* (Stockholm, 1799), 90.

32. Christian Georg Andreas Oldendorp, *Tillförlåtlig underrättelse om negrerne på Gvinea kusten, samt de derifrån hämtade slafvars närvarande belägenhet, medfart, seder och sinnelag* ... (Uppsala, 1784), n.p. foreword (ital. in original): "En Svensk Officerare, som med utmärkt heder gjort hela Sjö-Campagnen under sist slutade kriget i Vestindien, berättade, det han på Martinique sedt en Fransk Officerare på Billarden, med sin queue krossa huvudskålen på en Neger-gosse, blott för en ringa försummelse vid marqueringen. Negren stalp, och Officeraren sade dervid helt kallt: *Jag kan betala honom.*"

33. J. G. Stedman, *Capitain Johan Stedmans Dagbok öfwer sina fälttåg i Surinam...* (Stockholm, 1800), n.p. foreword: "Öfversättaren föreställer sig, at de fläste läsare skola anse många här förekommande och emot Surinams slafvar utöfvade grymheter öfverdrefna, naturstridiga, omöjeliga. Men en så tröstelig tanke vågar han dock icke understödja. De underrättelser han äger om Holländares och Ängelsmäns sätt att handtera sina slafvar på Wästindiska öarna, gifva sammanlagde en tafla, som gör desse olyckliga varelsers medfart på Surinam för ingen del otrolig."

34. August von Kotzebue, *Neger-slafvarne. Dramatiserad historie-målning* (Stockholm, 1796).

35. Sébastien-Roch Nicolas de Chamfort, *Slafhandlaren i Smirna* (Stockholm, 1774), 27 (the four periods are in the orig.): "Hvad vil han väl säga? Säljer Ni icke Negrer? Jag säljer Er på samma grund.... kommer det intet på et ut? Åtskilnaden består allenast deruti, at de äro svarta, och Ni äro hvita."

36. *Mirza och Lindor, Pantomime-Ballet uti Tre Acter. — Sammansatt af Herr Marcadet, Premier-Danseur vid Kongl. Operan...* (Stockholm, 1793), n.p.: "Scenen är på Ön S:t Barthelemy."

37. Jenna M. Gibbs, *Performing the Temple of Liberty: Slavery, Theater, and Popular Culture in London and Philadelphia, 1760–1850* (Baltimore, 2014); Sylvie Chalaye, *Du Noir au nègre: l'image de Noir au théâtre: de Marguerite de Navarre à Jean Genet (1550–1960)* (Paris, Montréal, 1998); Franca Dellarosa, *Slavery on Stage: Representations of Slavery in British Theatre, 1760s–1830s* (Bari, 2009).

38. Marie-Christine Skuncke & Anna Ivarsdotter, *Svenska operans födelse. Studier i gustaviansk musikdramatik* (Stockholm, 1998), 28f.

39. Kerstin Anér, *Läsning i blandade ämnen. Studier i 1790-talets svenska press- och litteraturhistoria* (Gothenburg, 1948), 211; Karin Dovring, "Till författarfrågan i Läsning i blandade ämnen," in *Scandia* 19:2 (1948): 284–98.

40. Stig Boberg, *Gustav III och tryckfriheten 1774–1787* (Stockholm, 1951); Elmar Nyman, *Indragningsmakt och tryckfrihet 1785–1810* (Stockholm, 1963).

41. Wadström, *An essay on colonization...*, 2:187.

42. Harald Elovson, *Amerika i svensk litteratur 1750–1820. En studie i komparativ litteraturhistoria* (Lund., 1930), 247.

43. Bengt Anders Euphrasén, *Beskrifning öfver svenska vestindiska ön St. Barthelemi, samt öarne St. Eustache och St. Christopher...* (Stockholm, 1795), 52–53: "straffet går merendels för sig på följande sätt. Den brottslige läggas framstupa på jorden, bindes med händerna fast vid hjulet under en Canon, fötterna utsträckes och fastbindes vi 2:ne pålar, som blifva nedslagna uti jorden, kläderne blifva borttagne, at kroppen blifver bar, den som skall slå honom, har en piska med kort skaft; men snärten och smällen är 6 eller 7 alnar lång; han ställer sig på något afstånd och med piskan slår knäppsmällar på slafvens bara kropp; hvarje slag smäller som et pistol-skott och stora skin- samt köttstycken följa ofta med ifrån kroppen; Slafven får uthärda 30, 50 eller 100 sådane slag, alt efter större eller mindre brott."

44. Fredrik Thomasson, "Raynal and Sweden. Royal Propaganda and Colonial Aspirations," in *Raynal's 'Histoire des deux Indes.' Colonialism, networks and global exchange,* Oxford University Studies in the Enlightenment (previously SVEC), eds. Cecil Courtney & Jenny Mander (Oxford, 2015), 201–15.

45. Ingegerd Hildebrand, *Den svenska kolonin S:t Barthélemy och Västindiska kompaniet fram till 1796* (Lund, 1951), 57.

Labor and Money

1. Erik W. Dahlgren, "Carl Bernhard Wadström: Hans verksamhet för Slafhandelns Bekämpande och de samtida Kolonisationsplanerna i Västafrika," in *Nordisk Tidskrift för Bok- och Biblioteksväsenden* (1915): 24–25. In other contexts, Nordenskiöld has presented the ideas that reappear in *Plan for a Free Community*. For example, they appear in *Afton-bladet: en vecko-skrift utgiven af et sälskap i Stockholm,* nos. 3 and 4 (Stockholm: Carlbohm, 1784); and they appear in Nordenskiöld's *Församlingsformen uti det Nya Jerusalem* (Copenhagen, 1790).

2. Ellen Hagen, *En frihetstidens son: Carl Bernhard Wadström* (Stockholm, 1946). See also Erik W. Dahlgren's bibliographic comments in his 1915 article in *Nordisk Tidskrift för Bok- och Biblioteksväsenden.*

3. August Nordenskiöld was born in 1754 on the Eriksnäs estate in the region of Nyland in Finland, then a Swedish province. He died in 1792 in the city of Freetown in Sierra Leone. For further information on him, see A. E. Arppe, "Anteckningar om Finska Alkemister," in *Bidrag till Kännedom om Finlands Natur och Folk* 16 (Helsinki/Helsingfors, 1870): 15–17. See also Gösta Bodman, "August Nordenskiöld, en Gustaf den Tredjes Alkemist," in *Lychnos: Årsbok för Idé- och Lärdomshistoria* (1943), as well as Ronny Ambjörnsson, "Guds Republique," in *Lychnos* (1975).

4. *Afton-bladet,* nos. 3 and 4; and Arppe, "Anteckningar om Finska Alkemister," 20.

5. Bodman, "August Nordenskiöld," 215.

6. Arppe, "Anteckningar om Finska Alkemister," 87.

7. August Nordenskiöld, *An Address to the True Members of the New Jerusalem Church, Revealed by the Lord in the Writings of Emanuel Swedenborg* (London, 1789), 7.

8. Martin Lamm, *Upplysningstidens romantik: den mystiskt sentimentala strömningen i svensk litteratur,* Part 2 (Stockholm: Geber, 1920), 43.

9. Swedenborg's pronouncements on Africa have been collected by J. J. G. Wilkinson, *The African and the True Christian Religion: his Magna Charta* (London, 1892). See also Sten Lindroth, "Adam Afzelius: en Linnean i England och Sierra Leone," in *Lychnos* (1944–45): 32.

10. Henry Smeathman, *Plan of Settlement to be Made near Sierra Leona, on the Grain Coast of Africa, Intended more particularly for the service and happy establishment of Blacks and People of Colour, to be shipped as freemen under the direction of the Committee for Relieving the Black Poor, and under the protection of the British Government* (London, 1786).

11. Martin Lamm, *Emanuel Swedenborg: The Development of His Thought*, translated by Tomas Spiers and Anders Hallengren (West Chester, PA: Swedenborg Foundation, 2000), 290–319.

12. *Afton-bladet*, no. 3, 10. Author's translation.

13. Ibid., 11.

14. August Nordenskiöld, Carl Bernhard Wadström, Colborn Barrell, and Johan Gottfried Simpson, *Plan for a Free Community upon the Coast of Africa, Under the Protection of Great Britain; But Intirely Independent of all European Laws and Governments. With an Invitation, under certain Conditions, to all Persons desirous of partaking the Benefits thereof.* . . . (London: R. Hindmarsh, printer 1789), chapter 11.

15. Ibid., chapter 8, 32ff. Nordenskiöld's underlining; author's translation.

16. Ibid., 20.

17. Carl Bernhard Wadström, *An Essay on Colonization, Particularly Applied to the Western Coast of Africa, with Some Free Thoughts on Cultivation and Commerce; also Brief Descriptions of the Colonies already Formed or Attempted in Africa, Including those of Sierra Leone and Bulama*, Part 1 (London: Darton and Harvey, 1794), 70.

18. Ibid., 72.

19. Granville Sharp, *A Short Sketch of Temporary Regulations (until Better Shall Be Proposed) for the Intended Settlement on the Grain Coast of Africa, near Sierra Leona* (London: H. Baldwin, 1786), 13.

20. Carl Bernhard Wadström, *Quelques Idées sur la Nature du Numéraire et sur la Nécessité de Combiner l'Intérêt du Cultivateur avec celui du Négociant au Moment où l'on Établit un Nouveau Plan de Finances* (Paris, 1796), 4.

21. Adam Smith, *The Wealth of Nations* (London: J. M. Dent, 1910), 110.

Enlightenment, Scientific Exploration, and Abolitionism

1. Christopher Leslie Brown, *Moral Capital: Foundations of British Abolitionism* (Chapel Hill: University of North Carolina Press, 2006), 17.

2. Brycchan Carey, *British Abolitionism and the Rhetoric of Sensibility: Writing, Sentiment, and Slavery, 1760–1807* (Basingstoke: Palgrave Macmillan, 2005).

3. Sverker Sörlin and Otto Fagerstedt, *Linné och hans apostlar* (Stockholm: Natur och Kultur, 2004), 175.

4. "Anders Sparrman," in *Biographiskt lexicon* 15 (1848); Sörlin and Fagerstedt, *Linné och hans apostlar*, 152–83; Kenneth Nyberg, "Anders Sparrman," in *Svenskt Biografiskt Lexikon* 33 (2007); Tony Rice, *Voyages of Discovery: A Visual Celebration of Ten of the Greatest Natural History Expeditions* (London: Natural History Museum, 2010 [1999]), 172–73.

5. "Carl Bernhard Wadström," in *Biographiskt lexicon* 19 (1852); Ellen Hagen, *En frihetstidens son. Carl Bernhard Wadström* (Stockholm: Gothia, 1946); Robert Rix, *William Blake and the Cultures of Radical Christianity* (Aldershot: Ashgate, 2007), 91–98.

6. Hagen, *En frihetstidens son,* 122–23; "Carl Bernhard Wadström," in *Biographiskt lexicon* 19 (1852); Jakob Christensson, *Lyckoriket: Studier i svensk upplysning* (Stockholm: Atlantis, 1996), 192; Philip Nelson, *Carl Bernhard Wadström. Mannen bakom myten* (Norrköping: Föreningen Gamla Norrköping, 1998), 37–39.

7. Sven Odén, "Carl Axel Arrhenius," in *Svenskt Biografiskt Lexikon* 2 (1920).

8. House of Commons, *Minutes of the evidence taken before a committee of the House of Commons ... appointed ... to take the examination of the several witnesses ...* (London, 1790), 19.

9. Ronny Ambjörnsson, "'Guds Republique,' En utopi från 1789," in *Lychnos* (1975–76): 12–16; Nelson, *Carl Bernhard Wadström,* 40; Nyberg, "Anders Sparrman." Economic motives were of central importance behind many of the journeys of Linnaeus's disciples; see, for example, Lisbet Koerner, *Linnaeus: Nature and nation* (Cambridge: Harvard University Press, 1999), Ch. 6; Sörlin and Fagerstedt, *Linné och hans apostlar,* 48.

10. Carl Bernhard Wadström, "Resa ifrån Stockholm genom Danmark, Tyskland och Frankrike till Senegal-länderna i Afrika, år 1787 och 88," in *Archiv för nyare resor: månads-skrift: med kartor och kopparstick* 6(3) (Stockholm: J. P. Marquard, 1811–15): 4.

11. "Carl Axel Arrhenius," in *Svenskt Biografiskt Lexikon – ny följd* (1857–58).

12. Thomas Clarkson, *The History of the rise, progress, and accomplishment of the abolition of the African slave-trade by the British Parliament,* vol. 1 (London, 1808), 489.

13. Thomas Clarkson, *An essay on the slavery and commerce of the human species, particularly the African, translated from a Latin dissertation, which was honoured ...* (London, 1786), 50–53.

14. A number of the primary sources used in this article have been accessed through the digitized collections in the database *The Making of the Modern World* (Gale, Cengage Learning) at Gothenburg University Library. These include: Clarkson, *Essay on the slavery and commerce of the human species* (London, 1786); Board of Trade, *Report of the Lords of the committee of council appointed for the consideration of all matters relating to trade and foreign plantations* ([London?], 1789); Thomas Clarkson, *The substance of the evidence of sundry persons on the slave-trade, collected in the course of a tour made in the autumn of the year 1788* (London, 1789); Carl Bernhard Wadström, *Observations on the slave trade, and a description of some part of the coast of Guinea, during a voyage, made in 1787, and 1788, in company with ...* (London, 1789); William Wilberforce, *The speech of William Wilberforce, Esq., representative for the County of York, on Wednesday the 13th of May, 1789, on the question of the ...* (London, 1789); Olaudah Equiano, *The Interesting Narrative of the Life of Olaudah Equiano; or, Gustavus Vassa, the African, written by himself,* vol. 1 (London, 1789); House of Commons, *Minutes of the evidence* (London, 1790); *An abstract of the evidence delivered before a Select Committee of the House of Commons in the*

years 1790 and 1791; on the part of the . . ., 2ⁿᵈ ed. (London, 1791); *Extracts from the evidence delivered before a Select Committee of the House of Commons in the years 1790 and 1791, on the part of the petitioners* . . . (London, 1791); John Ranby, *Observations on the evidence given before the Committees of the Privy Council and House of Commons in support of the Bill for abolishing the* . . . (London, 1791); Thomas Clarkson, *Letters on the slave-trade, and the state of the natives in those parts of Africa which are contiguous to Fort St. Louis and Goree, written at* . . . (London, 1791); *Abridgment of the minutes of the evidence, taken before a committee of the whole House, to whom it was referred to consider of the slave trade,* . . . ([n.p.], [1792?]); House of Commons, *The Parliamentary Register; or, History of the proceedings and debates of the House of Commons [and House of Lords]* . . ., vol. 26 (London, 1782–96); Clarkson, *History of the rise, progress, and accomplishment of the abolition of the African slave-trade,* vols. 1–2 (London, 1808); Bryan Edwards, *The history, civil and commercial, of the British West Indies. With a continuation to the present time.* 5ᵗʰ ed., vol. 4 (London, 1819); Prince Hoare, *Memoirs of Granville Sharp, Esq. composed from his own manuscripts, and other authentic documents in the possession of his family and of the* . . . (London, 1820).

15. Board of Trade, *Report of the Lords;* House of Commons, *Minutes of the evidence.*

16. House of Commons, *Minutes of the evidence,* 18.

17. All translations from this source, from Swedish into English, are made by the author of this article.

18. On the early cities and European settlements in West Africa, see Bill Freund, *The African city. A history* (Cambridge: Cambridge University Press, 2007), 51–55.

19. House of Commons, *Minutes of the evidence,* 39; Board of Trade, *Report of the Lords;* Wadström, "Resa ifrån Stockholm genom Danmark," 6(1): 57, 62.

20. House of Commons, *Minutes of the evidence,* 22. Wadström gave evidence concerning the same thing before the Board of Trade; see Clarkson, *Substance of the evidence,* 110.

21. House of Commons, *Minutes of the evidence,* 23; Ranby, *Observations on the evidence,* 146.

22. Wadström, *Observations on the slave trade,* 9, 14–15; Clarkson, *Substance of the evidence,* 112. The same stories also figure in Wadström's travel account: Wadström, "Resa ifrån Stockholm genom Danmark," 6(1): 61.

23. Wadström, *Observations on the slave trade,* 11–12.

24. House of Commons, *Minutes of the evidence,* 23.

25. Board of Trade, *Report of the Lords.*

26. House of Commons, *Minutes of the evidence,* 23. See also Clarkson, *Substance of the evidence,* 113; *Abstract of the evidence,* 18.

27. Clarkson, *Substance of the evidence,* 110–11; Wadström, *Observations on the slave trade,* 16–17.

28. Board of Trade, *Report of the Lords;* Clarkson, *Substance of the evidence,* 114; Wadström, *Observations on the slave trade,* 2–4; House of Commons, *Minutes of*

the evidence, 27; *Abridgment of the minutes*, 8; *Abstract of the evidence*, 18; Ranby, *Observations on the evidence*, 147; Edwards, *History, civil and commercial*, 334–35.

29. Wadström, *Observations on the slave trade*, 4; *Abridgment of the minutes*, 8–9; Clarkson, *Letters on the slave-trade*, 31–32.

30. House of Commons, *Minutes of the evidence*, 29.

31. Ibid.

32. Clarkson, *Substance of the evidence*, 114.

33. House of Commons, *Minutes of the evidence*, 30.

34. Wadström, *Observations on the slave trade*, 29.

35. Ibid., 28.

36. Board of Trade, *Report of the Lords*. Carl Bernhard Wadström gave a very similar witness on the same issue.

37. Wadström, "Resa ifrån Stockholm genom Danmark," 6(2): 65.

38. House of Commons, *Minutes of the evidence*, 31–32.

39. Wadström, "Resa ifrån Stockholm genom Danmark," 6(1): 56.

40. Clarkson, *Substance of the evidence*, 107–8; Board of Trade, *Report of the Lords*.

41. House of Commons, *Minutes of the evidence*, 32.

42. Ibid., 34.

43. *Abstract of the evidence*, 97; *Extracts from the evidence*, 20; *Abridgment of the minutes*, 9–11.

44. House of Commons, *Minutes of the evidence*, 40.

45. Ibid., 35–36.

46. Wadström, "Resa ifrån Stockholm genom Danmark," 6(1): 50–51, 54–55; 6(2): 65, 73.

47. Ibid., 6(2): 78.

48. Board of Trade, *Report of the Lords*.

49. Wilberforce, *Speech of William Wilberforce*, 10–11; House of Commons, *Parliamentary Register*, 133.

50. Clarkson, *History of the rise, progress, and accomplishment of the abolition of the African slave-trade*, vol. 1, 491.

51. Ibid. Ester Copley has in her history of the abolitionist movement, *A history of slavery and its abolition* (London, 1839), 269–70, recapitulated Clarkson's description almost exactly.

52. Hoare, *Memoirs of Granville Sharp*, 513; Equiano, *Interesting narrative*, Subscriber's list.

53. Clarkson, *History of the rise, progress, and accomplishment of the abolition of the African slave-trade*, vol. 2, 151.

54. Wadström, *Observations on the slave trade*, vii.

55. Society for the Abolition of the Slave Trade, *List of the Society* (London, 1788); Clarkson, *History of the rise, progress, and accomplishment of the abolition of the*

African slave-trade, vol. 2, 27.

56. Wadström, *Observations on the slave trade,* iv.

57. Ibid., vi.

58. Clarkson, *History of the rise, progress, and accomplishment of the abolition of the African slave-trade,* vol. 1, 565.

59. Philip Curtin, *The Image of Africa: British Ideas and Action, 1780–1850* (Madison: University of Wisconsin Press, 1965), 14–16.

60. Ranby, *Observations on the evidence.*

61. Clarkson, *History of the rise, progress, and accomplishment of the abolition of the African slave-trade,* vol. 1, 489.

62. Estimates of the TSTD2 from *The Trans-Atlantic Slave Trade Database,* http:// www.slavevoyages.org.

63. Philip Curtin, *Economic Change in Precolonial Africa: Senegambia in the Era of the Slave Trade* (Madison: University of Wisconsin Press, 1975), Ch. 4; James Searing, *West African Slavery and Atlantic Commerce: The Senegal River Valley, 1700–1860* (Cambridge: Cambridge University Press, 1993), Ch. 5; Boubacar Barry, *Senegambia and the Atlantic Slave Trade* (Cambridge: Cambridge University Press, 1998), Ch. 8; Martin Klein, *Slavery and Colonial Rule in French West Africa* (Cambridge: Cambridge University Press, 1998), 37–42; for an example of a part of Senegambia where the slave trade is claimed to not have had the effect of an increase in violence, see Donald Wright, *The World and a Very Small Place in Africa: A History of Globalization in Niumi, The Gambia* (Armonk: M. E. Sharpe, 2004), Ch. 4.

64. See, for example, Walter Rodney, *How Europe Underdeveloped Africa* (London: Bogle-L'Ouverture, 1972); Barry, *Senegambia,* Ch. 8; Nathan Nunn, "The Long-Term Effects of Africa's Slave Trades," in *Quarterly Journal of Economics* 123(1) (2008): 139–76.

65. See, for example, Timothy Garrard, *African Gold* (London: Prestel, 2011).

66. For a study of life at the British forts in Africa, including life for the castle slaves, see William St Clair, *The Door of No Return: The History of Cape Coast Castle and the Atlantic Slave Trade* (New York: Bluebridge, 2007).

67. Searing, *West African Slavery,* 44–52; Barry, *Senegambia,* 112–21; Klein, *Slavery and Colonial Rule,* Ch. 1; Paul Lovejoy, *Transformations in Slavery: A History of Slavery in Africa* (Cambridge: Cambridge University Press, 2000), 281–83.

68. Searing, *West African Slavery,* 63–71; Curtin, *Economic Change,* Chs. 7–8.

69. Searing, *West African Slavery,* 38.

70. P. J. Marshall and Glyndwr Williams, *The Great Map of Mankind: British Perceptions of the World in the Age of Enlightenment* (London: Dent, 1982), 33–37; 227–57.

71. Ibid., 37.

72. Mary Louise Pratt, *Imperial Eyes: Travel Writing and Transculturation* (London: Routledge, 1992), 24.

73. Ibid., 38–39.

74. Ibid., 48–52.

75. Ibid., 49–53.

76. Ibid., 52.

77. For a study of naturalist expeditions, see, for example, Rice, *Voyages of Discovery*.

78. Sverker Sörlin, *Världens ordning: Europas idéhistoria 1492–1918* (Stockholm: Natur och Kultur, 2004), 618.

79. William Beinart, "Men, science, travel and nature in the eighteenth and nineteenth-century Cape," in *Journal of Southern African Studies* 24(4) (1998): 778. See also William Beinart and Lotte Hughes, *Environment and Empire* (Oxford: Oxford University Press, 2009), 78–79.

80. Brown, *Moral Capital*, 51.

81. The only exception being that Wadström, in his travel accounts, complained that he was unable to bring "my good Negro Amargalle" when returning home to Europe; see Wadström, "Resa ifrån Stockholm genom Danmark," 6(3): 7.

82. Curtin, *Image of Africa*, 36–38; Peter Gay, *The Enlightenment: The Science of Freedom* (New York: Norton, 1969), 174–75, 319–23.

83. Curtin, *Image of Africa,* 23; Edward Said, *Orientalism: Western Conceptions of the Orient* (London: Penguin, 1995 [1978]), 49–73; Marshall and Williams, *Great Map,* 239; Tzvetan Todorov, *The Conquest of America: The Question of the Other* (Norman: University of Oklahoma Press, 1999 [1982]); Mary Campbell, *The Witness and the Other World: Exotic European Travel Writing, 400–1600* (Ithaca: Cornell University Press, 1988), 28, 42, 177, 260; Anthony Pagden, *European Encounters with the New World: From Renaissance to Romanticism* (New Haven: Yale University Press, 1993), 60; Philip Morgan, "Encounters between British and 'indigenous' peoples, c. 1500–c. 1800," in *Empire and Others: British Encounters with Indigenous Peoples, 1600–1850,* eds. Martin Dauton and Rick Halpern (Philadelphia: University of Pennsylvania Press, 1999), 42–78.

84. Beinart, "Men, science, travel and nature," 778, 781.

85. C. B. Wadström, *An Essay on Colonization particularly applied to the Western Coast of Africa with some free thoughts on Cultivation and Commerce* [New York: Kelley, 1968 [1794]]. See also Curtin, *Image of Africa,* 103–16.

86. For analyses of Linnaeus's classification of the human races, see Winthrop Jordan, *White Over Black: American Attitudes Toward the Negro, 1550–1812* (Williamsburg: University of North Carolina, 1968), 218–23; Sten Lindroth, *Svensk Lärdomshistoria: Frihetstiden* (Stockholm: Norstedt, 1978), 210–12; Curtin, *Image of Africa,* 36–38; Koerner, *Linnaeus: Nature and nation,* 9; Sörlin and Fagerstedt, *Linné och hans apostlar,* 116–29; Emmanuel Chukwudi Eze, ed., *Race and the Enlightenment: A Reader* (Malden, Mass.: Blackwell, 1997), Ch. 1; Marshall and Williams, *Great Map,* 245; Roy Porter, *Enlightenment: Britain and the Creation of the Modern World* (London: Allen Lane, 2000), 354–58.

87. Hanna Hodacs and Kenneth Nyberg, *Naturalhistoria på resande fot. Om att forska, undervisa och göra karriär i 1700-talets Sverige* (Stockholm: Nordic

Academic Press, 2007), 21–24; Nyberg, "Anders Sparrman"; Beinart, "Men, science, travel and nature," 786; Sten Selander, *Linnélärjungar i främmande länder* (Stockholm: Bonnier, 1960), 78–80; Sörlin and Fagerstedt, *Linné och hans apostlar*, 174.

88. Hagen, *En frihetstidens son*, 122–23; "Carl Bernhard Wadström," in *Biographiskt lexicon* 19 (1852); Nelson, *Carl Bernhard Wadström*, 37–39. For a description of Swedenborg's portrayal of Africans, see Curtin, *Image of Africa*, 26–27; Rix, *William Blake*, 96.

89. Hodacs and Nyberg, *Naturalhistoria på resande fot*, 213.

90. Quote from Brown, *Moral Capital*, 211. For some of the other more important works in a long scholarly debate, see Eric Williams, *Capitalism and Slavery* (London: Deutsch, 1964 [1943]); David Brion Davis, *The Problem of Slavery in Western Culture* (Ithaca: Cornell University Press, 1966); Roger Anstey, *The Atlantic Slave Trade and British Abolition, 1760–1810* (London: Macmillan, 1975); David Brion Davis, *The Problem of Slavery in the Age of Revolution* (Ithaca: Cornell University Press, 1975); Seymour Drescher, *Econocide: British Slavery in the Era of Abolition* (Chapel Hill: University of North Carolina Press, 2010 [1977]); Seymour Drescher, *Capitalism and Antislavery: British Mobilization in Comparative Perspective* (London: Macmillan, 1986); David Eltis, *Economic Growth and the Ending of the Transatlantic Slave Trade* (Oxford: Oxford University Press, 1987); Robin Blackburn, *The Overthrow of Colonial Slavery, 1776–1848* (London: Verso, 1988); John Oldfield, *Popular Politics and British Anti-Slavery: Mobilisation of Public Opinion Against the Slave Trade, 1787–1807* (Manchester: Manchester University Press, 1995); Selwyn Carrington, *The Sugar Industry and the Abolition of Slave Trade, 1775–1810* (Gainesville: University Press of Florida, 2002); David Brion Davis, *Inhuman Bondage: the Rise and Fall of Slavery in the New World* (Oxford: Oxford University Press, 2006), Ch. 12; David Beck Ryden, *West Indian Slavery and British Abolition, 1783–1807* (Cambridge: Cambridge University Press, 2009); Seymour Drescher, *Abolition: A History of Slavery and Antislavery* (Cambridge: Cambridge University Press, 2009), Ch. 8; Maurice Jackson, *Let This Voice Be Heard. Anthony Benezet, Father of Atlantic Abolitionism* (Philadelphia: University of Pennsylvania Press, 2009).

91. Drescher, *Abolition*, 209.

92. Curtin, *Image of Africa*, 53–57, 68. Quote on page 57.

93. Ernst Ekman, "Sweden, the Slave Trade and Slavery, 1784–1847," in *Revue française d'histoire d'outre-mer* 62 (1975): 221–31; Ingegerd Hildebrand, *Den Svenska Kolonin S:t Barthélemy och Västindiska Kompaniet fram till 1796* (Lund: Lindstedts, 1951).

94. See, for example, Gay, *Enlightenment*, 407–23; Davis, *Problem of Slavery*, Chs. 13–14; Louis Sala-Molins, *Dark Side of the Light: Slavery and the French Enlightenment* (Minneapolis: University of Minnesota Press, 2006); Christopher Miller, *The French Triangle: Literature and Culture of the Slave Trade* (Durham: Duke University Press, 2008), Ch. 3; Laurent Dubois, "An Enslaved Enlightenment: Rethinking the Intellectual History of the French Atlantic," in

Social History 31(1) (February 2006): 1–14; Porter, *Enlightenment*, 359–60. See also Ambjörnsson, "'Guds Republique,'" 39–40.

95. Gay, *Enlightenment*, 126–28; Porter, *Enlightenment*, Ch. 6. See also Sörlin, *Världens ordning*, 324; Tore Frängsmyr, *Sökandet efter upplysningen: Perspektiv på svenskt 1700-tal* (Stockholm: Natur och Kultur, 2006), 62–69.

96. Carey, *British Abolitionism.*

97. Brown, *Moral Capital*, 297. See also Sarah Thomas, "'On the Spot': Travelling Artists and Abolitionism, 1770–1830," in *Atlantic Studies* 8(2) (2011): 213–32, for a study of the contribution of visual representations of slavery.

98. Pagden, *European Encounters*, 54–56.

The Swedenborgian, or New Church, Foundations . . .

1. Carl Bernhard Wadström, *Plan for a free community at Sierra Leona, upon the coast of Africa, under the protection of Great Britain; with An Invitation to all Persons desirous of partaking the Benefits thereof . . .* , ECCO Print Edition (London: T. and J. Egerton, 1792).

2. Cyriel Odhner Sigstedt, *The Swedenborg Epic: The Life and Works of Emanuel Swedenborg* (London: The Swedenborg Society, 1981 [1952]), 276.

3. Carl Bernhard Wadström, Letter 1 in the *New-Jerusalem Magazine* (London, January 1790): 70.

4. Emanuel Swedenborg, *Conjugial Love,* translated by Samuel M. Warren and Louis H. Tafel (West Chester, PA: Swedenborg Foundation, 1998), §113.

5. Ibid.

6. Ibid., §114.

7. Emanuel Swedenborg, *Last Judgment (Posthumous),* translated by N. Bruce Rogers (Bryn Athyn, PA: General Church of the New Jerusalem, 1997), §118. It should be pointed out that Swedenborg's view of the Africans differed from that of most intellectuals at the end of the eighteenth century, who saw them as similar to beasts, lacking in intelligence, and definitely inferior to Europeans.

8. Wadström, Letter 1 in the *New-Jerusalem Magazine,* 70.

9. Ibid., 71. It should also be pointed out that this antislavery association predated both the Quaker antislavery society formed in 1783 and Clarkson's Society for the Abolition of Slavery organized in 1787.

10. Alfred Acton, "Carl Bernhard Wadström" (Unpublished paper held in Swedenborg Library, Bryn Athyn, PA, 1943), 10.

11. Ibid.

12. Carl Bernhard Wadström, *An Essay on Colonization, Particularly Applied to the Western Coast of Africa, with Some Free Thoughts on Cultivation and Commerce,* Part 2 (London: Darton and Harvey, 1795), 185.

13. Acton, "Carl Bernhard Wadström," 6.

14. Jane Williams-Hogan, "Swedenborgianism in Stockholm (1772–1795)" (Unpublished paper, written as part of a study presented at the Teologiska

Institutionen i Uppsala, Sverige, 1995, titled: "1700-talets svenska samhällsstruktur och swdenborgianismens utveckling i Göteborg, Skara, och Stockholm"), 3.

15. Harry Lenhammar, *Tolerans och Bekännelsetvång: Studier i den svenska swedenborgianismen 1765–1795* (Uppsala: Studia historico-ecclesiastica Upsaliensia 11, 1966), 275.

16. Ibid., 275–76.

17. Acton, "Carl Bernhard Wadström," 50.

18. Wadström, *Plan for a free community at Sierra Leona*, 1.

19. Ibid., 13.

20. Ibid., 38.

21. Ibid., 39.

22. Emanuel Swedenborg, *True Christianity*, translated by Jonathan S. Rose (West Chester, PA: Swedenborg Foundation, 2010), §4:3.

23. Ibid., §5.

24. Wadström, *Plan for a free community at Sierra Leona*, 40.

25. Ibid., 3.

26. Emanuel Swedenborg, *Married Love*, translated by N. Bruce Rogers (Bryn Athyn, PA: General Church of the New Jerusalem, 1995), §350.

27. Emanuel Swedenborg, *Conjugial Love*, translated by Alfred Acton (London: Swedenborg Society, 1953), §350.

28. Jane Williams-Hogan, "The Swedenborgian Perspective on the Social Ideal: Society in Human Form," in *Dialogue and Alliance* 10:1 (Spring/Summer 1996): 63.

29. Wadström, *Plan for a free community at Sierra Leona*, 4. It should be pointed out that Swedenborg frequently uses the concept of variety. In his writings, unity is founded on variety, not on uniformity or sameness.

30. Emanuel Swedenborg, *Heaven and Hell*, translated by George F. Dole (West Chester, PA: Swedenborg Foundation, 2010), §59.

31. Wadström, *Plan for a free community at Sierra Leona*, 4–5.

32. Ibid., 5.

33. Ibid., 26.

34. Ibid.

35. Ibid., 26–27.

36. Ibid., 27.

37. Emanuel Swedenborg, *Divine Providence*, translated by George F. Dole (West Chester, PA: Swedenborg Foundation, 2010), §129:3.

38. Swedenborg, *True Christianity*, §814.

39. Wadström, *Plan for a free community at Sierra Leona*, 6.

40. Emanuel Swedenborg, *Apocalypse Revealed*, translated by John Whitehead (West Chester, PA: Swedenborg Foundation, 1997), §459:1–2.

41. Wadström, *Plan for a free community at Sierra Leona,* 27.

42. Ibid.

43. Ibid., 28.

44. Ibid.

45. Ibid., 29–30.

46. Ibid., 29.

47. Wilson Van Dusen, "Usefulness" (West Chester, PA: Swedenborg Foundation), 4.

48. Emanuel Swedenborg, *Divine Love and Wisdom,* translated by George F. Dole (West Chester, PA: Swedenborg Foundation, 2010), §298. The Van Dusen translation of §298: "God as a man is the form itself of all uses, from which form all uses in the created universe derive their origin, thus the created universe, viewed as to uses, in an image of him" ("Usefulness," 4).

49. Wadström, *Plan for a free community at Sierra Leona,* vi.

50. Ibid., v–vi.

51. Ibid., vi, vii.

52. Swedenborg, *Conjugial Love* (1953), §115.

53. Ibid., §115:2.

54. Ibid., §115:3, 5.

55. Wadström, *Plan for a free community at Sierra Leona,* 28. Along with this contract to support the ideal of marriage, the concept of concubinage is discussed. The statement reads, "By *Anti-conjugal Life,* I do not here mean the attachment of one unmarried Man to one free Woman, and simply Concubinage, which under certain regulations never ought to be forbidden in a Free State; but I mean, (1.) Adultery. (2.) The Lust of Variety. (3.) The Lust of Defloration. (4.) The Lust of Violation. (5.) The Lust of Seducing the Innocent" (p. 31). All these concepts are discussed in the second part of *Conjugial Love,* which is called "The Pleasures of Insanity Pertaining to Scortatory Love." It is not my intention to do more than mention this. I will also point out that Nordenskiöld published material concerning this in London and that the matter of concubinage became an issue in the Great Eastcheap society. Since this was apparently raised by Nordenskiöld and not by Wadström, I am not addressing this matter either. The impact of this on the colonization project should at some point in the future be investigated.

56. Robert MacIver, *The Web of Government* (New York: The Free Press, 1965), 47.

57. "Anatomy," "Active power," and "Reactive power" are the sections that form the first (unpaginated) part of the 1792 Plan.

58. Andrew J. Cherlin, "The Deinstitutionalization of American Marriage," in *Journal of Marriage and Family* 66 (2004): 848.

59. Swedenborg, *Divine Love and Wisdom,* §47.

Building a New Jerusalem in Africa in the 1790s

1. See Appendix B on pages 217–19 of the present volume.

2. Carl Bernhard Wadström, *An Essay on Colonization, Particularly Applied to the Western Coast of Africa*, Part 1 (London: printed for the author, by Darton and Harvey, Gracechurch-Street, 1794).

3. Daniel Padenheim, *Bref till en Vän i Sverige, Innehållande Historisk och Geografisk Beskrifning öfver Colonien Sierra Leona i Afrika, jemte S. L. Compagniets och Coloniens Formerande, med Anmärkningar öfver Climatet, Producter &c, Colonisternas och de Inföddas Caracterer, Population, Religion, Seder, Gjöromål &c, Coloniens Tiltagande och dess Förstörande af en Fransk Esquadre i October 1794, samt Handlingar och Bref Rörande Följderna deraf* (Stockholm: Kumblinska tryckeriet, 1801).

4. Philip Beaver, *African Memoranda: Relative to an Attempt to Establish a British Settlement on the Island of Bulama, on the Western Coast of Africa, in the Year 1792, with a Brief Notice of the Neighbouring Tribes, Soil, Productions and some Observations on the Facility of Colonizing that Part of Africa, with a View to Cultivation and the Introduction of Letters and Religions to its Inhabitants, but More Particularly as the Means of Gradually Abolishing African Slavery* (London: C. & R. Baldwin, 1804).

5. Thomas Winterbottom, *An Account of the Native Africans in the Neighbourhood of Sierra Leone, to Which is Added an Account of the Present State of Medicine among them* (London: C. Wittingham, 1803).

6. Anna Maria Falconbridge, *Two Voyages to Sierra Leone during the Years 1791, 1792, 1793, in a Series of Letters* (London: Printed for the author, 1794).

7. Carl Bernhard Wadström, "Resa ifrån Stockholm genom Danmark, Tyskland och Frankrike till Senegal-länderna i Afrika, år 1787 och 88," in *Archiv för nyare resor: månads-skrift: med kartor och kopparstick* (Stockholm: J. P. Marquard, 1811–15).

8. Wadström, *Essay on Colonization*, Part 2 (1795), §612.

9. It was set to music by Hubert Parry in 1916 and entitled "Jerusalem."

10. Act of Parliament, July 1, 1791, for a period of thirty-one years, according to Padenheim's First Letter in *Bref till en Vän i Sverige* (p. 23).

11. Founded in July 1, 1791, and associated with John Wesley's colleague George Whitefield.

12. Cf. Ronny Ambjörnsson's article in this book entitled "Labor and Money: Wadström's and Nordenskiöld's Utopian Ideas."

13. S. Eakin and J. Logsdon, eds., *Solomon Northup's 1853 Autobiography: Twelve Years a Slave* (Baton Rouge: Louisiana State University Press, 1968).

14. Ulric Nordenskiöld, *Afhandling om Nyttan för Sverige af Handel och Nybyggen i Indierna och på Africa* (Stockholm: Peter Hesselberg, 1776).

15. Suzanne Schwarz, *Zachary Macaulay and the Development of the Sierra Leone Company 1793–1794: 1. Journal, June–October 1793* (Leipzig: University of Leipzig Papers on Africa, History and Culture, series no. 4, 2000), xii.

16. Alexander Peter Kup, *Adam Afzelius' Sierra Leone Journal* (Uppsala: Studia Ethnographica Upsaliensia #27, 1967).

17. Royal Botanical Gardens, Kew; Joseph Banks's correspondence, Volume 2, JBK/1/5 (p. 58).

18. Joshua Montefiore, *An Authentic Account of the Late Expedition to Bulam on the Coast of Africa, with a Description of the Present Settlement of Sierra Leone and the Adjacent Country* (London: J. Johnson, 1794).

19. Lasse Berg, *Ut ur Kalahari: Drömmen om det Goda Livet* (Stockholm: Ordfront, 2014).

20. John Clarkson, Journal 1791–1792, British Library Add MS 41,262–41,267.

21. Wadström gives an extensive account of the colonization plans regarding the "Bulama" island off the coast of Guinea in *An Essay on Colonization*, Part 2, Ch. XI, §§528–90.

22. Ibid., §604.

23. Henry Smeathman, *Plan of Settlement to be Made near Sierra Leona, on the Grain Coast of Africa, Intended more particularly for the service and happy establishment of Blacks and People of Colour, to be shipped as freemen under the direction of the Committee for Relieving the Black Poor, and under the protection of the British Government* (London, 1786).

24. R. J. Olu-Wright, "The Physical Growth of Freetown," in *Freetown: A Symposium,* eds. Christopher Fyfe and Eldred Jones (Freetown: Sierra Leone University Press, 1968).

25. Sylvie Kandé, *Terres, Urbanisme et Architecture "Créoles" en Sierra Leone XVIIIᵉ–XIXᵉ siècles* (Paris: L'Harmattan, 1998), 45.

26. Wadström, *Essay on Colonization*, Part 2, §532.

27. Padenheim, *Bref till en Vän i Sverige*, Second Letter, 39.

28. Schwarz, *Zachary Macaulay and the Development of the Sierra Leone Company 1793–1794: 1. Journal, June–October 1793*, 6.

29. Padenheim, *Bref till en Vän i Sverige*, Third Letter, 77. Author's translation.

30. Ibid., Fifth Letter, 120. Author's translation.

31. Aminatta Forna, *Ancestor Stones* (London: Bloomsbury, 2006), 83.

32. Padenheim, *Bref till en Vän i Sverige*, Third Letter, 73.

"The Little Black Boy"

1. The first essay to connect Blake with the abolitionist cause was David Erdman, "Blake's Vision of Slavery," in *Journal of the Warburg and Courtauld Institutes* 15 (1952): 242–52. See also Erdman, *Prophet against Empire: A Poet's Interpretation of the History of His Own Times,* rev. ed. (Princeton, NJ: Princeton University Press, 1977), 230–42.

2. *Morning Chronicle and London Advertiser* (June 20, 1788): 1.

3. It is important to note that the Blakes signed as sympathizers, not as Church members. Among the seventy-seven signers, fifty-six were actual members,

while the eighteen other names (among whom we find William and Catherine) did not commit themselves to membership. The documents are reprinted in Robert Hindmarsh, *Rise and Progress of the New Jerusalem Church in England, America, and Other Parts,* ed. Rev. Edward Madeley (London: n.p., 1861), 79–84 and 101–8.

4. All references to Blake's works are from David Erdman, ed., *The Complete Poetry and Prose of William Blake,* rev. ed. (New York: Doubleday, 1988); they will be indicated in parentheses as *E* for "Erdman" and will be preceded by page/plate/line numbers and followed by the page reference to Erdman's book.

5. Cf., however, the apparent parallels found among Swedenborg's *memorabilia* (which may have been discussed in Swedenborgian milieus): "There are some gentiles from those regions where the people are black who bring with them from life in the world the desire to be treated harshly, for they believe that nobody can enter heaven except through punishment and affliction, and that only after that will they receive more gladsome things which they call paradise-like. . . . They said that when they are being treated harshly they are black but that afterwards they cast away their blackness and take on a whiteness, for they know that their souls are white even though their bodies are black" (Emanuel Swedenborg, *Arcana Coelestia* [London, England: John Lewis, 1749–56], translated by John E. Elliott [London, England: The Swedenborg Society, 1983–99], §2603).

6. William Dickson, a collaborator Wadström used in preparing his tracts in English for publication, questioned Wadström's "colonialism" in this respect. See "Strictures on Miss Williams's Memoirs of Wadstrom," in *The Monthly Magazine* (December 1799): 862–69.

7. S. Foster Damon, *William Blake: His Philosophy and Symbols* (New York: Peter Smith, 1924), 269.

8. Anne K. Mellor, "Sex, Violence, and Slavery: Blake and Wollstonecraft," in *The Huntington Library Quarterly* 58.3/4 (1995): 359; Robert Earl Hood, *Begrimed and Black: Christian Traditions on Blacks and Blackness* (Minneapolis, Minn.: Augsburg Fortress, 1994), 136.

9. For these discourses, see Roxann Wheeler, "'Betrayed by Some of My Own Complexion': Cugoano, Abolition, and the Contemporary Language of Racialism," in *Genius in Bondage: Literature of the Early Black Atlantic,* eds. Vincent Carretta and Philip Gould (Lexington: University Press of Kentucky, 2001), 17–39.

10. This poem was first published in *Steps to the Temple. Sacred Poems, with Other Delights of the Muses* (1646). Eva Beatrice Dykes has compared this text to Blake's poem in her book *The Negro in English Romantic Thought; or, A Study of Sympathy for the Oppressed* (Washington, DC: Associated Publishers, 1942), 9.

11. In 1787, Blake was commissioned by Cugoano's employer, the painter Richard Cosway, to engrave the illustration "Venus Dissuades Adonis from Hunting"; see no. XXVIII in Robert N. Essick, *The Separate Plates of William Blake: A Catalogue* (Princeton: Princeton University Press, 1983), 145–49.

12. Ottobah Cugoano, *Thoughts and Sentiments on the Evil and Wicked Traffic of the Slavery and Commerce of the Human Species, Humbly Submitted to the Inhabitants of Great-Britain, by Ottobah Cugoano, a Native of Africa* (London, 1787), 46–47.

13. William Cowper, *Poems*, new ed., 2 vols. (London: J. Johnson, 1802), 1:402.

14. Mary Robinson, *The Poetical Works*, 3 vols. (London: Richard Philips, 1806), 2:172.

15. Stewart Crehan, *Blake in Context* (London: Gill and Macmillan, 1984), 99.

16. See, for example, Joseph Lavallée's *The Negro as There Are Few White Men*, translated by J. Trapp, 3 vols. (London, 1790), 1:15–18, in which Itanko is introduced to Christianity by his white master; or Olaudah Equiano's *The Interesting Narrative of the Life of Olaudah Equiano, or Gustavus Vassa, the African. Written by Himself*, 2 vols. (London, 1789), 1:171, in which his messmate, Daniel Queen, "took very great pains" to make him read the Bible.

17. Richard Nisbet, *The Capacity of Negroes for Religious and Moral Improvement [...] to Which Are Subjoined Short and Practical Discourses to Negroes, on the Plain and Obvious Principles of Religion and Morality* (London: James Phillips, 1789), 162.

18. Isaac Watts, *Divine Songs Attempted in Easy Language for the Use of Children*, 2nd ed. (London: M. Lawrence, 1716), 9.

19. Ibid., 8.

20. "That the Lord Now Establishes a Church in Africa," in *New-Jerusalem Magazine* (1790): 183.

21. Tudor Parfitt, *Black Jews in Africa and the Americas* (Cambridge, Mass.: Harvard University Press, 2013), 3–23.

22. Equiano, *Interesting Narrative*, 1:38.

23. Ibid., 1:27.

24. Ibid., 1:39. Equiano also refers to John Clarke's translation of Hugo Grotius's *The Truth of the Christian Religion* (1786) and Baptist minister John Gill's *An Exposition of the Old Testament, in which Are Recorded the Origin of Mankind, of the Several Nations of the World* (1788). In both of these, Africans are traced back to the Hebrew patriarchs with the help of genealogical ingenuity.

25. Morton Paley, "'A New Heaven Is Begun': William Blake and Swedenborgianism," in *Blake: An Illustrated Quarterly* 13.2 (1979): 64–90; Crehan, *Blake in Context*, 99; Camilla Townsend and Anne Rubenstein, "Revolted Negroes and the Devilish Principle: William Blake and Conflicting Visions of Boni's Wars in Surinam, 1772–1796," in *Blake, Politics, and History*, eds. Jackie DiSalvo, G. A. Rosso, and Christopher Z. Hobson (New York: Garland Publishing, 1998), 280–83; Deirdre Coleman, *Romantic Colonization and British Anti-Slavery* (Cambridge: Cambridge University Press, 2005), 104.

26. Kathleen Raine, *Blake and Tradition*, 2 vols. (Princeton, NJ: Princeton University Press, 1969), 10–14.

27. Emanuel Swedenborg, *The Wisdom of Angels concerning Divine Love and Divine Wisdom*, translated by N. Tucker (London: W. Chalken, 1788) [William Blake's

annotated copy in the British Library, shelf mark: C.45.e.1]. This is the same work that is most commonly known as *Divine Love and Wisdom*.

28. Hindmarsh, *Rise and Progress*, 81.

29. Emanuel Swedenborg, *A Treatise Concerning Heaven and Hell and of the Wonderful Things Within*, translated by William Cookworthy and Thomas Hartley, 2nd ed. (London: R. Hindmarsh, 1784), §117. For a similar formulation, see also Swedenborg, *Wisdom of Angels concerning Divine Love and Divine Wisdom*, §§112–13.

30. Emanuel Swedenborg, *The True Christian Religion, Containing the Universal Theology of the New Church*, translated by John Clowes (London: J. Phillips et al., 1781), §25. That the Divine appears as Christ is explained by the fact that Swedenborg is anti-Trinitarian, believing that the Lord is not three but one and manifests himself to man in the figure of Jesus.

31. Swedenborg, *Treatise Concerning Heaven and Hell and of the Wonderful Things Within*, §549, and *Wisdom of Angels concerning Divine Love and Divine Wisdom*, §138. See also *True Christian Religion*, §780.

32. *New-Jerusalem Magazine* (1790): 4–5. The scene was described in Swedenborg's tract on *Conjugial Love*, published in Latin in 1768. Cf. Coleman, *Romantic Colonization and British Anti-Slavery*, 73, on the Swedenborgians in London.

33. Roxann Wheeler, *The Complexion of Race: Categories of Difference in Eighteenth-Century British Culture* (Philadelphia: University of Pennsylvania Press, 2000), Chs. 1 and 4.

34. Carl Bernhard Wadström, *An Essay on Colonization, Particularly Applied to the Western Coast of Africa, with Some Free Thoughts on Cultivation and Commerce*, Part 1 (London: Darton and Harvey, 1794), §28.

35. Michael J. C. Echeruo, "Theologizing 'Underneath the Tree': An African 'Topos' in Ukawsaw Gronniosaw, William Blake, and William Cole," in *Research in African Literatures* 23:4 (1992): 51–58.

36. See, for example, Norma A. Greco, "Mother Figures in Blake's *Songs of Innocence* and the Female Will," in *Romanticism Past and Present* 10 (1986): 1–15.

37. Swedenborg, *Wisdom of Angels concerning Divine Love and Divine Wisdom*, §157.

38. Ibid., esp. §§93, 112, and 315.

39. Echeruo, "Theologizing 'Underneath the Tree,'" 51–58; Debbie Lee, "Black Single Mothers in Romantic History and Literature," in *Race, Romanticism, and the Atlantic*, ed. Paul Youngquist (Aldershot: Ashgate, 2013), 175–77.

40. Anna Laetitia Barbauld, *Hymns in Prose for Children* (London: J. Johnson, 1781), 98.

41. Swedenborg, *Treatise Concerning Heaven and Hell and of the Wonderful Things Within*, §333.

42. Ibid., §335.

43. For a description of the metaphor of the primitive "tent," see David Lyle Jeffrey, *A Dictionary of Biblical Tradition in English Literature* (Grand Rapids, Mich.: Eerdmans, 1992), 59–60.

44. Swedenborg, *True Christian Religion*, §§836, 838.

45. Ibid., §836.

46. Swedenborg, *Treatise Concerning Heaven and Hell and of the Wonderful Things Within*, §514.

47. Swedenborg, *Wisdom of Angels concerning Divine Love and Divine Wisdom*, §11.

48. Swedenborg, *True Christian Religion*, §840.

49. Carl Bernhard Wadström, *Plan for a free community at Sierra Leona, upon the coast of Africa, under the protection of Great Britain; with An Invitation to all Persons desirous of partaking the Benefits thereof . . .*, ECCO Print Edition (London: T. and J. Egerton, 1792), 40.

50. See "That the Lord Now Establishes a Church in Africa," in *New-Jerusalem Magazine* (1790): 183.

51. Carl Bernhard Wadström, *Observations on the Slave Trade, and a Description of some Part of the Coast of Guinea, during a Voyage, Made in 1787, and 1788, in Company with Doctor A. Sparrman and Captain Arrehenius* (London: James Phillips, 1789), 54, 55; the metaphor of Africans as children is elaborated in the section entitled "Reflections" (pp. 53–61).

52. John Coffey, *Exodus and Liberation: Deliverance Politics from John Calvin to Martin Luther King Jr.* (Oxford and New York: Oxford University Press, 2014), 117.

53. John Wesley, *Thoughts upon Slavery*, 3rd ed. (London: R. Hawes, 1774), 28.

54. Robert Hindmarsh, "Preface," in Emanuel Swedenborg, *A Brief Exposition of the Doctrine of the New Church, which is meant by the New Jerusalem in the Apocalypse* (London: Printed and sold by R. Hindmarsh, 1789), li–lii.

55. Alan Richardson, "Colonialism, Race, and Lyric Irony in Blake's 'The Little Black Boy,'" in *Papers on Language and Literature: A Journal for Scholars and Critics of Language and Literature* 26.2 (1990): 243, 245.

56. Joseph Proud, *Hymns and Spiritual Songs, for the Use of the Lord's New Church, Signified by the New Jerusalem in the Revelation* (London: Robert Hindmarsh, 1790), 59–60.

57. Carl Frederik von Breda may also have taken an interest in Swedenborgianism, since a painting of Swedenborg is known from his hand; see Ed Gyllenhaal "A 'New' Old Portrait of Emanuel Swedenborg," in *Glencairn Museum News* 28.1 (2006): 5–7.

58. From the reformed slave ship captain Harry Gandy's letter to Wadström dated Sept. 17, 1788 (printed in *New-Jerusalem Magazine*, p. 166). Panah should also "inspire the natives with a desire to follow the example, which would be a ready and honourable means to supply themselves, with those European articles, they are so excessively fond of, and thus a ground for civilization, would be laid, and through which, the arts and sciences might be gradually introduced."

59. The image made a general impact on the public and was reused as a 1792 abolitionist print engraved by "W. Pyott," which carried the generalizing title *The Benevolent Effects of Abolishing Slavery, or the Planter instructing His Negro*.

Swedenborg and Modernity

1. Ronny Ambjörnsson, "Guldmakarens hemlighet," in *Tiden ett äventyr. Om våghalsar, uppror och idéer* (Stockholm, 1980): 79–144.

2. Many examples of that are given in Inga Sanner's *Att älska sin nästa såsom sig själv. Om moraliska utopier under 1800-talet* (Stockholm, 1995) (utopian ideas); *Den segrande eros. Om kärleksföreställningar från Emananuel Swedenborg till Poul Bjerre* (Nora, 2003) (theories about love); and *Det omedvetna. Historien om ett utopiskt rum* (Nora, 2009) (ideas about the unconscious). Influences from Swedenborg on environmental ideas in later periods are treated by Devin Zuber in *A Language of Things: Swedenborg and the American Environmental Imagination* (Charlottesville: University of Virginia Press, 2017).

3. Several scholars have drawn attention to this and to Swedenborg's ideas of a correspondence between mind and matter. See, for instance, David Dunér, *The Natural Philosophy of Emanuel Swedenborg: A Study in the Conceptual Metaphors of the Mechanistic World-View,* translated by Alan Crozier (Dordrecht: Springer, 2013).

4. See, in particular, Emanuel Swedenborg, *Heaven and Hell* (West Chester, PA: Swedenborg Foundation, 2010).

5. Ibid., §§184, 387–94, 429, et passim. Swedenborg's concrete descriptions of the spiritual world make up an important theme in Colleen McDannell and Bernhard Lang, *Heaven: A History* (New Haven: Yale University Press, 1988), in the chapter entitled "Swedenborg and the Emergence of a Modern Heaven."

6. See Ambjörnsson, "Guldmakarens hemlighet."

7. Emanuel Swedenborg, *New Jerusalem* (West Chester, PA: Swedenborg Foundation, 2016), §§54–107.

8. Swedenborg, *Heaven and Hell,* §§457–59.

9. Ibid., §§461–62.

10. See Sanner, *Att älska sin nästa såsom sig själv;* and J. A. Passmore, *The Perfectibility of Man* (London, 1970).

11. Swedenborg, *Heaven and Hell,* §§502–5; Sanner, *Det omedvetna,* 70–72; Jan Häll, *I Swedenborgs labyrint. Studier i de gustavianska swedenborgarnas liv och tänkande* (Stockholm, 1995), 343–57. Regarding self-realization, see, for instance, Charles Taylor, *Sources of the Self: The Making of the Modern Identity* (Cambridge: Harvard University Press, 1989).

12. Sanner, *Det omedvetna,* 62f.

13. Several scholars have commented on similarities between the ideas of Swedenborg and ideas emerging within the tradition of psychoanalysis and the idea that he anticipated the concept of the unconscious: Sanner, *Det omedvetna,* 55–72; Olof Lagercrantz, *Epic of the Afterlife: A Literary Approach to Swedenborg* (West Chester, PA: Swedenborg Foundation, 2002), Ch. "Memory," 115ff; Häll, *I Swedenborgs labyrint,* 320. See also Lancelot Law Whyte, *The Unconscious before Freud* (New York, 1960), 96.

14. Swedenborg writes in many of his books about love between the sexes, but this theme is principally found in *Conjugial Love*. His ideas about love are dealt with by many scholars; for example, see Sverker Sieversen, *Sexualitet och äktenskap i Emanuel Swedenborgs religionsfilosofi* (Helsinki, 1993). For more on Swedenborg's ideas in connection with modern thinkers, see Sanner, *Den segrande eros,* 34–39.

15. Emanuel Swedenborg, *Conjugial Love* (West Chester, PA: Swedenborg Foundation, 1998), §§27–60.

16. See, for instance, Catherine Gallagher and Thomas Laqueur, eds., *The Making of the Modern Body: Sexuality and Society in the Nineteenth Century* (Berkeley and Los Angeles, CA: University of California Press, 1987).

17. Reinhart Koselleck, *Futures Past: On the Semantics of Historical Time* (New York: Columbia University Press, 2004 [1985]).

18. Jan Häll, among others, points out that these aspects of Swedenborg's worldview have inspired many thinkers after him (*I Swedenborgs labyrint,* 11).

A World Apart

1. See John R. McKivigan, "Series Introduction," in *Abolitionism and American Religion,* ed. John R. McKivigan (New York: Garland Publishing, Inc.), vii–xi; John R. McKivigan and Mitchell Snay, "Religion and the Problem of Slavery in Antebellum America," in *Religion and the Antebellum Debate over Slavery,* eds. John R. McKivigan and Mitchell Snay (Athens, GA: University of Georgia Press, 1998), 1–32; and Douglas M. Strong, *Perfectionist Politics: Abolitionism and the Religious Tensions of American Democracy* (Syracuse, NY: Syracuse University Press, 1999), 161–69.

2. The Quakers' legendary early antislavery discourse, preceding even the Revolutionary War period, never had the reach in national discourse that did the much larger and much more socially integrated Methodist and Baptist churches in the second antislavery wave. See Bertram Wyatt-Brown, "American Abolitionism and Religion," in *Divining America* (National Humanities Center, http://nationalhumanitiescenter.org/tserve/nineteen/nkeyinfo/amabrel.htm, accessed May 24, 2015).

3. "Most of Swedenborg's followers in the 1830s and 1840s were well-educated Protestants who were engaged in slipping their orthodox tethers," according to Alfred Habegger, the biographer of a famed free-thinking Swedenborgian, in *The Father: A Life of Henry James, Sr.* (New York: Farrar, Straus, and Giroux, 1994), 229.

4. Cited in Mark A. Noll, *The Civil War as a Theological Crisis* (Chapel Hill, NC: University of North Carolina Press, 2006), 12.

5. Carl Theophilus Odhner, "The Early History of the New Church in Sweden," in *New Church Life* 31:4 (April 1911): 269–80.

6. The Swedenborgian Library and Archives at Graduate Theological Union in Berkeley, California.

7. William Cooper Howells (1807–94), father of the eminent American man of letters William Dean Howells and ardent Swedenborgian, served as manager and possibly as founder of the Ohio branch of the American Anti-Slavery Society; a number of laypersons in Chicago and Boston Swedenborgian congregations actively supported the Underground Railroad.

8. See Marguerite Beck Block, *New Church in the New World: A Study of Swedenborgianism in America* (New York: Holt, Rhinehart, 1932), 85–86.

9. The original deed is located at the Gilder Lehrman Institute of American History in New York City. Photocopies of the original deed can be viewed at http://nominihallslavelegacy.com/the-deed-of-gift, accessed May 13, 2015.

10. See Block, *New Church in the New World*, 73–111, for the early formation of American organized Swedenborgianism and pages 130–69 for the intellectual environment of early American Swedenborgian reception.

11. Ibid., 170–204.

12. Ibid., 82–87, 115.

13. Quoted by Tisa M. Anders, "Three Decades in the Making: L. Maria Child's Surprising Convert to Reforms," paper presentation, Peace History Society (national meeting), Rock Hill, South Carolina, October 2009.

14. See Tisa M. Anders's unpublished manuscript entitled "Never Stifling the Voice of Conscience: L. Maria Child's Spiritual Journey in Nineteenth-Century America."

15. Though this figure is catalogued in Library of Congress systems as Richard De Charms (space), this essay will use Richard DeCharms (no space), a curious spelling that is universal in his extant writings as well as extensive writings about him during his lifetime. His name represents an English corruption of the original Norman and Huguenot family name Des Champs.

16. Scott Trego Swank, "The Unfettered Conscience: A Study of Sectarianism, Spiritualism, and Social Reform in the New Jerusalem Church, 1840–1870," Doctoral dissertation, University of Pennsylvania, 1970 [MS, microfilm, e-book], 78–79, 324–29.

17. Richard DeCharms, *A Discourse On The True Nature Of Freedom And Slavery: Delivered Before The Washington Society Of The New Jerusalem, In View Of The One Hundred And Eighteenth Anniversary Of Washington's Birth* (Philadelphia: J. H. Jones, 1850).

18. Richard DeCharms, letter 18, November 5, 1850, in the 1850 volume of personal correspondence of George Bush (Swedenborgian Research Collection located in Berkeley, California).

19. Brown is noted in numerous current articles as having formed America's first professional dental association as well as founded its first professional journal of dentistry practice. See M. E. Ring, "Solyman Brown: A Giant of Dentistry and Its Poet Laureate," in *Journal of the California Dental Association* 30:3 (March 2002): 216–24; Caryn Hannan, *Connecticut Biographical Dictionary* (Hamburg, MI: State History Publications, 2008), 175–76; and Leonard Elkins,

"Solyman Brown: A Biography," in *New York State Dental Journal* 27:8 (Oct. 1961): 379–89. (Editor's note: In 1850, pastor Solyman Brown ordained a fellow dentist, Elijah Bryan, to the priesthood. Bryan served as minister for the dissident mixed-race Swedenborgian congregation in the Danish Virgin Islands until his death in 1867. George Bush corresponded with that distant island church and argued with Ralph Waldo Emerson on topical Swedenborgian issues.)

20. Solyman Brown, *Union of Extremes: A Discourse on Liberty and Slavery, as They Stand Related to the Justice, Prosperity, and Perpetuity of the United Republic of North America* (New York: D. Fanshaw, n.d.).

21. See George Bush, "Editorial Items," in *The New Church Repository and Monthly Review* 4 (July 1851): 339. Bush is warmly complimentary, but he calls "gratuitous" Brown's claim that his antislavery arguments are uniquely Swedenborgian, even though Brown's deployment of the "celestial attributes of black Africans" argument is peculiar to Swedenborgian thought.

22. George Bush, ed., *New Church Miscellanies; or, Essays Ecclesiastical, Doctrinal and Ethical* (New York: Wm. McGeorge, 1855), 165–238.

23. See Woodbury M. Fernald, *Memoirs and Reminiscences of the Late Prof. George Bush* (Boston: Otis Clapp, 1860), 362–64.

24. George Bush, *The New Church Repository and Monthly Review* 5:6 (June 1852): 266–67.

25. See http://homenewshere.com/wilmington_town_crier/news/article_2a867148-fb7f-11e1-8a46-001a4bcf887a.html, accessed May 24, 2015.

26. For discussion of Scammon and Dyer, see Rudolph Williams, *The New Church and Chicago: A History* (Chicago: W. B. Conkey Co., 1906), 28, 149–50, respectively.

27. Kenneth S. Lynn, *William Dean Howells: An American Life* (New York: Harcourt, Brace, Jovanovich, 1970), 35–41.

28. For more on the father's antislavery commitment, see Susan Goodwin and Carl Dawson, *William Dean Howells: A Writer's Life* (Berkeley: University of California Press, 2005), 12–13, 284.

29. For Bolles's biographical details, see William Lloyd Garrison, *Letters of William Lloyd Garrison: I Will Be Heard (1822–1835),* vol. 1, ed. Walter M. Merrill (Cambridge: Harvard University Press, 1971), 306; and for the data citation that Bolles was manager of a branch of the American Anti-Slavery Society from 1840 to 1846, see John R. McKivigan, *The War against Proslavery Religion: Abolitionism and the Churches, 1830–1865* (Ithaca and London: Cornell University Press, 1984), 204.

30. John Rogers Bolles and Anna Bolles Williams, *The Rogerenes: Some Hitherto Unpublished Annals Belonging to the Colonial History of Connecticut* (Boston: Stanhope Press, 1904), 306–7.

31. William B. Hayden, *The Institution of Slavery: Viewed in the Light of Divine Truth* (Portland, ME: David Tucker, 1861), 3.

32. Chauncey Giles in a letter dated April 10, 1862, *The Life of Chauncey Giles,* ed. Carrie Giles Carter (Boston: Massachusetts New-Church Union, 1920), 193.

33. Sampson Reed, *A Biographical Sketch of Thomas Worcester* (Boston: Massachusetts New Church Union, 1880), 102.

34. Thomas Worcester, *A Discourse Delivered in the New Jerusalem Church* (Boston: William Carter & Brother, 1861).

35. See the full proceedings of the convention published in *New-Jerusalem Magazine* 35:1 (July 1862): 1–59. "The President's Address" concerning the war and the evils of slavery is found on pages 14–25.

36. Benjamin F. Barrett, "Dr. Worcester's Address before the General Convention," part 1, in *The Crisis* 11:10 (Aug. 15, 1862): 78.

37. Giles, *Life of Chauncey Giles,* 179–81.

38. Chauncey Giles, *The Problem of American Nationality and the Evils which Hinder Its Solution* (Cincinnati: n.p., 1863).

39. Ibid., 16.

40. Ibid., 17, 18.

41. Ibid., 23–24.

42. Swedenborg claimed to have witnessed the biblical Last Judgment, which unfolded in 1757 throughout the whole of the earth as a drama conducted entirely in the spiritual world and undetected in the natural world, though its effects would lead to a transformation of spiritual life throughout the natural world. See Emanuel Swedenborg, *Last Judgment,* translated by George F. Dole and Jonathan S. Rose (West Chester, PA: Swedenborg Foundation, 2018), §45.

43. Henry Weller, "1860. 1861.," in *The Crisis* 10:1 (Jan. 1, 1861): 4.

44. J. P. Stuart, "Address of the General Convention of the New Church in the United States of America to the General Conference of the New Church in Great Britain, 1862," in *New-Jerusalem Magazine* 36:1 (July 1863): 47–49.

45. See James Lawrence, "Was Lincoln a Discreet Swedenborgian? Assessing Honest Abe's Engagements with Swedenborg and Illinois Swedenborgians," in *The Messenger* 236:4 (April 2014): 48–49, 53.

46. J. R. Hibbard, *A Sermon on the Causes and Uses of the Present Civil War* (Chicago: New Jerusalem Temple, April 12, 1862).

47. Parsons was the author of at least two dozen published works on Swedenborgian thought. He wrote one of the finest overview volumes of Swedenborg's theology, *Outlines of the Religion and Philosophy of Swedenborg* (1876), which was reprinted twice and in use well into the twentieth century.

48. Theophilus Parsons, *Slavery: Its Origin, Influence and Destiny* (Boston: W. Carter and Brother, 1863).

49. See Benjamin F. Barrett, *Love toward Enemies and the Way to Manifest It: A Sermon Delivered in the New Church Temple, corner of Broad and Brandywine Streets, Sunday June 12th, 1864* (Philadelphia: J. B. Lippincott & Co., 1864).

50. See Kathryn Gin Lum, *Damned Nation: Hell in America from Revolution to Reconstruction* (Oxford and New York: Oxford University Press, 2014), 147–52; and Drew Gilpin Faust, *This Republic of Suffering: Death and the American Civil War* (New York: Random House, 2008), 178–82.

51. Barrett, *Love toward Enemies,* 19.

52. Benjamin F. Barrett, "Loyal Resolutions of General Convention," in *The Crisis* 12:9 (Sept. 1, 1864): 142.

53. James Walvin, "Black People in Britain: The Eighteenth Century," in *History Today* 31:9 (Sept. 1981).

A Story without End

1. Sven Lindqvist, *The Skull Measurer's Mistake: And Other Portraits of Men and Women Who Spoke Out Against Racism,* translated from the Swedish by Joan Tate (New York: The New Press, 1997); Susanne Everett, *History of Slavery: An Illustrated History of the Monstrous Evil* (New York: Chartwell Books, 2014); *The Trans-Atlantic Slave Trade Database,* accessed December 19, 2018, http://www.slavevoyages.org.

2. From *Global Estimates of Modern Slavery: Forced Labour and Forced Marriage* (Geneva: ILO, Walk Free Foundation, and International Organization for Migration, 2017), accessed August 29, 2018, http://www.ilo.org/global/topics/forced-labour/lang--en/index.htm.

3. There are two international reports by the International Labour Organization (ILO) that are of particular value: *Global Estimates of Modern Slavery: Forced Labour and Forced Marriage* (Geneva: ILO, Walk Free Foundation, and International Organization for Migration, 2017); and *Global Estimates of Child Labour: Results and Trends, 2012–2016* (Geneva: ILO, 2017).

4. Anders Hallengren, "Russia, Swedenborg, and the Eastern Mind," Hulme Hall Lecture (Manchester, 1991). This article was published with a bibliography in the American journal *The New Philosophy,* vol. XCIII, no. 4 (Oct.–Dec. 1990): 391–407. Another version was delivered as "Religion and Politics: Radical Humanism and New Church Spirituality—From the Decembrist Conspiracy to the Emancipation of the Serfs" at the conferences in St. Petersburg and Moscow, Sept 7–14, 1991, on "The Recovery of the Russian Philosophical Tradition" (Transcript, with a Russian summary [Moscow: The Transnational Research Association and Norwich, Vermont: The Transnational Institute, 1991]). A revised and developed account is found in the author's more recent *Gränszon: Swedenborgessäer* (Stockholm: Poetria, 2017), Ch. "Ryssland utan gräns," with an extensive bibliography.

5. Anders Hallengren, "Swedenborgianism in the Caribbean: A Social Force in the Nineteenth Century West Indies," in *Annual Journal of the New Church Historical Society for the Year 2005* (Chester, England: The New Church Historical Society, 2005): 21–50. This includes a full bibliography.

6. *A Directory of Churches World Wide Based on the Writings of Emanuel Swedenborg* (The New Church of the New Jerusalem—The Lord's New Church, 2015).

7. "Speech on the Past, Present, and Future of the African," in *Morning Light* [a General Conference journal published in London] (1892): 261–65.

8. The author of *A Historical Account of St. Thomas, W. I.* (New York: Negro Universities Press, 1970).

9. Edward Wilmot Blyden is the author of such notable titles as *From West Africa to Palestine* (Freetown, 1873) and *Christianity, Islam and the Negro Race* (London: W. B. Whittingham & Co., 1888).

10. *The African and the True Christian Religion, His Magna Charta: A Study in the Writings of Emanuel Swedenborg* (London, 1892).

11. Cf., for example, Sally McKee, "Domestic Slavery in Renaissance Italy," in *Slavery & Abolition* 29 (2008): 305–26; and the "Chronology" in Edgcumbe Staley, *Guilds of Florence* (London: Methuen & Co., 1906). Petrarch's witness report of the late 1360s is found in his autobiographical letters of old age, the *Epistolae Seniles* X.2. "Whereas huge shipments of grain used to arrive by ship annually in [Venice], now they arrive laden with slaves."

Appendix A

1. *Sine*, or *Siin*, a kingdom of the Serer people existing since pre-colonial times.

2. This occasional English spelling of his name originally stemmed from one of Wadström's passports.

3. Anders Sparrman, famous Swedish physician, botanist, and explorer, who traveled with James Cook on the second voyage (1772–75). The misspelling of his name (Spaarman) in the handwritten protocols from the hearing has here been corrected, as was done by Wadström himself in his records.

4. *"Sir, I have been honored with a fresh letter from you, on the 16th of this month on behalf of Mess. Sparrman, Arrhenius, and Wadstrom, who wish to sail to Africa. They can only trade with the natives, by means of goods. But, as they may meet with some difficulties in this respect on the coast between Cape Blanco and Cape Verd, the trade of which is reserved for the Senegal Company, I have, in agreement with your request, written to the Company, to remove those difficulties. And I doubt not that they will be ready to contribute everything within their province, to the success of the voyage of those gentlemen. I have the honor to be, with sincere attachment, Sir, your most obedient, and most humble servant.* —The Marchal DE CASTRIES"

5. *"Mr. Ambassador, THE COMPANY anxiously wishes to offer the most extensive services to Messrs. Sparrman, Arrhenius, and Wadstrom. The orders they have received on that subject, from the Marshal De Castries, and the recommendation which you have done them the honor to address to him, at once recompense their zeal, and are motives for their activity. The Company had many conferences with these learned gentlemen respecting the means of rendering their journey into the interior of Africa as secure and easy as possible. They will find at the factories, and with the Company's agents, the directions, assistance, and resources, which the settlements can afford; and, in the meantime, they will be treated with great attention on board the ship which is to convey them to Senegal. The Company is extremely happy in having this opportunity of showing your*

Excellency how much they desire to be agreeable to you. I am, with respect, Mr. Ambassador, Your most humble and obedient servant. For the Senegal Company: —FRAISE, Acting Director."

6. "I have the honor to send you, Sir, the answer of Mr de Fraisse, by which you will see that there will be no more difficulties for your passage and that those that were raised came from a misunderstanding. I only have time to renew my assurances to you and your compatriots of my best wishes for the success of your trip. Will you please, Sir, let them know, and accept the feelings I have expressed. —Baron Staël von Holstein" [= the husband of the influential woman of letters, Anne Louise Germaine de Staël-Holstein, commonly known as Madame de Staël].

7. A commercial center in Western Senegal during the age of sail, Joal was to become the birthplace of the first president of Senegal in the modern era, Léopold Sédar Senghor, one of the major poets and intellectuals of the twentieth century and an initiator of the transnational *Négritude* movement. Joal today is named Joal-Fadiouth.

8. *Île de Gorée,* a forty-five-acre island two kilometers off the coast of present-day Dakar.

9. Franco-African Creole merchants.

10. I.e., the French bastion with its officers, sailors, and Afro-European merchants and interpreters.

11. The domain of the traditional *Damel* (= "ruler," or "king") of the long-lasting Wolof kingdom of Cayor [Kajoor] was extended by the colonial power to include the Serer kingdom of Baol and parts of the ancient Serer kingdom of Sine, its southern neighbors. This does not mean that the *damel* Birima Fatim-Penda of Cayor (1777–90) had any say in Sine when Wadström was there. *Tin* was the hereditary name of the ruler of Baol. In a similar fashion, *Bursin* and *Bursallum* were hereditary titles of the kingdoms of Sine and Saloum, whereas *Cayor, Baol, Sine,* and *Saloum* were names of territories.

12. *Captiverie* (Fr.), large building [*bâtiment*] in Senegal containing captives before shipping, in our times memorialized as *La Maison des Esclaves.*

13. Rufisque is a coastal city in the Dakar region, Senegal, at the base of the Cap-Vert Peninsula, the harbor of which faces the small Goree Island.

14. = Cap Rouge, by the southern coast of Senegal.

15. Dakar.

16. Marabout, *Murâbit* (Arab.), learned religious leader of the Muslim brotherhoods of Senegal.

17. Gambia River and *Le Fleuve Sénégal.*

18. Referring to the emirates of Waala and their trade with the British port.

19. *Le royaume du Galam.*

20. May sometimes refer to dark Hassaniyya-speaking Muslims of Maghreb descent.

21. Should refer to M. Jean-Gabriel Pelletan, born in Marseille in 1747, who arrived at Senegal at the same time as Wadström, in 1787; *Administrateur et directeur*

général de la compagnie royal du Sénégal à Paris. The French Revolution of 1789 put an end to his business, and he was incarcerated and ended up an abolitionist as did Wadström and Sparrman. He published *Mémoire sur la colonie français du Sénégal: avec quelques considérations historiques et politiques sur la traite des nègres* (Paris: Chez Le Ve Panckoucke, An. IX, i.e., 1800), which contained critical reflections on the slave trade. (His life story is outlined in *Biographie Universelle et portative de Contemporains ou Dictionnaire historique* [Paris: Au Bureau de la biographie, 1826].)

22. The kingdom of Saloum, or Saluum, a pre-colonial state like the kingdoms of Sine and Baol.

23. Dutch daalder and guilder in silver and the Spanish Peso de Ocho ("piece of eight"), a silver coin worth eight *reales.*

24. Filigree, *filigrane* (Fr.), ornamental work in fine wire formed into delicate tracery.

25. Le Havre ("The Harbor"), major seaport in Normandy, France, at the English Channel.

26. And he had no plans to return.

27. Gustav III, ultimately responsible for the slave trade route that was still passing the Swedish harbor at Saint Barthélemy in transit. Obviously, Wadström is no longer communicating with his employer or the royal court on a regular basis. That contact was never to be resumed. This is the first part of the interview where his answers turn evasive and vague.

28. Carl Axel Arrhenius, famous Swedish chemist and mineralogist. That he is not mentioned by name in this context may be due to growing political disagreement.

29. Among mariners, these merchant and cargo ships trafficking the Guinea coast were known as *Guinea-men.*

30. Hubert Le Loup de Beaulieu, French naval officer.

31. French military port in Brittany.

32. Wadström finds all these questions embarrassing since he has greater plans than just repeating the trip of exploration and reconnaissance he has recently done. He has collected the alarming facts needed to make a radical difference and has already published his groundbreaking *Observations on the Slave Trade, and a Description of some part of the Coast of Guinea* (1789) with the purpose of "exposing to the world the atrocious acts committed in that part of the globe to which I have been eye-witness," coauthored *Plan for a Free Community upon the Coast of Africa, Under the Protection of Great Britain; But Intirely Independent of all European Laws and Governments. . . .* (1789), and is working on his persuasive abolitionist classic, *An Essay on Colonization, particularly applied to the Western Coast of Africa, with some Free Thoughts on Cultivation and Commerce* (1794–95).

Bibliography

Abridgment of the minutes of the evidence, taken before a committee of the whole House, to whom it was referred to consider of the slave-trade [House of Commons Proceedings, 1789–91].

An abstract of the evidence delivered before a Select Committee of the House of Commons in the years 1790 and 1791; on the part of the petitioners for the abolition of the slave-trade. 2nd ed. London, 1791.

ACTON, Alfred. "Carl Bernhard Wadström." Unpublished paper held in Swedenborg Library (Bryn Athyn, PA, 1943): 1–64.

AHLSKOG, Jonas. "The Political Economy of Colonisation: Carl Bernhard Wadström's Case for Abolition and Civilisation." *Sjuttonhundratal: Nordic Yearbook for Eighteenth-Century Studies* 7 (2010): 146–67.

AMBJÖRNSSON, Ronny. *Fantasin till makten!: utopiska idéer i västerlandet under fem hundra år.* Stockholm: Ordfront, 2004.

———. "'Guds Republique,' En utopi från 1789." *Lychnos: Årsbok för Idé- och Lärdomshistoria* (1975–76): 1–57.

———. "Guldmakarens hemlighet." *Tiden ett äventyr: Om våghalsar, uppror och idéer* (Stockholm: Liber, 1980): 79–144.

ANDERS, Tisa M. "Never Stifling the Voice of Conscience: L. Maria Child's Spiritual Journey in Nineteenth-Century America." Unpublished manuscript.

———. "Religion and advocacy politics in the career of L. Maria Child." PhD thesis, Iliff School of Theology and The University of Denver (Colorado Seminary), 2002.

———. "Three Decades in the Making: L. Maria Child's Surprising Convert to Reforms," paper presentation, Peace History Society (national meeting), Rock Hill, South Carolina, October 2009.

"Anders Sparrman." *Biographiskt lexicon öfver namnkunnige svenska män* 15 (1848).

Annual Report of the Inter-Departmental Ministerial Group on Human Trafficking. Norwich and London: Home Office, 2012.

ANSTEY, Roger. *The Atlantic Slave Trade and British Abolition, 1760–1810.* London: Macmillan, 1975.

APPELGREN, Göran. *Ett urval ur Emanuel Swedenborgs 1758 "Det Nya Jerusalem – De Nova Hierosolyma et Ejus Doctrina Coelesti ex Auditis e Coelo."* Stockholm: Swedenborgsällskapet, 2011.

ARBUTHNOTT, George. "The slaves in your weekly shop." *The Sunday Times Magazine* (October 6, 2013).

ARPPE, A. E. "Anteckningar om Finska Alkemister." *Bidrag till Kännedom om Finlands Natur och Folk* 16 (Helsingfors/Helsinki, 1870): 1–110.

BARRETT, Benjamin F. "Dr. Worcester's Address before the General Convention," part 1. *The Crisis* 11:10 (Aug. 15, 1862): 77–79.

———. *Love toward Enemies and the Way to Manifest It: A Sermon Delivered in the New Church Temple, corner of Broad and Brandywine Streets, Sunday June 12th, 1864.* Philadelphia: J. B. Lippincott & Co., 1864.

———. "Loyal Resolutions of General Convention." *The Crisis* 12:9 (Sept. 1, 1864): 141–42.

BARRY, Boubacar. *Senegambia and the Atlantic Slave Trade.* Cambridge: Cambridge University Press, 1998.

BEARD, Morgan, ed. *Divine Love: Lessons from Emanuel Swedenborg.* West Chester, PA: Swedenborg Foundation, 2015.

BEAVER, Philip. *African Memoranda: Relative to an Attempt to Establish a British Settlement on the Island of Bulama, on the Western Coast of Africa, in the Year 1792, with a Brief Notice of the Neighbouring Tribes, Soil, Productions and some Observations on the Facility of Colonizing that Part of Africa, with a View to Cultivation and the Introduction of Letters and Religions to its Inhabitants, but More Particularly as the Means of Gradually Abolishing African Slavery.* London: C. & R. Baldwin, 1804.

BEINART, William, "Men, science, travel and nature in the eighteenth and nineteenth-century Cape." *Journal of Southern African Studies* 24(4) (1998): 775–99.

BEINART, William, and Lotte Hughes. *Environment and Empire.* Oxford: Oxford University Press, 2009.

BELL, Richard. "Slave Suicide, Abolition and the Problem of Resistance." *Slavery & Abolition* 33:4 (2012): 525–49.

BERG, Lasse. *Ut ur Kalahari: Drömmen om det Goda Livet.* Stockholm: Ordfront, 2014.

BERGQUIST, Lars. *Swedenborg's Dream Diary,* translated by Anders Hallengren. West Chester, PA: Swedenborg Foundation, 2001.

———. *Swedenborg's Secret: The Meaning and Significance of the Word of God, the Life of the Angels, and Service to God: a Biography.* London: The Swedenborg Society, 2005.

BEZERRA, Nielson Rosa. *Escravidão, Farinha e Comércio no Recôncavo do Rio de Janeiro, século 19.* Duque de Caxias, Rio de Janeiro: APPH-CLIO, 2011.

BJÖRKAS, Mattias. "Bref från Colonien." Avhandling pro gradu, Åbo akademi, 2008.

BLACKBURN, Robin. *The Overthrow of Colonial Slavery, 1776–1848.* London: Verso, 1988.

Blake, Politics, and History, eds. Jackie DiSalvo, G. A. Rosso, and Christopher Z. Hobson. New York: Garland Publishing, 1998.

BLOCK, Marguerite Beck. *New Church in the New World: A Study of Swedenborgianism in America.* New York: Holt, Rhinehart, 1932. New ed., with an introduction by Robert H. Kirven, New York: Octagon Books, 1968.

BLYDEN, Edward Wilmot. *Christianity, Islam and the Negro Race.* London: W. B. Whittingham & Co., 1888.

———. *From West Africa to Palestine.* Freetown, 1873.

————. "Speech on the Past, Present, and Future of the African," delivered by the Liberian minister to England at the Annual Meeting of the Swedenborg Society in London 1892, published in *Morning Light* [a General Conference journal published in London] (1892): 261–65.

Board of Trade. *Report of the Lords of the committee of council appointed for the consideration of all matters relating to trade and foreign plantations . . . and particularly the trade in slaves; . . .* London: House of Commons, Proceedings, 1789-04-25.

BODMAN, Gösta. "August Nordenskiöld, en Gustaf den Tredjes Alkemist." *Lychnos: Årsbok för Idé- och Lärdomshistoria* (1943): 189–229.

BOLLES, John Rogers, and Anna Bolles Williams. *The Rogerenes: Some Hitherto Unpublished Annals Belonging to the Colonial History of Connecticut.* Boston: Stanhope Press, 1904.

BOOTH, Robert. "Children lost from care in human trafficking cases, says Council." *The Guardian* (October 18, 2011).

BRAIDWOOD, Stephen J. *Black Poor and White Philanthropists: London's Blacks and the Foundation of the Sierra Leone Settlement 1786–1791.* Liverpool: Liverpool University Press, 1994.

Britain's Forgotten Slave Owners, I–II. BBC Two documentary film by David Olusoga, 2015.

BROBERG, Gunnar, David Dunér, and Roland Moberg, eds. *Anders Sparrman: Linnean, världsresenär, fattigläkare.* Uppsala: Svenska Linnésällskapet, 2012.

BROWN, Christopher Leslie. *Moral Capital: Foundations of British Abolitionism.* Chapel Hill: University of North Carolina Press, 2006.

BROWN, Solyman. *Union of Extremes: A Discourse on Liberty and Slavery, as They Stand Related to the Justice, Prosperity, and Perpetuity of the United Republic of North America.* New York: D. Fanshaw, n.d.

BUSH, George, ed. *New Church Miscellanies; or, Essays Ecclesiastical, Doctrinal and Ethical.* New York: Wm. McGeorge, 1855.

The Cambridge World History of Slavery, vols. 1–4. Cambridge University Press, 2011–17.

CAMPBELL, Mary. *The Witness and the Other World: Exotic European Travel Writing, 400–1600.* Ithaca: Cornell University Press, 1988.

CAREY, Brycchan. *British Abolitionism and the Rhetoric of Sensibility: Writing, Sentiment and Slavery, 1760–1807.* Basingstoke: Palgrave Macmillan, 2005.

"Carl Bernhard Wadström." *Biographiskt lexicon öfver namnkunnige svenska män* 19 (1852).

CARLBOHM, Johan Arvid. *Afton-bladet, en vecko-skrift af et sälskap i Stockholm.* Stockholm: Carlbohm, 1784.

CARRINGTON, Selwyn. *The Sugar Industry and the Abolition of Slave Trade, 1775–1810.* Gainesville: University Press of Florida, 2002.

CASTRIES, René de La Croix, duc de. *Le maréchal de Castries (1727–1800)* / préf. du duc de Lévis Mirepoix. Paris, 1956.

CHALAYE, Sylvie. *Du noir au nègre: l'image de Noir au théâtre: de Marguerite de Navarre à Jean Genet (1550–1960).* Paris: L'Harmattan, 2002.

CHERLIN, Andrew J. "The Deinstitutionalization of American Marriage." *Journal of Marriage and the Family* 66 (2004): 848–61. Accessed May 17, 2015. http://www.jstor.org/stable/3600162.

CHRISTENSSON, Jakob. *Lyckoriket: Studier i svensk upplysning*. Stockholm: Atlantis, 1996.

CLARKSON, John. Journal 1791–1792. British Library Add MS 41,262–41,267.

CLARKSON, Thomas. *An Essay on the Slavery and Commerce of the Human Species, Particularly the African . . .*, 2nd ed. London, 1788 [1786] [Cites Sparrman's account (1783) of how the Dutch colonists hunted Hottentots to enslave them].

———. *The History of the Rise, Progress, and Accomplishment of the Abolition of the African Slave-Trade by the British Parliament*, 2 vols. London: Longman, Hurst, Rees, and Orme, 1808.

———. *Letters on the slave-trade, and the state of the natives in those parts of Africa which are contiguous to Fort St. Louis and Goree, written at . . .* London, 1791.

———. *The Substance of the Evidence of sundry persons on the Slave-trade, collected in the course of a tour made in the autumn of the year 1788*. London, 1789.

CLIFFORD, Marie Louise. *From Slavery to Freetown: Black Loyalists after the American Revolution*. Jefferson, NC: McFarland & Company, 1999.

COFFEY, John. *Exodus and Liberation: Deliverance Politics from John Calvin to Martin Luther King Jr.* Oxford and New York: Oxford University Press, 2014.

COLEMAN, Deirdre. *Romantic Colonization and British Anti-Slavery*. Cambridge: Cambridge University Press, 2005 [Reviewed in ROTBERG (2005); see below].

COPLEY, Ester. *A History of Slavery and Its Abolition*. London: Houlston & Stoneman, 1839.

CREHAN, Stewart. *Blake in Context*. London: Gill and Macmillan, 1984.

CUGOANO, Ottobah. *Thoughts and Sentiments on the Evil and Wicked Traffic of the Slavery and Commerce of the Human Species, Humbly Submitted to the Inhabitants of Great-Britain, by Ottobah Cugoano, a native of Africa*. London, 1787.

———. *Thoughts and Sentiments on the Evil of Slavery and Other Writings*, edited with an introduction and notes by Vincent Carretta. New York, NY: Penguin Books, cop. 1999.

CULLEN-DUPONT, Kathryn. *Human Trafficking*. New York, NY: Facts On File, 2009.

CURTIN, Philip. *Economic Change in Precolonial Africa: Senegambia in the Era of the Slave Trade*. Madison: University of Wisconsin Press, 1975.

———. *The Image of Africa: British Ideas and Action, 1780–1850*. Madison: University of Wisconsin Press, 1965.

———. "The White Man's Grave:" Image and Reality, 1780–1850. *Journal of British Studies* 1:1 (November 1961): 94–110.

DAHLGREN, Erik Wilhelm. "Carl Bernhard Wadström: Hans verksamhet för Slafhandelns Bekämpande och de samtida Kolonisationsplanerna i Västafrika." *Nordisk Tidskrift för Bok- och Biblioteksväsen*. Utgiven af Isak Collijn, Stockholm (Upsala & Stockholm: Almqvist & Wiksell, 1915): 1–52.

DAMON, S. Foster. *William Blake: His Philosophy and Symbols*. New York: Peter Smith, 1924.

DAVIS, David Brion. *Inhuman Bondage: The Rise and Fall of Slavery in the New World*. Oxford: Oxford University Press, 2006.

————. *The Problem of Slavery in the Age of Revolution*. Ithaca: Cornell University Press, 1975.

————. *The Problem of Slavery in Western Culture*. Ithaca: Cornell University Press, 1966.

DECHARMS, Richard. *A Discourse On The True Nature Of Freedom And Slavery: Delivered Before The Washington Society Of The New Jerusalem, In View Of The One Hundred And Eighteenth Anniversary Of Washington's Birth*. Philadelphia: J. H. Jones, 1850.

————. Letter 18, to Professor Geo. Bush, Nov. 5, 1850, Letter Book Vol. 5, 1850, Box 3, George Bush Archives, Swedenborgian Library and Archives, Berkeley, California.

DELLAROSA, Franca. *Slavery on Stage: Representations of Slavery in British Theatre, 1760s–1830s: with an anthology of texts*. Bari: Edizioni del Sud, 2009.

DEWDNEY, J. C., and M. Harvey. "Planning Problems in Freetown." *Freetown: A Symposium*, eds. Christopher Fyfe and Eldred Jones. Freetown: Sierra Leone University Press, 1968.

DICKSON, William. "Strictures on Miss Williams's Memoirs of Wadstrom." *The Monthly Magazine* (December 1799): 862–69.

A Directory of Churches World Wide Based on the Writings of Emanuel Swedenborg. The New Church of the New Jerusalem—The Lord's New Church, 2015.

DRESCHER, Seymour. *Abolition: A History of Slavery and Antislavery*. Cambridge: Cambridge University Press, 2009.

————. *Capitalism and Antislavery: British Mobilization in Comparative Perspective*. London: Macmillan, 1986.

————. *Econocide: British Slavery in the Era of Abolition*. Chapel Hill: University of North Carolina Press, 2010 [1977].

DUBOIS, Isaac. "Journal from my Departure from the Colony 16th July 1793." British Library, Add MS 41,263, vol. 3.

DUBOIS, Laurent. "An Enslaved Enlightenment: Rethinking the Intellectual History of the French Atlantic." *Social History* 31:1 (February 2006): 1–14.

DUNÉR, David. *The Natural Philosophy of Emanuel Swedenborg: A Study in the Conceptual Metaphors of the Mechanistic World-View*, translated by Alan Crozier. Dordrecht: Springer, 2013.

DYKES, Eva Beatrice. *The Negro in English Romantic Thought; or, A Study of Sympathy for the Oppressed*. Washington, DC: Associated Publishers, 1942.

EAKIN, S., and J. Logsdon, eds. *Solomon Northup's 1853 Autobiography: Twelve Years a Slave*. Baton Rouge: Louisiana State University Press, 1968.

EARLY, Mary W. "Some Reminiscences of the Warminster Society." *New-Church Messenger* 107 (July 8, 1914): 26–27.

ECHERUO, Michael J. C. "Theologizing 'Underneath the Tree': An African Topos in Ukawsaw Gronniosaw, William Blake, and William Cole." *Research in African Literatures* 23:4 (1992): 51–58.

EDWARDS, Bryan. *The history, civil and commercial, of the British West Indies. With a continuation to the present time*. 5th ed., 5 vols. London: For G. and W. B. Whittaker, 1819.

EKMAN, Ernst. "Sweden, the Slave Trade and Slavery, 1784–1847." *Revue française d'histoire d'outre-mer* 62 (1975): 221–31.

ELTIS, David. *Economic Growth and the Ending of the Transatlantic Slave Trade.* Oxford: Oxford University Press, 1987.

EMERSON, Ralph Waldo. *The Complete Works* (Concord ed., 1903–4), vol. XI, Miscellanies: "Emancipation in the British West Indies" (1844); "The Fugitive Slave Law" (1851); "John Brown" 1–2 (1859); "The Emancipation Proclamation" (1862).

EQUIANO, Olaudah. *The Interesting Narrative of the Life of Olaudah Equiano; or, Gustavus Vassa, the African, written by himself,* 2 vols. London, 1789 [Scholarly edition: *The Interesting Narrative,* edited by Brycchan Carey. Oxford University Press, 2018].

ERDMAN, David. "Blake's Vision of Slavery." *Journal of the Warburg and Courtauld Institutes* 15 (1952): 242–52.

———. *Prophet against Empire: A Poet's Interpretation of the History of His Own Times,* rev. ed. Princeton, NJ: Princeton University Press, 1977.

ERDMAN, David, ed. *The Complete Poetry and Prose of William Blake,* rev. ed. New York: Doubleday, 1988.

ESSICK, Robert N. *The Separate Plates of William Blake: A Catalogue.* Princeton: Princeton University Press, 1983.

EUPHRASÉN, Bengt Anders. *Beskrifning öfver svenska vestindiska ön St. Barthelemi, samt öarne St. Eustache och St. Christopher . . .* Stockholm: Anders Zetterberg, 1795.

EVERETT, Susanne. *History of Slavery: An Illustrated History of the Monstrous Evil.* New York: Chartwell Books, 2014.

Extracts from the evidence delivered before a Select Committee of the House of Commons in the years 1790 and 1791, on the part of the petitioners . . . London, 1791.

EZE, Emmanuel Chukwudi, ed. *Race and the Enlightenment: A Reader.* Malden, Mass.: Blackwell, 1997.

FALCONBRIDGE, Anna Maria. *Two Voyages to Sierra Leone during the Years 1791, 1792, 1793, in a Series of Letters.* London: Printed for the author, 1794.

FARA, Patricia. *Sex, Botany and Empire.* New York: Columbia University Press, 2003.

FERNALD, Woodbury M. *Memoirs and Reminiscences of the Late Prof. George Bush.* Boston: Otis Clapp, 1860.

FINLEY, Cheryl. *Committed to Memory: The Art of the Slave Ship Icon.* Princeton University Press, 2018.

"Forced labour, modern slavery and human trafficking." International Labour Organization (ILO) update 2018. http://www.ilo.org/global/topics/forced-labour/lang--en/index.htm.

FORNA, Aminatta. *Ancestor Stones.* London: Bloomsbury, 2006.

FRAISSE, Ch. *Précis pour la Compagnie du Sénégal.* [Paris], 1790.

FRÄNGSMYR, Tore. *Sökandet efter upplysningen: Perspektiv på svenskt 1700-tal.* Stockholm: Natur och Kultur, 2006.

FREUND, Bill. *The African City: A History.* Cambridge: Cambridge University Press, 2007.

FYFE, Christopher, ed. *Our Children Free and Happy: Letters from Black Settlers in Africa in the 1790s.* Edinburgh: Edinburgh University Press, 1991.

FYFE, Christopher, and Eldred Jones, eds. *Freetown: A Symposium*. Freetown: Sierra Leone University Press, 1968.

GAINOT, Bernard. "La Décade et la «colonisation nouvelle»." *Annales historiques de la Révolution française* 339 (Janvier/Mars 2005): 99–116.

GALLAGHER, Catherine, and Thomas Laqueur, eds. *The Making of the Modern Body: Sexuality and Society in the Nineteenth Century*. Berkeley and Los Angeles, CA: University of California Press, 1987.

GARRARD, Timothy. *African Gold*. London: Prestel, 2011.

GARRISON, William Lloyd. *Letters of William Lloyd Garrison: I Will Be Heard (1822–1835)*, vol. 1, ed. Walter M. Merrill. Cambridge: Harvard University Press, 1971.

GAY, Peter. *The Enlightenment: The Science of Freedom*. New York: Norton, 1969.

GIBBS, Jenna M. *Performing the Temple of Liberty: Slavery, Theater, and Popular Culture in London and Philadelphia, 1760–1850*. Baltimore: Hopkins University Press, 2014.

GILES, Chauncey. *The Life of Chauncey Giles*, ed. Carrie Giles Carter. Boston: Massachusetts New-Church Union, 1920.

———. *The Problem of American Nationality and the Evils which Hinder Its Solution*. Cincinnati: n.p., 1863.

GILL, John. *An Exposition of the Old Testament, in which Are Recorded the Origin of Mankind, of the Several Nations of the World, and of the Jewish nation in particular . . .* London: Printed for the author and sold by George Keith, 1763–65.

GIN LUM, Kathryn. *Damned Nation: Hell in America from Revolution to Reconstruction*. Oxford and New York: Oxford University Press, 2014.

Global Estimates of Child Labour: Results and Trends, 2012–2016. Geneva: ILO, 2017.

Global Estimates of Modern Slavery: Forced Labour and Forced Marriage. Geneva: ILO, Walk Free Foundation, and International Organization for Migration, 2017.

GROTIUS, Hugo. *The Truth of the Christian Religion*. London, 1786 [= *De veritate religionis Christianæ*].

Guidance on Slavery and Trafficking Prevention Orders and Slavery and Trafficking Risk Orders under Part 2 of the Modern Slavery Act 2015. London: Home Office, 2017.

GURA, Philip F. *Man's Better Angels: Romantic Reformers and the Coming of the Civil War*. Harvard University Press, 2017.

HAGEN, Ellen. *En frihetstidens son: Carl Bernhard Wadström*. Stockholm: Gothia, 1946.

HÄLL, Jan. *I Swedenborgs labyrint: studier i de gustavianska swedenborgarnas liv och tänkande*. Stockholm: Atlantis, 1995.

HALLENGREN, Anders. *The Code of Concord*. Acta Universitatis Stockholmiensis, Stockholm Studies in History of Literature 34. Stockholm: Almqvist & Wiksell International, 1994, Part III: "Laws of Society," 117–253.

———. *Gallery of Mirrors: Reflections of Swedenborgian Thought*. West Chester, PA: Swedenborg Foundation, 1998. Reissued as e-book in 2014.

———. *The Garment of Love: Charity is the Bond of Perfection*. London: The Swedenborg Society, 2013.

———. *The Grand Theme and Other Essays*. London: The Swedenborg Society, 2013. Reissued as e-book in 2014.

———. *Gränszon: Swedenborgessäer*. Stockholm: Poetria, 2017.

———. *Nobel Laureates in Search of Identity and Integrity: Voices of Different Cultures.* Hackensack, NJ, and Singapore: World Scientific Publishing; and London: Imperial College Press, 2004, 2011.

———. "Russia, Swedenborg, and the Eastern Mind." *The New Philosophy*, vol. XCIII, no. 4 (Oct.–Dec. 1990): 391–407.

———. "Swedenborgianism in the Caribbean: A Social Force in the Nineteenth Century West Indies." *Annual Journal of the New Church Historical Society for the Year 2005* (Chester, England: The New Church Historical Society, 2005): 21–50.

HARRISON, Dick. "Prolog – En resa med Carl Bernhard Wadström." *Slaveri: Från 1800 till nutid* (Lund: Historiska Media, 2008): 11–16.

HAYDEN, William B. *The Institution of Slavery, Viewed in the Light of Divine Truth.* Portland, ME: David Tucker, 1861.

HIBBARD, J. R. *A Sermon on the Causes and Uses of the Present Civil War.* Chicago: New Jerusalem Temple, April 12, 1862.

HILDEBRAND, Ingegerd. *Den Svenska Kolonin S:t Barthélemy och Västindiska Kompaniet fram till 1796.* Lund: Lindstedts, 1951.

HINDMARSH, Robert. *Rise and Progress of the New Jerusalem Church in England, America and Other Parts*, ed. Rev. Edward Madeley. London, 1861.

HOARE, Prince. *Memoirs of Granville Sharp, Esq.: composed from his own manuscripts, and other authentic documents in the possession of his family and of the African Institution . . .* London: Printed for H. Colburn, 1820.

HODACS, Hanna, and Kenneth Nyberg. *Naturalhistoria på resande fot. Om att forska, undervisa och göra karriär i 1700-talets Sverige.* Stockholm: Nordic Academic Press, 2007.

HOLCOMBE, William. "The Alternative: A Separate Nationality, Or The Africanization Of The South." *Southern Literary Messenger* (Richmond, Virginia, Feb. 1861); also issued in Waterproof, Tensas Parish, Louisiana, 1860.

———. *Suggestions as to the Spiritual Philosophy of African Slavery.* New York: Mason Brothers, 1861.

HOOD, Robert Earl. *Begrimed and Black: Christian Traditions on Blacks and Blackness.* Minneapolis, Minn.: Augsburg Fortress, 1994.

HOTSON, Clarence Paul. "Prof. Bush's reply to Emerson on Swedenborg." *The New-Church Magazine* 51 (1932): 175–84; 213–23.

———. "Sampson Reed, A Teacher of Emerson." *The New England Quarterly* II.2 (1929): 249–77.

House of Commons. *Minutes of the evidence taken before a committee of the House of Commons . . . appointed . . . to take the examination of the several witnesses . . .* London, 1790.

———. *The Parliamentary Register; or, History of the proceedings and debates of the House of Commons [and House of Lords]; containing an account of the most interesting speeches and motions . . .*, 45 vols. London: Printed for J. Debrett, 1782–96.

ILLIFE, John. *Africans: The History of a Continent*, 2nd ed. Cambridge University Press, 2007 [1995].

It Happens Here: Equipping the United Kingdom to Fight Modern Slavery: A Policy Report. London: Centre for Social Justice, 2013.

JACKSON, Maurice. *Let This Voice Be Heard. Anthony Benezet, Father of Atlantic Abolitionism*. Philadelphia: University of Pennsylvania Press, 2009.

JEFFREY, David Lyle. *A Dictionary of Biblical Tradition in English Literature*. Grand Rapids, Mich.: Eerdmans, 1992.

JOHANSÉN, Anders [Johansen, Andrew]. *A Geographical and Historical Account of the Island of Bulama, with Observations on its Climate, Productions &c and an Account of the Formation and Progress of the Bulam Association and of the Colony Itself, to which are Added a Variety of Authentic Documents and a Description Map of the Island and Adjoining Continent*. London: Martin and Bain, 1794.

JOHNSON, Patrick L. *Carl Bernhard Wadström: In Search of the New Jerusalem*. Swedenborg Society Transactions, no. 9. London: The Swedenborg Society, 2013. With a preface by Anders Hallengren.

JORDAN, Winthrop D. *White Over Black: American Attitudes Toward the Negro, 1550–1812*. Williamsburg: University of North Carolina, 1968.

KALM, Pehr. *En resa till norra America . . .*, 3 vols. Stockholm: Salvius, 1753–61.

KANDÉ, Sylvie. *Terres, Urbanisme et Architecture "Créoles" en Sierra Leone XVIIIᵉ–XIXᵉ siècles*. Paris: L'Harmattan, 1998.

KARA, Siddharth. *Modern Slavery: A Global Perspective*. New York: Columbia University Press, 2017.

KELLGREN, Johan Henric. "Förslag, Til Nybyggens anläggande i Indien, och på Africanska Kusten." *Nya Handelsbibliotheket* (Stockholm, 1784): 65–80.

KENNEDY, Deborah. *Helen Maria Williams and the Age of Revolution*. Lewisburg, PA: Bucknell University Press, 2002.

KLEIN, Herbert S. *The Atlantic Slave Trade*, new ed. Cambridge: Cambridge University Press, 2010.

KLEIN, Martin. *Slavery and Colonial Rule in French West Africa*. Cambridge: Cambridge University Press, 1998.

KNOX, John P. *A Historical Account of St. Thomas, W. I.* New York: Negro Universities Press, 1970.

KOERNER, Lisbet. *Linnaeus: Nature and Nation*. Cambridge: Harvard University Press, 1999.

KOSELLECK, Reinhart. *Futures Past: On the Semantics of Historical Time*, translated and with an introduction by Keith Tribe. New York: Columbia University Press, 2004 [original title: *Vergangene Zukunft*].

KOTISWARAN, Prabha, ed. *Revisiting the Law and Governance of Trafficking, Forced Labor and Modern Slavery*. New York, NY: Cambridge University Press, 2017.

KUP, Alexander Peter. *Adam Afzelius' Sierra Leone Journal*. Uppsala: Studia Ethnographica Upsaliensia #27, 1967.

LAGERCRANTZ, Olof. *Epic of the Afterlife: A Literary Approach to Swedenborg*, translated by Anders Hallengren. West Chester, PA: Swedenborg Foundation, 2002.

LAMM, Martin. *Emanuel Swedenborg: The Development of His Thought*, translated by Tomas Spiers and Anders Hallengren. West Chester PA: Swedenborg Foundation, 2000.

———. *Upplysningstidens romantik: den mystiskt sentimentala strömningen i svensk litteratur*. Stockholm: Geber, 1918 (Part 1) and 1920 (Part 2).

LAVALLÉE, Joseph. *The Negro as There Are Few White Men,* translated by J. Trapp, 3 vols. London, 1790 [= *Le nègre comme il y a peu de blancs*].

LENHAMMAR, Harry. *Tolerans och Bekännelsetvång: Studier i den svenska swedenbor-gianismen 1765–1795.* Uppsala: Studia historico-ecclesiastica Upsaliensia 11, 1966.

LÉOUZON LE DUC, Louis Antoine, ed. *Correspondance diplomatique du baron de Staël-Holstein, ambassadeur de Suède en France, et de son successeur comme chargé d'affaires, le baron Brinkman: documents inédits sur la révolution (1783–1799) /* recueillis aux archives royales de Suède et publiés avec une introduction par L. Léouzon Le Duc. Paris: Hachette, 1881.

LEVY, Andrew. *The First Emancipator: The Forgotten Story of Robert Carter, the Founding Father Who Freed His Slaves.* NY: Random House, 2006.

LINDQVIST, Sven. *The Skull Measurer's Mistake: And Other Portraits of Men and Women Who Spoke Out Against Racism,* translated from the Swedish by Joan Tate. New York: The New Press, 1997.

LINDROTH, Sten. "Adam Afzelius: a Swedish botanist in Sierra Leone, 1792–1796." *Sierra Leone Studies* 4 (1955): 194–207.

———. "Adam Afzelius: en Linnéan i England och Sierra Leone." *Lychnos: Årsbok för Idé- och Lärdomshistoria* (1944–45 [reprint 1945]): 28–43.

———. *Svensk Lärdomshistoria: Frihetstiden.* Stockholm: Norstedt, 1978.

List of the Society, instituted in 1787, for the purpose of effecting the Abolition of the Slave Trade. London, 1788.

LOVEJOY, Paul. *Transformations in Slavery: A History of Slavery in Africa.* Cambridge: Cambridge University Press, 2000.

LOVEJOY, Paul, and Suzanne Schwarz, eds. *Slavery, Abolition and the Transition to Colonialism in Sierra Leone.* Trenton, New Jersey: Africa World Press, 2015.

MACIVER, Robert. *The Web of Government.* New York: The Free Press, 1965.

The Making of the Modern World (Gale Digital Collections). Boston: Gale, Cengage Learning.

MALMBERG, Carl-Johan. *Stjärnan i foten: dikt och bild, bok och tanke hos William Blake.* Stockholm: Wahlström & Widstrand, 2013.

MARSHALL, P. J., and Glyndwr Williams. *The Great Map of Mankind: British Perceptions of the World in the Age of Enlightenment.* London: Dent, 1982.

MCDANNELL, Colleen, and Bernhard Lang. "Swedenborg and the Emergence of a Modern Heaven." *Heaven: A History* (New Haven: Yale University Press, 1988).

MCKEE, Sally. "Domestic Slavery in Renaissance Italy." *Slavery & Abolition* 29 (2008): 305–26.

MCKIVIGAN, John R. *The War against Proslavery Religion: Abolitionism and the Churches, 1830–1865.* Ithaca and London: Cornell University Press, 1984.

MELLOR, Anne K. "Sex, Violence, and Slavery: Blake and Wollstonecraft." *The Huntington Library Quarterly* 58.3/4 (1995): 345–70.

MERCIER, Louis-Sébastien. *Westindie-fararen, eller Dygdens belöning: drame i 3 akter,* translated by Didric Gabriel Björn [= *L'Habitant de la Guadeloupe,* first staged in Paris in 1786, by Mercier]. Stockholm: Kongl. tryckeriet, 1791.

MILLER, Christopher. *The French Triangle: Literature and Culture of the Slave Trade.* Durham: Duke University Press, 2008.

Modern Slavery Act 2015 maritime enforcement powers (England and Wales): Code of practice. London: Home Office, 2016. National government publication.

Modern Slavery Strategy. London: Home Office, 2014. National government publication.

MONTEFIORE, Joshua. *An Authentic Account of the Late Expedition to Bulam on the Coast of Africa, with a Description of the Present Settlement of Sierra Leone and the Adjacent Country.* London: J. Johnson, 1794.

MORGAN, Philip. "Encounters between British and 'indigenous' peoples, c. 1500–c. 1800." *Empire and Others: British Encounters with Indigenous Peoples, 1600–1850,* eds. Martin Dauton and Rick Halpern. Philadelphia: University of Pennsylvania Press, 1999, 42–78.

MORRISON, Toni. *The Origin of Others.* The Charles Eliot Norton Lectures. Cambridge, MA: Harvard University Press, 2017.

MORTON, Louis. *Robert Carter of Nomini Hall: A Virginia Tobacco Planter of the Eighteenth Century.* Williamsburg, VA: Colonial Williamsburg, Inc., 1941.

NAUM, Magdalena, & Jonas M. Nordin, eds. *Scandinavian Colonialism and the Rise of Modernity: Small Time Agents in a Global Arena.* New York: Springer, 2013.

NELSON, Philip. *Carl Bernhard Wadström: mannen bakom myten.* Norrköping: Föreningen Gamla Norrköping, 1998.

New-Jerusalem Magazine, or a treasury of celestial, spiritual, and natural knowledge by several members of the London Universal Society for Promotion of the New Church. London, 1790–91.

NISBET, Richard. *The Capacity of Negroes for Religious and Moral Improvement [...] to Which Are Subjoined Short and Practical Discourses to Negroes, on the Plain and Obvious Principles of Religion and Morality.* London: James Phillips, 1789.

NOLL, Mark A. *The Civil War as a Theological Crisis.* Chapel Hill, NC: University of North Carolina Press, 2006.

"Nordenskiöld, August." *Svenskt Biografiskt Handlexikon.* http://runeberg.org/sbh/b0198.html. Accessed Jan. 6, 2018.

NORDENSKIÖLD, August. *An Address to the True Members of the New Jerusalem Church, Revealed by the Lord in the Writings of Emanuel Swedenborg.* London, 1789.

NORDENSKIÖLD, August, Carl Bernhard Wadström, Colborn Barrell, and Johan Gottfried Simpson. *Plan for a Free Community upon the Coast of Africa, Under the Protection of Great Britain; But Intirely Independent of all European Laws and Governments. With an Invitation, under certain Conditions, to all Persons desirous of partaking the Benefits thereof. Embellished with a . . . View of Sierra Leone, on the Coast of Guinea.* London: R. Hindmarsh, printer 1789. (Reviewed in the 1790 *New-Jerusalem Magazine.*)

NORDENSKIÖLD, Carl Fredrik, ed. *Samlingar för philantroper.* Stockholm: Anders Jac. Nordström, 1–4, 1787.

NORDENSKIÖLD, Ulric. *Afhandling om Nyttan för Sverige af Handel och Nybyggen i Indierna och på Africa.* Stockholm: Peter Hesselberg, 1776.

NUNN, Nathan. "The Long-Term Effects of Africa's Slave Trades." *Quarterly Journal of Economics* 123(1) (2008): 139–76.

NYBERG, Kenneth. "Anders Sparrman." *Svenskt Biografiskt Lexikon* 33 (2007).

ODÉN, Sven. "Carl Axel Arrhenius." *Svenskt Biografiskt Lexikon* 2 (1920).

ODHNER, Carl Theophilus. "The Early History of the New Church in Sweden." *New Church Life* 31:4 (April 1911): 269–80.

OLDENDORP, Christian Georg Andreas. *Geschichte der Mission der evangelischen Brüder auf den caribischen Inseln S. Thomas, S. Croix und S. Jan.* Leipzig: Barby, 1777.

———. *Tillförlåtlig underrättelse om negrerne på Gvinea kusten, samt de derifrån hämtade slafvars närvarande belägenhet, medfart, seder och sinnelag . . .* Upsala: Johan Edman, 1784.

OLDFIELD, John. *Popular Politics and British Anti-Slavery: Mobilisation of Public Opinion Against the Slave Trade, 1787–1807.* Manchester: Manchester University Press, 1995.

OLU-WRIGHT, R. J. "The Physical Growth of Freetown." *Freetown: A Symposium,* eds. Christopher Fyfe and Eldred Jones. Freetown: Sierra Leone University Press, 1968.

OLUSOGA, David. *Black and British: A Forgotten History.* London: Macmillan, 2016.

OXENSTIERNA, Johan Gabriel. *Skördarne* ["The Harvests"]. *Poëme i nio sånger.* Stockholm: J. P. Lindh, 1796.

PADENHEIM, Daniel Wilhelm. *Bref till en Vän i Sverige, Innehållande Historisk och Geografisk Beskrifning öfver Colonien Sierra Leona i Afrika, jemte S. L. Compagniets och Coloniens Formerande, med Anmärkningar öfver Climatet, Producter &c, Colonisternas och de Inföddas Caracterer, Population, Religion, Seder, Gjöromål &c, Coloniens Tiltagande och dess Förstörande af en Fransk Esquadre i October 1794, samt Handlingar och Bref Rörande Följderna deraf.* Stockholm: Kumblinska tryckeriet, 1801.

PAGDEN, Anthony. *European Encounters with the New World: From Renaissance to Romanticism.* New Haven: Yale University Press, 1993.

PALEY, Morton. "'A New Heaven Is Begun': William Blake and Swedenborgianism." *Blake: An Illustrated Quarterly* 13.2 (1979): 64–90.

PARFITT, Tudor. *Black Jews in Africa and the Americas.* Cambridge, Mass.: Harvard University Press, 2013.

PARSONS, Theophilus. *Slavery: Its Origin, Influence and Destiny.* Boston: W. Carter and Brother, 1863.

PASSMORE, J. A. *The Perfectibility of Man.* London, 1970.

PELLETAN, Jean-Gabriel. *Mémoire sur la colonie français du Sénégal: avec quelques considérations historiques et politiques sur la traite des nègres.* Paris: Chez La Veuve Panckoucke, An. IX, i.e., 1800.

PORTER, Roy. *Enlightenment: Britain and the Creation of the Modern World.* London: Allen Lane, 2000.

POTTS, J. F. *The Swedenborg Concordance,* vols. I–VI. Compiled, edited, and translated by Rev. John Faulkner Potts. London: Swedenborg Society, 1888–1902.

PRATT, Mary Louise. *Imperial Eyes: Travel Writing and Transculturation.* London: Routledge, 1992.

PROUD, Joseph. *Hymns and Spiritual Songs, for the Use of the Lord's New Church, Signified by the New Jerusalem in the Revelation.* London: Robert Hindmarsh, 1790.

RABBE, Alphonse, ed. et al. *Biographie Universelle et portative des Contemporains ou Dictionnaire historique,* 5 vols. Paris, 1826–34.

Race, Romanticism, and the Atlantic, ed. Paul Youngquist. Farnham: Ashgate, 2013.

RAINE, Kathleen. *Blake and Tradition*. 2 vols. Princeton, NJ: Princeton University Press, 1969.

RANBY, John. *Observations on the evidence given before the Committees of the Privy Council and House of Commons in support of the Bill for abolishing the slave trade.* London: printed for John Stockdale, 1791.

RAWLEY, James A., with Stephen D. Behrendt. *The Transatlantic Slave Trade: A History*, 2nd revised edition. Lincoln: University of Nebraska Press, 2005.

REED, Sampson. *A Biographical Sketch of Thomas Worcester.* Boston: Massachusetts New Church Union, 1880.

Religion and the Antebellum Debate over Slavery, eds. John R. McKivigan and Mitchell Snay. Athens, GA: University of Georgia Press, 1998.

Report of the Inter-Departmental Ministerial Group on Modern Slavery. Norwich: The Stationery Office, 2014.

RICE, Tony. *Voyages of Discovery: A Visual Celebration of Ten of the Greatest Natural History Expeditions.* London: Natural History Museum, 2010 [1999].

RIX, Robert. *William Blake and the Cultures of Radical Christianity.* Aldershot: Ashgate, 2007.

RIX, Robert William. "Carl Bernhard Wadström (1746–1799)." http://www.brycchancarey.com/abolition/wadstrom.htm. Accessed on Jan. 6, 2018.

———. "William Blake and Radical Swedenborgianism." *Esoterica* 5 (2003): 73–94.

RODNEY, Walter. *How Europe Underdeveloped Africa.* London: Bogle-L'Ouverture, 1972.

ROTBERG, Robert I. "The Swedenborgian Search for African Purity." *Journal of Interdisciplinary History* (M.I.T.) 36:2 (Autumn 2005): 233–40 [Review of Deirdre Coleman, *Romantic Colonization and British Anti-Slavery*].

RYDEN, David Beck. *West Indian Slavery and British Abolition, 1783–1807.* Cambridge: Cambridge University Press, 2009.

RYDÉN, Göran, ed. *Sweden in the 18th Century World: Provincial Cosmopolitans.* Farnham: Ashgate, 2013.

SAID, Edward. *Orientalism: Western Conceptions of the Orient.* London: Penguin, 1995 [1978].

SALA-MOLINS, Louis. *Dark Side of the Light: Slavery and the French Enlightenment.* Minneapolis: University of Minnesota Press, 2006.

SANNER, Inga. *Att älska sin nästa såsom sig själv. Om moraliska utopier under 1800-talet.* Stockholm: Carlsson, 1995.

———. *Den segrande eros: Om kärleksföreställningar från Emanuel Swedenborg till Poul Bjerre.* Nora: Nya Doxa, 2003.

———. *Det omedvetna: historien om ett utopiskt rum.* Nora: Nya Doxa, 2009.

SCARPA, Silvia. *Trafficking in Human Beings: Modern Slavery.* Oxford: Oxford University Press, 2008.

SCHWARZ, Suzanne. *Commerce, Civilisation and Christianity: The Development of the Sierra Leone Company.* Liverpool: Liverpool University Press, 2007.

———. *Zachary Macaulay and the Development of the Sierra Leone Company 1793–1794: 1. Journal, June–October 1793.* Leipzig: University of Leipzig Papers on Africa, History and Culture, series no. 4, 2000.

————. *Zachary Macaulay and the Development of the Sierra Leone Company 1793–1794: 2. Journal, October–December 1793.* Leipzig: University of Leipzig Papers on Africa, History and Culture, series no. 4, 2002.

SEARING, James. *West African Slavery and Atlantic Commerce: The Senegal River Valley, 1700–1860.* Cambridge: Cambridge University Press, 1993.

SELANDER, Sten. *Linnélärjungar i främmande länder.* Stockholm: Bonnier, 1960.

SHARP, Granville. *A Short Sketch of Temporary Regulations (until Better Shall Be Proposed) for the Intended Settlement on the Grain Coast of Africa, near Sierra Leona.* London: H. Baldwin, 1786.

A Short Account of the Honourable Emanuel Swedenborg, and his Theological Writings. Printed and sold by R. Hindmarsh, printer to His Royal Highness the Prince of Wales, No. 32, Clerkenwell-Close, London, 1787.

Sierra Leone Company. "Orders and regulations from the directors of the Sierra Leone Company to the superintendent and council for the settlement, 1791." London: British Library, Endangered Archives Programme 284/5/1.

————. *Substance of the Report Delivered by the Court of Directors of the Sierra Leone Company to the General Court of Proprietors on Thursday the 29th March 1798.* London: James Phillips, 1798.

SIEVERSEN, Sverker. *Sexualitet och äktenskap i Emanuel Swedenborgs religionsfilosofi.* Schriften der Luther-Agricola-Gesellschaft 27. Helsinki, 1993.

SIGSTEDT, Cyriel Odhner. *The Swedenborg Epic: The Life and Works of Emanuel Swedenborg.* London: The Swedenborg Society, 1981 [1952].

Slave Trade Evidence (1789–91). Minutes of Evidence touching the Slave Trade. Taken between 26 May 1789 and 18 April 1791. Records of the House of Lords: Main Papers 1750–99. [File.] Parliamentary Archives, United Kingdom.

SLOAN, Donna J. "The Swedenborgian Church and the Issue of Slavery: A Study of the Pro-Slavery and Anti-Slavery Activities, Involvement and Perspectives of the Swedenborgian Denomination." Master's thesis, Harvard Divinity School, 1990.

SMEATHMAN, Henry. *Plan of Settlement to be Made near Sierra Leona, on the Grain Coast of Africa, Intended more particularly for the service and happy establishment of Blacks and People of Colour, to be shipped as freemen under the direction of the Committee for Relieving the Black Poor, and under the protection of the British Government.* London, 1786.

SMITH, Adam. *The Wealth of Nations.* London: J. M. Dent, 1910.

SÖRLIN, Sverker. *Världens ordning: Europas idéhistoria 1492–1918.* Stockholm: Natur och Kultur, 2004.

SÖRLIN, Sverker, and Otto Fagerstedt. *Linné och hans apostlar.* Stockholm: Natur och Kultur, 2004.

SPARRMAN, Anders. *Resa till Goda Hopps-udden, södra pol-kretsen och omkring jordklotet, samt till hottentott- och caffer-landen, åren 1772–76, af Anders Sparrman . . .* Stockholm, I–III, 1783–1818.

SPRINCHORN, Carl. "Sjuttonhundratalets planer och förslag till svensk kolonisation i främmande världsdelar." *Historisk tidskrift* (1923): 109–62.

ST. CLAIR, William. *The Door of No Return: The History of Cape Coast Castle and the Atlantic Slave Trade.* New York: Bluebridge, 2007.

STALEY, Edgcumbe. *Guilds of Florence*. London: Methuen & Co., 1906.

STRAND, Jakob. "Journal, April–September 1792." British Library, Add MS 12,131.

STRONG, Douglas M. *Perfectionist Politics: Abolitionism and the Religious Tensions of American Democracy*. Syracuse, NY: Syracuse University Press, 1999.

STUART, J. P. "Address of the General Convention of the New Church in the United States of America to the General Conference of the New Church in Great Britain, 1862." *New-Jerusalem Magazine* 36:1 (July 1863): 47–49.

SUNDELIN, Rob. *Swedenborgianismens Historia i Sverige: Under Förra Århundradet*. Upsala: W. Schultz, 1886.

SWANK, Scott Trego. "The Unfettered Conscience: A Study of Sectarianism, Spiritualism, and Social Reform in the New Jerusalem Church, 1840–1870." Doctoral dissertation, University of Pennsylvania, 1970 [MS, microfilm, e-book].

SWARTZ, Olof. *Inträdes-Tal Innehållande Anmärkningar om Vestindien; hållet för Kongl. Vetenskaps Academien, den 18 martii 1789* ... Stockholm: Johan Georg Lange, 1790.

SWEDENBORG, Emanuel. *Apocalypse Revealed*, translated by John Whitehead. West Chester, PA: Swedenborg Foundation, 1997.

———. *Arcana Coelestia* [London, England: John Lewis, 1749–56], translated by John E. Elliott. London, England: The Swedenborg Society, 1983–99.

———. *A Brief Exposition of the Doctrine of the New Church, which is meant by the New Jerusalem in the Apocalypse*. London: Printed and sold by R. Hindmarsh, 1789.

———. *Conjugial Love*, translated by Alfred Acton. London: Swedenborg Society, 1953.

———. *Conjugial Love*, translated by Samuel M. Warren and Louis H. Tafel. West Chester, PA: Swedenborg Foundation, 1998.

———. *De coelo et ejus mirabilibus, et de inferno*. London, 1758.

———. *De Nova Hierosolyma et ejus doctrina cælesti*. London, 1758.

———. "The delights of wisdom respecting conjugal love," translated by Carl Bernhard Wadström. Published in the *New-Jerusalem Magazine* (1790–91) by installments.

———. *Delitae Sapientiae de Amore Conjugiali. Post quas sequuntur voluptates insaniae de Amore Scortatorio*. Amsterdam, 1768.

———. *Divine Love and Wisdom*, translated by George F. Dole. West Chester, PA: Swedenborg Foundation, 2003.

———. *Divine Providence*, translated by George F. Dole. West Chester, PA: Swedenborg Foundation, 2003.

———. *Doctrina Novae Hierosolymae de Charitate: opus posthumum Emanuelis Swedenborgii*. New York: American Swedenborg Printing and Publishing Society, 1906 [= *Charity or the Practice of Neighborliness*, a translation from the Latin by William F. Wunsch of Emanuel Swedenborg's "De charitate." Philadelphia, 1931]. New edition by William Ross Woofenden, West Chester, PA: Swedenborg Foundation, 1995.

———. *The Doctrine of Life for the New Jerusalem, from the Commandments of the Decalogue. Translated from the Latin of the Hon. Emanuel Swedenborg*, 2nd ed. London: R. Hindmarsh, 1786.

———. *The Doctrine of Uses. Being a translation of "De divino amore, De divina sapientia," a Latin manuscript* [Translated by E. C. Mongredien]. London: Swedenborg Society, 1944.

————. *The Doctrine of Uses: From the Latin of E- S-. Being a translation of "De divino amore et de divina sapientia," contained in his posthumous work entitled "Apocalypsis explicata"* [Translated by J. Pansley]. London: Swedenborg Society, 1901.

————. *Heaven and Hell,* translated by George F. Dole. West Chester, PA: Swedenborg Foundation, 2010.

————. *Heaven and Hell,* translated by John C. Ager. West Chester, PA: Swedenborg Foundation, 1995.

————. *Last Judgment (Posthumous)* [Written in 1762, not published by the author], translated by N. Bruce Rogers. Bryn Athyn, PA: General Church of the New Jerusalem, 1997.

————. *Last Judgment / Supplements,* translated by George F. Dole and Jonathan S. Rose. West Chester, PA: Swedenborg Foundation, 2018.

————. *Life / Faith,* translated by George F. Dole. West Chester, PA: Swedenborg Foundation, 2014.

————. *The Lord,* translated by George F. Dole. West Chester, PA: Swedenborg Foundation, 2014.

————. *Married Love,* translated by N. Bruce Rogers. Bryn Athyn, PA: General Church of the New Jerusalem, 1995.

————. *A sketch of the chaste delights of conjugal love, and the impure pleasures of adulterous love. Translated from the "Apocalypsis explicata," a manuscript of the posthumous works of the Hon. Emanuel Swedenborg.* London: printed by J. Denew, 1789.

————. *Spiritual Experiences,* translated by A. W. Acton, Rev. George Bush, Rev. John H. Smithson, and James F. Buss. New York: Swedenborg Foundation, n.d.

————. *A Treatise Concerning Heaven and Hell and of the Wonderful Things Within,* translated by William Cookworthy and Thomas Hartley, 2nd ed. London: R. Hindmarsh, 1784.

————. *True Christian Religion,* translated by William C. Dick. London: Swedenborg Society, 1954.

————. *The True Christian Religion, Containing the Universal Theology of the New Church,* translated by John Clowes. 2 vols. London: J. Phillips et al., 1781.

————. *True Christianity,* translated by Jonathan S. Rose. West Chester, PA: Swedenborg Foundation, 2010.

————. *The Wisdom of Angels concerning Divine Love and Divine Wisdom,* translated by N. Tucker. London: W. Chalklen, 1788 [William Blake's annotated copy in the British Library, shelf mark: C.45.e.1].

SYNNESTVEDT, Dan A., ed. *The World Transformed: Swedenborg and the Last Judgment.* Bryn Athyn, PA: Bryn Athyn College Press, 2011.

TAFEL, Rudolf L. *Documents concerning the Life and Character of Emanuel Swedenborg,* collected, translated, and annotated by R. L. Tafel. Bound in 3 vols. London: Swedenborg Society, British and Foreign, 1875–77. I–II:1–2.

TAYLOR, Andrew. "Nineteenth-century America (1843–1870)." *Henry James in Context,* ed. David McWhirter. Cambridge: Cambridge University Press, 2010, 3–13.

TAYLOR, Charles. *Sources of the Self: The Making of the Modern Identity.* Cambridge: Harvard University Press, 1989.

"That the Lord Now Establishes a Church in Africa." *New-Jerusalem Magazine* (London, 1790): 181–86.

THOMAS, Sarah. "'On the Spot': Travelling Artists and Abolitionism, 1770–1830." *Atlantic Studies* 8:2 (2011): 213–32.

TODOROV, Tzvetan. *The Conquest of America: The Question of the Other.* Norman: University of Oklahoma Press, 1999 [1982].

TOMKINS, Stephen. *William Wilberforce: A Biography.* Grand Rapids, MI: William B. Eerdmans Publishing Co., 2007.

"The Trade in Human Beings: Human Trafficking in the UK, Sixth Report of Session 2008–09, Volume 1." Report, together with formal minutes. London: The Stationery Office, 2009. House of Commons Papers (series).

The Trans-Atlantic Slave Trade Database. http://www.slavevoyages.org. Accessed Dec. 19, 2018.

VAN DUSEN, Wilson. "Usefulness." West Chester, PA: Swedenborg Foundation.

———. *Uses: A Way of Personal and Spiritual Growth.* New York, NY: Swedenborg Foundation, 1983 [1981].

"Wadström, Carl Bernhard." *Svenskt Biografiskt Handlexikon.* http://runeberg.org/sbh/b0671.html. Accessed Jan. 6, 2018.

WADSTRÖM, Carl Bernhard. *Adresse au Corps législatif et au Directoire exécutif de la République française: Par C.B. Wadstrom, Suédois . . .* Paris, 1795.

———. *Anmärkningar rörande slaf-handeln på kusten af Guinea; upsatte af Carl Bernhard Wadström . . .* Norrköping: Adolf Fred. Raam, 1791. [Swedish translation printed at his own expense].

———. *An Essay on Colonization particularly applied to the Western coast of Africa, with some free thoughts on cultivation and commerce; also brief descriptions of the colonies already formed, or attempted, in Africa, including those of Sierra Leona and Bulama. By C. B. Wadström. In two parts,* 2 vols. London: printed for the author, by Darton and Harvey, Gracechurch-Street, 1794–95 (reprinted New York: Augustus M. Kelley, Publishers, 1968).

———. Letter 1 in the *New-Jerusalem Magazine* (January 1790): 70–73.

———. *Observations on the slave trade, and a description of some part of the coast of Guinea, during a voyage, made in 1787, and 1788, in company with Doctor A. Sparrman and Captain Arrehenius.* London: printed and sold by James Phillips, 1789 [The Royal Library, Stockholm, and The Cornell University Library Digital Collection].

———. *Plan for a free community at Sierra Leona, upon the coast of Africa, under the protection of Great Britain; with an invitation to all persons desirous of partaking the benefits thereof. . . . By Charles Bernard Wadstrom.* Printed for T. and J. Egerton, London, 1792.

———. *Précis sur l'établissement des colonies de Sierra Léona et de Boulama: A la côte occidentale de l'Afrique. Contenant: 1° exposé des vraies causes qui ont donné lieu à leur formation, 2° anecdotes sur l'attaque de Sierra Léone par l'escadre francaise en 1794; 3° lettres du célèbre naturaliste docteur Adam Afzélius sur ses nouvelles découvertes dans cette partie du globe, les productions tropicales la plupart inconnues jusqu'ici et l'usage dont elles pourroient etre relativement au commerce avec l'Europe; 4° lettre sur la situation politique de S. Léona par C. B. Wadstrom, . . .* Paris, Ch. Pougens, imprimeur-libraire, rue St.-Thomas-du-Louvre, n°. 246. L'an VI, 1798.

————. *Propositions for Consideration, laid before the Subscribers of the Bulam Association, at a Meeting held on the 29th of April 1794* [Conference Publication]. London, 1794.

————. *Quelques Idées sur la Nature du Numéraire et sur la Nécessité de Combiner l'Intérêt du Cultivateur avec celui du Négociant au Moment où l'on Établit un Nouveau Plan de Finances*. Paris, 1796.

————. "Resa ifrån Stockholm genom Danmark, Tyskland och Frankrike till Senegal-länderna i Afrika, år 1787 och 88." *Archiv för nyare resor: månads-skrift: med kartor och kopparstick* (Stockholm: J. P. Marquard, 1811–15).

————. *Strödda tankar uti philosophiska ämnen*. Stockholm: A. J. Nordström, 1787.

WALKER, J. W. St. G. *The Black Loyalists: The Search for a Promised Land in Nova Scotia and Sierra Leone, 1783–1870*. London: Longman, 1976.

WALVIN, James. "Black People in Britain: The Eighteenth Century." *History Today* 31:9 (Sept. 1981).

WÄSTBERG, Per. *The Journey of Anders Sparrman* [a biographical novel, translated by Tom Geddes]. London: Granta, 2010.

WELLER, Henry. "1860. 1861." *The Crisis* 10:1 (Jan. 1, 1861): 4–5.

WESLEY, John. *Thoughts upon Slavery*, 3rd ed. London: R. Hawes, 1774.

WHEELER, Roxann. "'Betrayed by Some of My Own Complexion': Cugoano, Abolition, and the Contemporary Language of Racialism." *Genius in Bondage: Literature of the Early Black Atlantic,* eds. Vincent Carretta and Philip Gould. Lexington: University Press of Kentucky, 2001, 17–39.

————. *The Complexion of Race: Categories of Difference in Eighteenth-Century British Culture*. Philadelphia: University of Pennsylvania Press, 2000.

WHYTE, Lancelot Law. *The Unconscious before Freud*. London: Friedmann, 1978 [New York, 1960].

WILBERFORCE, William. *The speech of William Wilberforce, Esq., representative for the County of York, on Wednesday the 13th of May, 1789, on the question of the Abolition of the Slave Trade . . .* London: Logographic Press, 1789.

WILKINSON, James John Garth. *The African and the True Christian Religion, his Magna Charta: A Study in the Writings of Emanuel Swedenborg*. London, 1892.

WILLIAMS, Eric. *Capitalism and Slavery*. London: Deutsch, 1964 [1943].

WILLIAMS, Helen Maria. "Memoirs of the Life of Charles Berns Wadstrom." *The Monthly Magazine* 7 (July 1799): 462–65. [Obituary first published in French in the journal *La Décade philosophique, littéraire et politique / par une société de républicains* (April 29, 1799).]

WILLIAMS-HOGAN, Jane. "The Swedenborgian Perspective on the Social Ideal: Society in Human Form." *Dialogue and Alliance* 10:1 (Spring/Summer 1996): 61–77.

————. "Swedenborgianism in Stockholm (1772–1795)." Unpublished paper, written as part of a study presented at the Teologiska Institutionen i Uppsala, Sweden, 1995, titled: "1700-talets svenska samhällsstruktur och swedenborgianismens utveckling i Göteborg, Skara och Stockholm."

WILSON, Ellen Gibson. *John Clarkson and the African Adventure*. London: Macmillan, 1980.

WINTERBOTTOM, Thomas. *An Account of the Native Africans in the Neighbourhood of Sierra Leone, to Which is Added an Account of the Present State of Medicine among them.* London: C. Wittingham, 1803.

WOOFENDEN, William Ross. *Swedenborg's Concept of Love in Action: A Study of the Ethics of Emanuel Swedenborg.* Boston: Massachusetts New Church Union, 1971.

WORCESTER, Thomas. *A Discourse Delivered in the New Jerusalem Church.* Boston: William Carter & Brother, 1861.

WRIGHT, Donald. *The World and a Very Small Place in Africa: A History of Globalization in Niumi, the Gambia.* Armonk: M. E. Sharpe, 2004.

WRIGHT, E. J. "Granville Town." *Sierra Leone Studies* 12 (1956).

ZUBER, Devin. *A Language of Things: Swedenborg and the American Environmental Imagination.* Monograph in Studies in Religion and Culture series. Charlottesville: University of Virginia Press, 2017.

Contributors and Participants

Ronny Ambjörnsson was a professor of intellectual history at the University of Umeå from 1970 to 2001. He has published books on utopian ideas, Swedish working-class culture, and ideas on the concept of Europe. He has also published essays on gender history and a biography on the Swedish writer Ellen Key (1849–1926), *Ellen Key: An European Intellectual* (Stockholm, 2012).

Mark Florman has advised a wide variety of governments and industries. He is also an entrepreneur, having founded businesses in technology, media, transportation, publishing, private equity, banking and leisure, as well as think tanks, school building and international development programs, charities, and political campaigns. Mark is chairman and CEO of Time Partners; chair of the City of London Corporation Development Finance High-Level Steering Group; author of "The External Rate of Return" with the London School of Economics; visiting senior fellow at LSE's Institute of Global Affairs; visiting professor at The Policy Institute at King's College London; distinguished fellow at INSEAD's Global Private Equity Initiative; and co-founder of the Centre for Social Justice, the Early Intervention Foundation, and other not-for-profit organizations working for better societies and better business.

Sir Roger Gifford is a senior banker at SEB, where he has worked for more than thirty-five years, and he is chairman of the UK's Green Finance Initiative. He was the Lord Mayor of London from 2012 to 2013 and lived in the historic Mansion House during that year. In that role, he promoted the UK and the city of London as a global hub for banking, insurance, maritime, and other professional and financial services. Roger is a strong believer in the importance of culture and the arts in people's lives, and he supports a number of arts charities as trustee. He also believes in the importance of education about religious tolerance and diversity and he is a trustee of Co-Exist House and St Paul's Cathedral Foundation.

Anders Hallengren (editor) is a former Harvard history fellow, a research affiliate of Stockholm University in the Department of Culture and Aesthetics, and a fellow of the Linnean Society of London. He served as president of the Swedenborg Society of London from 2011 to 2013, and he was vice president from 2013 to 2015. Anders has published books on Swedenborgian thought (*Gallery of Mirrors*, 1998; *The Grand Theme*, 2013), ethics and natural law (*The Code of Concord*, 1994, doctoral dissertation), international law and African affairs (*Kuba i Afrika*, 1984), and integration in a multicultural world of change (*Nobel Laureates in Search of Identity and Integrity*, 2004); and he is internationally renowned for his Nobel essay "Nelson Mandela and the Rainbow of Culture," first published on September 11, 2001, by Nobelprize.org.

Jonathan Howard is a Swedish architect who grew up in Britain. After graduating from Cambridge in 1956, he worked in Canada, Africa, and Sweden, where he now lives. During the last five years, he has researched the late-eighteenth-century European settlements in West Africa, in which a dozen Swedes were involved.

Neil Kent is an associate of the Scott Polar Research Institute at the University of Cambridge; an associate professor at the École Speciale Militaire de St-Cyr, France; and a member of the council of the Anglo-Swedish Society, London. He was formerly professor of European history and culture at the St. Petersburg State Academic Institute of Fine Arts, Sculpture and Architecture; fellow of the Cyber Conflict Documentation Project, Washington, DC; and a member of the board of the Finnish Institute, London. Neil's publications include *The Triumph of Light and Nature: Nordic Art 1740–1940* (London: Thames and Hudson,

1987); *The Soul of the North: A Social, Cultural and Architectural History of the Nordic Countries* (London: Reaktion Books, 2000); *A Concise History of Sweden* (Cambridge: Cambridge University Press, 2008); *Crimea. A History* (Hurst and Company, 2016); *Italia Rediviva. A Social and Cultural History of Italy. 1740–1900* (Washington, DC, and London: Academica Press, 2017); and *St. Petersburg* (Northampton, Massachusetts: Interlink Books, 2018). Forthcoming are *Denmark and its Imperial Legacy* (Hurst and Company, 2019) and *A History of the Russian Orthodox Church* (Washington, DC, and London: Academica Press, 2020).

James F. Lawrence teaches in historical and cultural studies of religion at the Graduate Theological Union in Berkeley, California. His research areas include new religious movements, Christian spirituality, and Swedenborgian studies. His publications include "An Extraordinary Season in Prayer: Warren Felt Evans's Journey into 'Scientific' Swedenborgian Spiritual Practice," in *Studia Swedenborgiana* 12:3 (2002); "Swedenborgian Spirituality," in *The New Westminster Dictionary of Christian Spirituality* (Louisville: Westminster John Knox Press, 2005); "Telling the Old, Old Story Anew: George Dole's Developmentalist Reading of the Bible," in *Principles in Play: Essays in Honor of George Dole's Contributions to Swedenborgian Thought,* ed. James Lawrence (Berkeley: Studia Swedenborgiana Press, 2012); and "Correspondentia: A Neologism in Aquinas Attains Its Zenith in Swedenborg," in *Correspondence: Journal for the Study of Esotericism* (v. 5, 2017).

Anders Mortensen (conference organizer) is associate professor of comparative literature at Lund University; director of the Centre for Scandinavian Studies Copenhagen–Lund; a member of the Committee for Swedish Studies Abroad at the Swedish Institute, Stockholm; and former editor of the Scandinavian humanist journal *Res Publica*. His fields of research are aesthetics and economy in European romanticist and modernist literature; processes of canon formation in Scandinavian literature; and Carl Jonas Love Almqvist and Gunnar Ekelöf, on whose writings he has published a large number of studies and editions. At present, he is working on a book dealing with the *Abolitionist Economics* of Carl Bernhard Wadström and late-eighteenth-century poets William Blake, Samuel Taylor Coleridge, Thomas Thorild, and Johan Gabriel Oxenstjerna.

Robert W. Rix is associate professor at the University of Copenhagen. He has published widely in several areas relating to the eighteenth century: politics, language, book history, nationalism, and religion. Rix has written a number of articles on William Blake and his connections with the milieu that included C. B. Wadström and other Swedenborgians. He is also the author of the monograph *William Blake and the Cultures of Radical Christianity* (2007). Rix has published *The Barbarian North in Medieval Imagination: Ethnicity, Legend, and Literature* (Routledge, 2014) and edited a volume of essays on Romantic-era print history (MT Press, 2015). In recent years, his research interests have also included Scandinavian Romanticism, on which he has published several articles.

Klas Rönnbäck is professor of economic history at the University of Gothenburg, Sweden. His research interests include the transatlantic trade in slaves and commodities and the socioeconomic impact that this had on Africa, the Americas, and Europe. He has published a number of articles in various academic journals, including *Slavery & Abolition, History in Africa, Economic History Review, African Studies, European Review of Economic History,* and *Itinerario.* He is the author of *Labour and Living Standards in Pre-Colonial West Africa: The Case of the Gold Coast* (Routledge, 2015).

Inga Sanner is a professor of the history of ideas at the University of Stockholm. Her research is centered around the process of secularization in Sweden during the nineteenth and twentieth centuries, with a special focus on the different efforts to formulate alternatives to traditional Christianity. From this perspective, she has explored utopian ideas and theories about love and the unconscious in her monographs: *Att älska sin nästa såsom sig själv: om moraliska utopier under 1800-talet* (Carlssons, 1995), *Den segrande eros: kärleksföreställningar från Emanuel Swedenborg till Poul Bjerre* (Nora: Nya Doxa, 2003), and *Det omedvetna: historien om ett utopiskt rum* (Nora: Bokförlaget Nya Doxa, 2009).

Fredrik Thomasson is a researcher at the Department of History, Uppsala University. His present research project concerns the legal system of the Swedish Caribbean colony, Saint Barthélemy; and he is the first historian to systematically investigate the Swedish court of justice records in the Archives nationales d'outre mer in Aix-en-Provence. He is the author of *The Life of J. D. Åkerblad: Egyptian Decipherment and Orientalism in Revolutionary Times* (Leiden and Boston: Brill Academic Publishers, 2013).

Jane Williams-Hogan (1942–2018) attended the University of Pennsylvania, earning a BA in English literature in 1964, an MA in human relations in 1969, and a PhD in sociology in 1985. Her doctoral dissertation on the early formations of the Swedenborgian Church movement in England—*A New Church in a Disenchanted World: A Study of the Formation and Development of the General Conference of the New Church in Great Britain*—contained several ideas that she would continue to refine and develop in a vast array of papers and lectures. Serving as professor at Bryn Athyn College in Pennsylvania, being the primary administrator of the MA program of religious studies, and teaching sociology and history, she also served as organizer and chair of international Swedenborg research conferences, from the ground-breaking symposium Swedenborg and His Influence (1988) to the Swedenborg and the Arts International Conference (2017), contributing widely to a scholarly understanding of Swedenborg.

Index

279